More Praise for This Book

"A brilliantly accessible guide to developing training that works! This book brings the best of current academic thought to the practitioner in a conversational, practical, and usable format. The endnotes are a phenomenal resource for anyone who wants to dig deeper. Simply superb."

Bonnie Beresford
Vice President, Client Services, Capital Analytics

"I've been recommending this book for years to my staff, my students, and friends who work for nonprofits. It's the most accurate and easy-to-read book for anyone who wants to help someone learn. The new section on technology is especially helpful for those of us involved in online learning. And my doctoral students will love this updated version with more than 300 references."

Petti Van Rekom
Professor, Training and Performance Improvement, Capella University
Director of Online Learning, Iowa Writers Online

"It is hard to improve on their original, wonderful training guide, but Stolovitch and Keeps have managed to do just that. This edition of *Telling Ain't Training* identifies changes organizations must make to meet modern workplace skill and knowledge improvement challenges. The endnotes are exceptional. What a treasure trove of scientific and professional resources for additional research and reading! *Telling Ain't Training* is an essential resource for trainers."

Connie Denicola
Instructor Development Manager,
National Center for Biomedical Research and Training

Praise for the First Edition

"A critical topic delivered in a compelling way. I can see how this book will elevate the conversation about learning and performance."

Allison Rossett
Professor of Educational Technology, San Diego State University

"This practical, innovative, and well-researched book on how we all learn is an invaluable tool for all learning and performance professionals. As a former vice president of training and change management, I would have made the book mandatory reading for trainers, coaches, and managers, had it existed. Well done!"

Michel Desjardins
Senior Vice President, BDC Consulting Group,
Business Development Bank of Canada

"This is a great book that will change your perceptions about teaching. I have always listened carefully to what Harold and Erica have to say on this subject. Now I have what I always wanted—a readily accessible Harold and Erica. A convincing, fun, and interesting read."

J. Kimball Dietrich
Associate Professor, Finance and Business Economics,
University of Southern California

"I believe in *Telling Ain't Training* so much that I have ordered five copies and am going to do a book study with the five trainers we have in our district. I am so excited to get the opportunity to share the information from your book with my trainers. I feel they will benefit and be brought up to the next level."

Kenyon Boswell
Technology Training Supervisor, Katy Independent School District

"I wanted to let you know how your book, *Telling Ain't Training*, has positively transformed a company's training program and me! The most exciting part has been the comments from the new hires who have gone through the training: 'It's so organized,' 'It's so easy to understand,' 'This is the best training I've ever been through….' The most incredible part is the feedback from the current staff concerning the high level of the new hires after training and also the fact that the current employees are so intrigued with the new training that they want to go through it themselves! Thank you for such an enlightening, easy-to-understand, transformational book!"

Pamela Sullivan
Recognition and Retention Consultant, PS Sullivan & Co.

"I have just finished reading your book *Telling Ain't Training,* and I wanted to drop you a note to commend you on an excellent book. I have been reviewing considerable literature for the past few years, and I think your publication is one of the clearest, most straightforward publications I have come across in a long time. I am recommending that everyone in our training organization review it because it serves as a great tool to 'bring everything together.'"

Steve Sniderman
Performance Improvement Consultant, Global Education & Training,
Global Sales Division, Amway

Readers Share How *Telling Ain't Training,* First Edition, Was Used in Their Organizations

"At Merck Sharp and Dohme (New Zealand), we drew together a group of people who are involved in the training and education of others and began monthly forum sessions based around *Telling Ain't Training* and *Training Ain't Performance.* The main changes have come from the growing awareness within the group that they should be performance based and learner centered. It has significantly changed the way they see their roles, and, in particular, caused them to go back to the drawing board to look at what they are trying to achieve and why. In almost all cases, my group has changed its approach from being 'trainers' to 'improvers of performance.' When they do put together training they now carefully consider how to best enable people to learn as opposed to just attending a course.

"We used to have a calendar of typical training workshops that either consisted of too much material being transmitted or too many activities that were superfluous and didn't result in performance improvement. So our trainers are now starting with the learners and what they need to know and do and are then designing training and other performance support to enable it. The result has been less but more relevant training, less money, and the content and structure match the performance outcomes required.

"I laminated a simple, brightly colored card for each person that simply reads 'Performance Based and Learner Centered.' I've noticed that everyone has it above their desk as a reminder for their educational efforts and workplace conversations. We've already seen new learner-centered materials being produced together with shorter modules in formats that maximize retention and learning. Thank you for a couple of outstanding books that have been written in a way that walks the talk!"

Rob Bialostocki
Learning and Development Manager, Merck Sharp and Dohme (New Zealand)

"I am a teacher of developmental English at Baltimore City Community College. My students often have deficits in more areas than just grammar and mechanics. Their skill deficits often include the behavioral—not so much bad behavior, but lack of self-esteem. Few of my students feel comfortable working in a group. Even fewer know how to address a speaker or form a good question.

"When I returned from the Arlington, Virginia, *Telling Ain't Training* workshop, I immediately employed the 'Press Conference' technique in my class. The only modification I made was that I coached students on taking turns to ask questions and in ways to pose questions politely.

"The technique demonstrated a remarkable amount of potential in my students. They were far more comfortable working in groups and asking questions after they participated in the exercise. I feel that, with more practice, I will be able to apply the technique in my class with aplomb. Thank you for teaching me how to conduct Press Conferences in the training/instructional classroom."

Carole Quine
Associate Professor, English, Baltimore City Community College (USA)

"I organized a book club for about 25 trainers dispersed throughout my company. Because training is very decentralized here, we don't really have many opportunities to share experiences or learn from one another. By choosing *Telling Ain't Training* for our inaugural meeting, I hoped to instill a foundation for future discussions. We had a lively dialogue around this relevant book. I am currently designing a class that is 'PowerPoint free' where the focus is on the learner. Less is indeed more! Thanks for the inspiration."

Janet DiVincenzo
Senior Instructional Designer, Fulfillment Training,
New Century Mortgage (USA)

"I have used what I have learned from *Telling Ain't Training* in perhaps more subtle ways than changes to 'training courses' themselves:

▶ I have purchased copies for members of the corporate learning leadership team to open their thinking to fundamentals and challenge the way we often think about training (for example, basic understanding of when training is even relevant or the most effective means of addressing performance gaps or knowledge/skill gaps).

▶ I created my own four-page summary and share it with colleagues when certain topics come up (for example, someone recently stressed the importance of just-in-time training and that a little of the right stuff is more effective and often much cheaper to create than large volumes of content).

▶ Two key overall messages that I have promoted are
— the concept of 'learner-centered'—simple but powerful, easy to explain and have others think differently about what training should provide and how we offer it
— the understanding of 'the human learner' and the way our senses work, including filter mechanisms; it explains so much.

"Thanks for the book—I use it weekly in many ways!"

Mick Thomas
Learning Leader, Dow Chemical

Telling Ain't Training

Updated, Expanded, and Enhanced

Harold D. Stolovitch and Erica J. Keeps

With contributions from Marc J. Rosenberg

Alexandria, Virginia

ASTD Press is an internationally renowned source of insightful and practical information on workplace learning and performance topics, including training basics, evaluation and return on investment, instructional systems development, e-learning, leadership, and career development.

Ordering information: Books published by ASTD Press can be purchased by visiting ASTD's website at store.astd.org or by calling 800.628.2783 or 703.683.8100.

Library of Congress Control Number: 2009903513

ISBN-10: 1-56286-701-6
ISBN-13: 978-1-56286-701-0

ASTD Press Editorial Staff:

Director: Anthony Allen
Manager, ASTD Press: Larry Fox
Project Manager, Content Acquisition: Justin Brusino
Senior Associate Editor: Tora Estep
Associate Editor: Ashley McDonald
Editorial Assistant: Stephanie Castellano

Copyeditor: Tora Estep
Indexer: April Michelle Davis
Proofreader: Kris Patenaude
Interior Design and Production: Kathleen Schaner
Cover Design: Ana Ilieva Foreman

Contents

Dedication

For the pleasure of sharing in your growth and learning, we dedicate this book to

Ryan Samuel Bender

Shelby Anne Bender

Francesca Ruth Barlin

You always keep us aware that *telling truly ain't training.*

Preface

It is difficult to believe that nearly 10 years have passed since we sat down to write the first edition of *Telling Ain't Training*. We thought then that we were done. However, when we were approached to produce an updated, expanded, and enhanced version of *Telling Ain't Training*, ideas began to bubble to the surface. How could we decline such a tempting offer? So much has happened since *Telling Ain't Training* was first published. Yet, so much still remains the same. What to say? What choices to make?

Response to the first edition of *Telling Ain't Training* was overwhelming. We heard from hundreds of readers about how the book had affected the way they and their organizations approach training. We also heard from school teachers, professors, and parents who saw how the principles and strategies of *Telling Ain't Training* could be applied in their settings. Examples and testimonials poured in. We were so pleased when our readers asked for more. And more is what they got!

In 2004, the American Society for Training & Development (ASTD) published our companion book, *Training Ain't Performance,* which addresses the more expansive nature of what we do to improve human performance in the workplace. In 2005 and 2006, respectively, we launched our two fieldbooks, *Beyond Telling Ain't Training Fieldbook* and *Beyond Training Ain't Performance Fieldbook*. These publications further supported the implementation of our approach in organizations worldwide.

The *Ain't* series of books (which is what the group of four is often called) were not the only means of spreading the word. In fact, based on the popularity of *Telling Ain't Training*, ASTD invited us to conduct *Telling Ain't Training* mini conferences throughout the United States. This then led to *Telling Ain't Training* events in ASTD and International Society for Performance Improvement (ISPI) chapters; the Canadian Society for Training and Development (CSTD); and corporations, government agencies, and nonprofits throughout the world. Who could have imagined that *Telling Ain't Training* would be delivered live, on average, 20 times a year?

The first edition of *Telling Ain't Training* was a wonderfully enjoyable book to write. It wasn't a typical book for us but more of a conversation about training. We have devoted our professional lives—approximately 80 years combined—to teaching, designing instruction, helping organizations create learning and performance support solutions, and conducting research on learning and workplace performance. We have spent these years in both the academic and corporate worlds. We've produced many professional and scientific publications. *Telling Ain't Training* was totally different from anything else we had ever written. This edition of *Telling Ain't Training*—updated, expanded, and enhanced—remains true to the approach and style set in the original publication.

As with the first edition, we have done away with many of the conventions we normally apply to our writing. Except for a few references to specific individuals from whom we have directly borrowed ideas or words, we have eliminated the usual citation practices. Instead, we have placed at the end of the book a section called For Further Reading (updated and greatly expanded in this edition) that you can consult to dig more deeply into some aspect of what we present. In this second edition, we also provide endnotes to not only cite references, but also position them. The endnotes expand *Telling Ain't Training*'s depth. Hunting for research references and citations to bring the new edition up to date, enhance it, and add more evidence to support or update its content was an intensive two-year activity. But what an exciting and enlightening one it was! Reading articles, manuscripts, reports, research abstracts, meta-analysis studies, books, and even interview summaries significantly expanded our own horizons. We are happy to share what we discovered as we scoured the universe for new material.

Just as in the first edition, we have maintained a conversational—almost speaking—tone in our writing. We've also used contractions, dialogue, asides, fun exercises, teasers, challenges, and any other technique we felt would keep this book as reader-friendly as possible.

To create *Telling Ain't Training: Updated, Expanded, and Enhanced,* we took what accumulated research and well-documented professional procedure have demonstrated to be sound and desirable practices for training-learning (that is, the deliberate actions taken to trigger desirable skill/knowledge acquisition and the outcomes of these actions) and made them more approachable than typically presented in the scientific and professional journals. Our purpose was to make the best principles of training available to both newly appointed trainers and more experienced practitioners searching for explanation and confirmation on why certain things work (or perhaps don't). In no case have we "dumbed down" the research findings. We have worked diligently to maintain the integrity of the various researchers' and authors' works while modifying the language (never the ideas or findings) to make their discoveries accessible to a broad training audience. In this latest edition, we also spend more time and space on how the basic principles of training-learning play out in a changing world—one that has experienced the terrorist attacks on September 11, 2001; a major economic downturn; and the advent of many technological advances such as e-learning, webinars, social media, e-readers, and virtual worlds. Workplace learning has been transformed in ways we could have not imagined when we wrote the first edition.

With respect to technology and training, we felt that the best way to include content about this ever-changing scene would be by deferring to someone with greater expertise than we possess. Fortunately, our colleague and friend, Marc J. Rosenberg, who has authored excellent books on e-learning and the use of technology to improve human performance at work, accepted our invitation to become part of the writing team. He co-authored the section of this book called "Training-Learning With Technology and Beyond." This section consists of two chapters. The first provides a historical perspective and conceptual framework for using technology in training-learning. The second is more pragmatic and includes rich examples of technology at work. We are extremely grateful for the knowledge and wisdom he has shared to expand and enhance this second edition of *Telling Ain't Training*.

You will notice that we have divided the book into five sections containing 13 chapters. The first two chapters describe the contents and lay out a road map for what lies ahead. The ensuing chapters provide you with both substance and tools to bring *Telling Ain't Training: Updated, Expanded, and Enhanced* to life. Each chapter starts with a brief overview of its highlights to help you prepare yourself for the content that follows. To avoid too much "telling," which is almost inevitable in a book, and one-way communication, which is what we're asking *you* not to do, every chapter contains activities that are meant to engage you in meaningful ways. The exercises—many of them fun, several of them timed to increase the challenge—offer opportunities for you to interact with the learning content. All of the chapters (except the first one) conclude with brief, summary exercises and activities that prompt you to recall what you've learned and help you retain key points when you've finished reading the book. Along the way you will encounter the following icons:

 This icon signals an important fact for the reader.

 This icon identifies key points for using the information we've supplied.

This icon accompanies a review of the major takeaway knowledge in each chapter.

We would like to thank former ASTD Press acquisitions editor Mark Morrow for inviting us to create the original *Telling Ain't Training* and for supporting us so enthusiastically through its preparation and the other books in the *Ain't* series, including this updated, expanded, and enhanced edition.

Our thanks also go to Justin Brusino, ASTD Press acquisitions editor, who was the project manager for the second edition of *Telling Ain't Training*. His assistance, guidance, and support were most appreciated.

Our sincere appreciation goes to Tora Estep, former ASTD Press senior associate editor, for cleaning up our text beautifully without straying from our central message or style.

There is no way we could have completed this book without the constant support of our very dear right and left hand, Barbra Hellwig, who took care of all the hard stuff while we wrote. Barbra, we are eternally in your debt.

We have no words to express our deepest appreciation to Samantha Greenhill, who collaborated on this fifth book in the *Ain't* series. Her ability to work with us, tolerate our unending demands, and not flinch from our tight timelines never ceases to amaze us. Calmly, she absorbs what we send her, along with our cryptic instructions, and turns it all into something coherent. Astonishing!

In creating this book, we thought especially about the countless workers and managers who find themselves thrust into the role of trainer, often with no formal background in training and learning. Our hope is that these individuals feel guided and supported by this publication.

One of the greatest joys of writing a book in which you share what you have learned with readers is that of sharing the experience with a co-author you admire. We are not just co-authors; we are also professional colleagues and life partners. To each other, then, thanks for continuing the journey together.

Harold D. Stolovitch and Erica J. Keeps
Los Angeles, May 2011

Section 1

The Human Learner—
What Research Tells Us

Chapter 1

Learning Is Not Easy (Especially When Others Make It So Hard)

Chapter highlights:

▶ Opening teaser
▶ Set of challenges
▶ Discussion of what this book is about.

Most books start—logically, we might add—with an introduction that sets the stage for what's to come and then lays out, in overview, the contents of the volume. We'll get around to that soon enough. You have our word on this. However, we've always enjoyed the openings to thriller movies that hit you with a teaser to arouse your interest before moving on to the title, opening credits, and the rest of the movie. Prepare yourself, then, for a couple of challenging teasers.

Challenge 1

You've got 60 seconds to learn the following 18-digit sequence. One error and the bomb explodes. Time yourself. Ready? Go!

4 1 2 5 2 7 2 4 6 0 6 0 3 1 3 0 2 8

Now, cover the number sequence. You have 30 seconds to write down all 18 digits, in order, with no errors in the following box. Go!

How well did you do? How easy or hard was it? Almost no one can do it, especially under time pressure. Is there any way we can make the learning task easier? Here, once more, is our number:

4 1 2 5 2 7 2 4 6 0 6 0 3 1 3 0 2 8

And here are clues to accompany it. Please pay close attention. Your life depends on it!

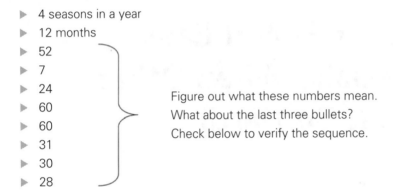

- ▶ 4 seasons in a year
- ▶ 12 months
- ▶ 52
- ▶ 7
- ▶ 24
- ▶ 60
- ▶ 60
- ▶ 31
- ▶ 30
- ▶ 28

Figure out what these numbers mean. What about the last three bullets? Check below to verify the sequence.

Read the sequence again as you try to retain the numbers. The total of the two readings should take about 60 seconds.

Now, once more, cover the numbers. Take 30 seconds—no more—to write down the sequence in the space below. Go!

And here's the correct answer:

4 seasons in a year; 12 months in a year; 52 weeks in a year; 7 days in a week; 24 hours in a day; 60 minutes in an hour; 60 seconds in a minute; 31, 30, or 28 days in a month

How did you do this time? In our tests with various learners, most do far better when they actively work out the clues than when they just study the numbers. There's a reason for this—one that we'll explain later.

Challenge 2

Up for another challenge? The other day we received the following invitation to a party in a city we had never visited. Please read it through without trying to memorize it. You should spend about 30 to 45 seconds on it. Then cover the note and answer the questions that follow the invitation.

Hi, here are the directions:

From the airport, take the road that leads out of the rental lot and follow it past the barrier around the lot until you get to the end where you connect up with the road out. Take the road, and just before it veers right, you'll see a triple fork. If you take the left branch, you'll head west and away from the lake. Don't do that! Straight puts you under the viaduct and really off track. Take the right branch and bear right at the next fork to the roundabout where you go not quite halfway around to the second road. It's 379 East, although it really goes south, so don't worry. From then on, it's a straight shot.

Cheers, André

Answer these questions without referring to the note:

1. Where's the parking lot?

2. Where are the rental cars?

3. What do you have to pass to get out of the parking lot?

4. What do you see just before the road veers right out of the parking lot?

5. After the second fork, what do you watch for?

6. Do you go over or under the viaduct?

7. Which highway do you take?

We asked for clearer directions. Our friend's sister sent us the map you'll find on the next page (figure 1-1).

Study this map for about 30 to 45 seconds. Then, come back to this page and without referring to the map, answer the same seven questions as before:

1. Where's the parking lot?

2. Where are the rental cars?

3. What do you have to pass to get out of the parking lot?

4. What do you see just before the road veers right out of the parking lot?

5. After the second fork, what do you watch for?

6. Do you go over or under the viaduct?

7. Which highway do you take?

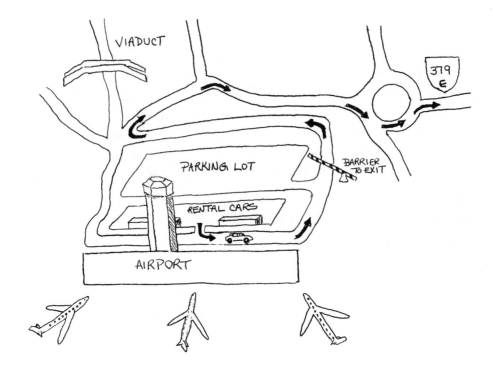

Turn the book over to find the correct answers.

Answer Key:

1. In front of the airport
2. At the front of the parking lot (or just in front of the parking lot)
3. A barrier
4. A triple fork
5. A roundabout
6. Neither
7. 379 east

Was it easier that time? Once again, in our trials we found that almost everyone had errors in the first attempt. However, nearly no one erred once they had seen the diagram.

 We presented these two learning challenges for the following reasons:

▶ To demonstrate that the same content, presented differently, creates a different impact on learning and retention.

▶ To get you to participate, respond, and receive feedback—all key to creating excellent learning events.

▶ To give you a taste of this book's style—fun, easy to read, challenging, a bit tongue in cheek, but focused on a serious theme.

Before we give away too much of the story, why don't you participate once more?

> In table 1-1 are sets of paired statements. Please check the statement in each pair that most closely corresponds to your personal experience of learning (check only one from column A or column B each time).

From our own experience in learning and from trying out these statement pairs with a lot of adults, we suspect that you checked most of the statements in column B and few to none in column A. No surprise. What does astonish us, however, is that those who teach for a living (instructors, teachers, professors, trainers) also check almost all the column B statements, but when we observe them teaching or training, they act as though column A statements were true!

Table 1-1. Paired Statements

Column A	Column B
☐ Someone who knows something I don't tells me about it.	☐ I discuss with someone who knows something I don't.
☐ I watch someone perform a full demonstration.	☐ I get involved and try things out during a demonstration.
☐ I attend lectures in which an instructor presents information to me.	☐ I attend sessions in which an instructor engages me in a two-way interaction.
☐ I see what's in it for the organization.	☐ I see what's in it for me.
☐ The content has a lot of detail.	☐ The content is minimal and meaningful.
☐ What is presented to me is organized according to the logic of the content.	☐ What is presented to me is organized according to the logic of how I learn things.
☐ I am shown how things are done.	☐ I get to try things for myself as I am being guided.
☐ I attend long learning sessions.	☐ I attend shorter spaced learning sessions.
☐ I am in a formal instructional setting.	☐ I am in an informal work and learning setting.
☐ I am told how things work.	☐ I experience how things work.

Time and again, we see almost a complete reversal between what people say about how they learn and how they try to help others learn. Quite the paradox! It's also one of the main reasons for writing this book.

What Is This Book About?

Enough teasing. Let's see what this book is all about. A lot of traditions, myths, and misguided—although well-intentioned—principles and activities in training create barriers to effective learning. We have produced this book for two main reasons: to dispel these counterproductive beliefs and practices that harm the instructional process and to help you to be the most effective trainer or instructor you can be. Here then is what *Telling Ain't Training: Updated, Expanded, and Enhanced* offers you:

- ▶ *Separation of myths from research-based findings about learning and training.* We have done this in a nonacademic way using lots of examples and exercises. The goal is to make you reflect upon and reject the ill-founded myths that many people in the teaching-learning world perpetuate.

- ▶ *A breezy and friendly style that we believe will get our message across better than a formal approach.* But don't let the style fool you. Everything in this book is based on what the best research evidence tells us about how to help people learn.

- ▶ *Lots of endnotes that offer additional reading and useful references to support what we have covered in the book.* As you read, you will come across numbers in superscript. These refer to the endnotes at the back of the book. They serve four purposes: to be as inobtrusive as possible and hence not interfere with your reading; to substantiate what we say and allow you to back up any arguments you may make to others based on this book; sometimes to elaborate on what is in the text; and, finally, to suggest additional readings if you wish to pursue a particular topic.

- ▶ *Lots of interaction.* As you've already seen, you get to do things and think about them, not just read words. To make our message meaningful and credible, we want to use an approach that is consistent with what we are proposing. All human beings—and that includes you and us—learn through active mental engagement. In this book, we make every effort to engage you mentally in meaningful ways.

- ▶ *Practical and down-to-earth counsel.* One of us authors has devoted his almost 50-year career to studying and conducting research about learning and then translating findings into practical application. The other one of us has spent close to 40 years in business managing the learning and performance of people. Together, the two of us focus on what it really takes to help people learn.

- ▶ *Above all, a sharing with you of what we have learned in our lifetimes.* The goal is for you to become highly effective trainers much more quickly than we did by interacting with the contents of this book.

Are you convinced? Even fired up? Then let us turn to the beginning—the introduction.

Chapter 2

An Introduction to Some "Familiar Terms"

Chapter highlights:

▶ Vocabulary lesson on "familiar terms"
▶ Underlying philosophy of the book
▶ Application to various media
▶ Overview of the book's contents.

Basic Vocabulary—The Terms of the Trade

Training … instruction … education … learning. These are words we often use interchangeably. When we analyze the words, however, we discover that each conveys a unique meaning. Individually and combined, these four activities give us power to build different types of skills and knowledge. Let's examine each of these words and begin to build a valuable vocabulary.

Training

You are trying to get your dog to sit at your command. Check off the expression below that best describes what you are doing:

☐ training your dog
☐ instructing your dog
☐ educating your dog.

You probably chose "training your dog" because it seems to fit best. The other two sound somewhat strange when applied to animals. If we dig deeper, we realize that when training a dog what we want is for it to perform something specific and precise.

We also want the dog to do it on command and without variation. You say, "sit," and the dog sits. The more effective the training, the more accurately and rapidly the dog responds. In "training," our purpose is to create a change in learners (including dogs) that they consistently reproduce without variation. Through intense training, the learner becomes increasingly able to reproduce the learned behavior with fewer errors, greater speed, and under more demanding conditions. Examine the list below and check all the items for which you believe training is appropriate:

- ☐ typing
- ☐ assembling a rifle
- ☐ stating a rule
- ☐ executing a complex skating maneuver
- ☐ reciting multiplication tables
- ☐ selecting the right icon on a screen
- ☐ applying all the steps of the emergency shutdown procedure.

If you checked all the items, you were right. Sounds mechanical? That's all right. Learning things that you apply automatically and invariably is often a necessary part of learning. How much variation do you want in naming objects, slicing a tomato, or logging on to a computer? Being able to execute mental or physical procedures without thinking is important in our lives (for example, shifting gears in a car, brushing our teeth, and recognizing letters and words). It cuts down on our cognitive (thinking) load. Training helps make our lives easier.

Instruction

"Instruction" helps learners generalize beyond the specifics of what is taught. The ability to reproduce unconsciously what we have learned is absolutely insufficient to make us complete as human beings. Therefore, we add instruction.

Here's an example: In French, the infinitive forms of regular verbs always end in "er." For instance, the verb *donner* (to give) is a regular verb. So is *demander* (to ask). Which of these verbs are French regular verbs?

- ☐ *choisir* (to choose)
- ☐ *chanter* (to sing)
- ☐ *nommer* (to name)
- ☐ *vendre* (to sell)
- ☐ *apporter* (to bring)
- ☐ *vouloir* (to want)

Even though you may not know much about French, you probably were able to take the rule and the two examples above and generalize to new instances. If you checked *chanter, apporter,* and *nommer, félicitations* (congratulations)!

In work settings, we require a lot of instruction. Let's take, for example, safety issues. We provide examples of workplace hazards and means for dealing with different types of dangerous situations. But no matter how many examples and rules we provide, we all know that we may run into many novel instances not covered during instruction. The expectation is that learners will be able to generalize beyond what was taught.

Just as for training, the purpose of instruction is to build new skills and knowledge. The key differences are presented in table 2-1.

Table 2-1. Differences Between Training and Instruction

Training allows you to	Instruction allows you to
• reproduce exactly what has been taught • act automatically • apply learning without variation, regardless of conditions.	• generalize beyond what has been taught • act thoughtfully • adapt learning to each new set of conditions.

Just to be sure you've got it, place a "T" beside each action below that you believe to require training and an "I" beside those that seem to fit with instruction.

1. _____ Light a lighter.
2. _____ Pronounce the French word *manger*.
3. _____ Select an appropriate product for a customer.
4. _____ Respond to a complaint.
5. _____ Place a specific component in the motherboard.
6. _____ Tie a reef knot.

Items 1, 2, 5, and 6 are all tasks for training (reproduce without variation). Items 3 and 4 require instruction because each new customer will be different, as will each complaint. Those actions demand generalization of learning and adaptation of behaviors.

Education

The third key vocabulary term is "education." As you probably already sense, education conveys a more long-term and broader connotation than do training and instruction, which are generally short-term and narrowly focused. Education is the result of a variety of life experiences and highly generalized learning principles and events. Much education derives from implicit messages transmitted through the behaviors of role models rather than from explicitly stated ones. The purpose of education is to build general mental models and value systems.

Let's place this in a work context and continue with the safety example: Training enables us to build specific safety behaviors, such as set off an alarm, activate a fire extinguisher, or select the right number to call. Instruction allows us to acquire the skills to identify new safety hazards or to act when an emergency occurs that we have not encountered before. Finally, education enables us to adopt a safety outlook on life. We automatically take precautions and proactively apply measures to avoid accidents. We foresee possible dangers, and we advocate safe working conditions and behaviors.

In our work as parents, teachers, and workplace training professionals, we do all three: train, instruct, and educate. All three activities have their place. One is not more important than another. All three work together. Imagine, for example, that you are responsible for building skills and knowledge in a technical service center where customer support specialists help callers solve technical problems. Consider the list of relevant tasks presented below and place a "T" beside each item requiring training, an "I" beside the instruction items, and an "E" beside those appropriate for education.

1. _____ Log a call.
2. _____ Probe to clarify the problem.
3. _____ Fill in fields in a customer record.
4. _____ Display empathy for customers' frustrations.
5. _____ State steps for a specific troubleshooting procedure.
6. _____ Draw out from the customer what she or he already has done in attempting to correct the problem.
7. _____ Select type of call code before filing the report.

Items 1, 3, 5, and 7 are most likely tasks to be trained. Item 2 probably is one best handled through instruction. Item 6 is largely instruction but has some aspects of education in it. You have to learn how to go about drawing information from a customer and applying listening skills. The rapport you create can make all the difference in the quality of customer responses you obtain. You can acquire the techniques through instruction, but the nuances of helpfully interacting with the customer draw from the education of the customer support specialist. Finally, item 4, displaying empathy, is a subtle skill not inherent in everyone. Empathy derives from the support specialist's own life experiences plus the models and implicit messages he or she communicates through actions. A person requires education to become empathic with customers.

To conclude our vocabulary drill, training, instruction, and education all aim to build knowledge and skills in learners. Each offers a unique and distinct approach, and all are necessary to help people learn. They seldom remain "pure." They can be mixed so that even while training for a specific behavior, we may be educating by attitude and by the example we create for our learners.

Learning

Learning is change. Don't forget that the whole reason for training, instruction, and education is to enable people to learn. In chapter 3, we will investigate learning more deeply. Suffice it to say at this point that we are seeking to "transform" our learners. If we train—the general term commonly used in the work setting for all three sets of activities—we do not simply transmit information. We change people. We transform learners in ways that are desirable both for them and for organizations.

Today, most organizations have moved from traditional "training" departments to "learning and development" groups or even "workplace learning and performance" teams. The emphasis on training has given way to a clear focus on learning and its impact on producing better results.[1]

Two Key Principles: Your Mantra as a Trainer (Instructor, Educator)

We are seated in a circle on the floor with our legs crossed. Our eyes are closed, and we are relaxed. The light is dim. We repeat over and over again, "learner centered… performance based… learner centered… performance based…." Why this mantra? Because these two terms are the keys to transforming learners. Let's examine each of the terms individually.

Learner Centered

Imagine you are an accountant and have been asked to conduct a session next week for a group of technical and professional personnel recently promoted to managers. Your mandate is to teach cash flow management to these nonfinancial managers. What will you do to prepare? Be honest and check off which of the following two scenarios more closely describes actions you would take.

☐ **A.** Gather materials on cash flow management. Examine documents for key concepts and terms. Create an outline of the content in logical sequence so that you ensure you hit all the fundamentals. Study up and rehearse so that you appear credible and can answer any content questions the learners raise. Put together information and exercises that clarify what cash flow is and how it works. Verify that all of your content is accurate and state of the art.

☐ **B.** Gather information on the prospective learners' jobs with respect to cash flow. Gather information on the learners' backgrounds and experiences concerning cash flow management. Investigate to identify problems new managers encounter and create with respect to cash flow. Gather a list of organizational expectations of these newly appointed managers concerning cash flow management. Create realistic scenarios and tools to help the learners acquire expected competencies. Create a list of benefits to them and to the organization when they manage cash flow well.

From experience, we have found that the overwhelming majority of people, when placed in this position, opt for A. They go for the content. The more appropriate answer, however, is B. Focus on the learners with their needs, concerns, desires, fears, frustrations, and characteristics. Option A leads to telling and transmission. The emphasis is on the instructor's ability to present a great deal of information. Option B leads to training and transformation. The focus is on the learner.

Performance Based

If you examine most course notes, either those of the trainer or instructor or of the participants, you likely will find them filled with lots of content. There is an impression that more is better. How often do you hear trainers complain, "I didn't have enough time to cover the content"?

Here's a simple choice: You have a group of technicians who have to learn about a totally new approach to diagnosing a problem. Check off your response below. Do you want them to

- ☐ know about the new approach?
- ☐ do the job correctly?

The obvious choice is "do the job correctly." You probably wouldn't mind them "knowing about the approach," but the priority is clear. We want them to be able to perform, not merely to know and talk about. The first choice leads to a content-based approach. The second is performance based—being able to act and to achieve worthwhile, verifiable results.[2]

"Learner centered... performance based...." That's the mantra of this book and the heart of our message. Instructor-centered and content-based efforts lead to telling and transmission. Learner-centered and performance-based efforts result in training and transformation.

Live or Technology Based: It's All the Same

Perhaps your impression is that everything we have included thus far applies exclusively to live, face-to-face instruction. One area of research on learning has not varied in its findings for more than 50 years—media and instructional delivery options. To summarize hundreds of studies, the effectiveness of messages aimed at learning is not bound up in the delivery vehicle but rather in how the message itself is designed.[3] The message developed to transform you will either succeed or fail based on how well we have designed it, not on whether we bring it to you live, through the pages of this book, in a video, or via computer.[4]

The message and principles of *Telling Ain't Training: Updated, Expanded, and Enhanced* are equally valid for e-learning, live instruction, or any form of mediated instruction (for example, video based, computer based, or simulation lab). Telling in any form engenders passivity. It is one-way communication. It is content focused. It is transmission. True learner-centered and performance-based training, instruction, or education requires dialogue and experience—engaging conversation[5] and meaningful interaction[6]—to transform. Self-paced print or sophisticated, electronically delivered instruction is only as effective as the instructional design principles that are applied.

Later, in chapters 10 and 11, we will focus specifically on training with technology. We will bring you up to date on the latest trends in technology use for learning and help you wisely select the form of technology that makes sense to use in your setting.

What's in This Book and Why?

We have given a great deal of thought to the content of this book and to the way we've presented it. The following points have been our guiding principles in choosing material to discuss and in selecting the means to portray that material:

- ▶ Start with the learner and never lose that focus. We assume that you are interacting with this book because you want to learn something. We're excited about this. You are the reason for our efforts, and we never forget that. Thanks for continuing the conversation.

- ▶ Present principles that apply to all types of learning: mental (cognitive), physical (psychomotor), emotional (affective), and, of course, combinations and mixtures of these. Although the emphasis may vary from chapter to chapter, we recognize that all types of learning are important. You will find numerous examples for each type of learning, alone or in combination.

- ▶ Provide a training session structure that you can apply universally and that is based on learning research. As an added bonus, this user-friendly model even lets you retrofit existing training programs and instructional materials. Chapter 6 is devoted to this model and returns to it from time to time.

▶ Include learning strategies and activities, complete with examples, that you can apply and adapt right away. You will notice that we prefer the simple. If "cheap" can do the job, why complicate things? However, some circumstances require more sophisticated tools and technologies. Complex decision making, handling of delicate or dangerous equipment, or life-or-death procedures are instances that may demand training tools and methods that employ resources far beyond the usual.

▶ Lay out practical tools for designing your next training session with a high probability of success. Almost all of these are easy to apply or adapt to meet your needs.

▶ Present helpful ways to evaluate your training effectiveness. There's a complete chapter (chapter 9) on testing, along with job aids for selecting and creating tests that verify learning.

▶ Provide access to the world of technology for learning in a manner that is easy to understand and allows for integration of training-learning fundamentals. A complete chapter on this (chapter 11) gets you started on considering technology for your setting.

▶ Present both myths and science-based findings about training and learning so that you can separate ineffective (and often counterproductive) lore from what research has shown leads to a high probability of learning success. This differentiation of truth and falsehood should help strengthen your own competence and confidence and should provide you with ammunition to combat practices that waste organizational time, energy, and resources.

▶ Conclude with some practical wisdom and thoughts about applying and maintaining what you gain from this book in your practice—that telling really ain't training and that your goal is transformation of the learner rather than transmission of the information.

 Remember This

▶ Training, instruction, education… use all of these to trigger learning.
▶ The whole purpose of training, instruction, and education is to enable people to learn. Your mission is not to transmit information but to transform your learners.

▶ Your mantra as a trainer, instructor, or educator is "learner centered... performance-based." Any approach short of this leads to one-way transmission and uncertain results.

▶ Live or technology based, it's all the same. The medium is not the message. The principles in this book are valid regardless of the delivery vehicle you select. Focus on meaningful interaction to transform your learners.

Chapter 3

The Human Learner

Chapter highlights:

▶ Trip through the body and brain of the learner

▶ Explanation of what learning is

▶ Capacity and limitations of the human learner.

W elcome to a voyage through the body and brain of your learner. Why undertake such a voyage? Two reasons. First, if you are really dedicated to transforming people in ways that benefit them and those they serve, doesn't it make sense to know as much as possible about the characteristics and capabilities of these individuals? This chapter offers you information and insights into the human learner.[1] It increases your ability to adapt your instructional efforts for maximum effect. Second, most writings about training focus on instructional stimulus elements, that is, what you should do to be a great trainer or designer of instruction. They rarely explain how the learner deals with and internalizes these stimuli. Without a clear understanding of how humans access, treat, and retrieve what we transmit to them, we decrease the probability of successful learner transformation. Let's begin our study of the learner by defining "learning."

What Is Learning?

Before we share our definition, stop here for a moment and come up with your own words to describe "learning." Write them here:

Basically, learning is change, adaptation. All organisms are genetically coded to reproduce the essential characteristics of their species: Daffodils beget other daffodils. Humans are no different. We are all more or less the same. We discriminate easily between ourselves and nonhumans because, as humans, we share so many characteristics. But each individual member of a species is different from all other members of the species in subtle ways. These variations are critical to our survival. As environmental conditions change, the individual variations result in some members of the species adapting better than others. This allows species to survive and evolve over time.

Humans have an enormous capacity for learning, a capacity genetically coded into us. This learning capability permits us to change as we receive information from the environment. The most adaptable individuals, especially in primitive times, learned more rapidly than did others about the opportunities and dangers surrounding them, and they passed this learning ability on to their offspring, who eventually passed it on to us. Today, we humans are incredible learning organisms. No other species on earth does it better. That's the good news.

The bad news is that we are genetically programmed for an environment that no longer exists. In the natural world, it takes thousands of generations to alter a species significantly. (We can speed things up through deliberate breeding programs, but this is not how it works in nature.) Think about it. At 25 years per generation (the average time to reproduce and grow a replacement human), how many generations have there been since the year 1 A.D.?

$$2{,}000 \text{ years} \div 25 = \underline{\hspace{2cm}}$$

Eighty generations! Not enough to make even a mild dent in our evolution. But imagine how different the world facing today's youngsters is from that of 2,000 years ago. Even 10,000 years represents only 400 generations. Hardly a drop in the evolutionary bucket.

Remember that we are speaking of learning as change—the ability to adapt to new information. Learning is an innate capability of all humans, but like height or body build, it varies by individual. This is key to your work as a trainer, instructor, educator, instructional designer, or training manager. Your job is to help people learn—to help them change. Your job is to facilitate that transformation, not to transmit information.

Here are the results of three training sessions. In your view, which one was the most successful? Place a checkmark in that session's box.

- [ ] **Session 1:** The trainees left the session chuckling over what the trainer had told them about the new products. They thought she was witty and had been entertaining and fun.
- [ ] **Session 2:** The trainees left the session with an armload of manuals and a strong impression that soon they would be dealing with a lot of new products.
- [ ] **Session 3:** The trainees left the session able to position the array of new products and sell them to their customers.

Session 1 apparently was fun, but the only change noted was a new memory of an entertaining presenter. Session 2 suggests that the change wrought was "an impression" of a lot of new products. In Session 3, trainees leave usefully transformed. They can do two things they weren't capable of doing prior to the session: They can position the new products, and they can sell them. Applause for the Session 3 trainer!

How We Learn: Senses, Filters, and Memory

Now we begin our guided tour of the human body and brain with some fascinating pauses to view learning in action. Let's start with the senses.[2]

Senses and Perception

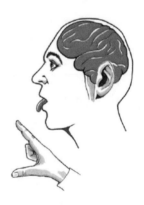

Imagine yourself as a learner. There you are, surrounded by the universe. Just you and the universe.

What connects the internal you to the external universe? How does information from the outside world get in? Answer: It enters through your senses. How many senses? Please insert your number in the box below.

Your guess:

Answer: five.

Take a moment now to do two things. In table 3-1, write the names of the five senses. These five provide us with all of our sensory inputs—every piece of information we obtain from the outside world. Then estimate what percentage of all the sensory information we receive comes to us through each sense and write that number to the right of the sense. Another way of answering this is to estimate the processing capability of each sense compared with that of the others (how much information we can gather from each sense in the same unit of time relative to one another). Assume all senses are working perfectly, with no impairments.

Table 3-1. Senses Percent of Information, Estimated

Sense	Percentage of Information
	Total: 100%

The answers are in table 3-2.

Table 3-2. Senses Percent of Information, Actual

Senses	Percent
Sight	83.0%
Hearing	11.0%
Smell	3.5%
Touch	1.5%
Taste	1.0%
	Total: 100%

Surprised? You won't be after you reason it out. Imagine that you're in an open field. It's a calm, clear day. How far can you see? Probably 50 miles, maybe more.

Hear? A mile or two. Smell? Ten to 20 yards if no wind is blowing. Touch? Arm's length. Taste? A couple of inches.

Let's try a simple demonstration. Close your eyes. Open them for one second. Note how much you saw (shape, color, texture, depth, space, position, and so forth). If you listened to an orchestra playing, would you perceive as much complexity and individuality in the same one second? What about smell? Touch? Taste? This demonstrates how powerful our sense of sight is. Hearing processes less information in the same timeframe. Smell, less than hearing. Touch, even less. Taste is very limited.

It's important to remember that the human learner has multiple senses, each with different processing capacities. Sight, obviously, is extremely important for learning because it is such a major sense. Hearing is also enormously important because through our hearing we acquire language, especially in early childhood. Language provides us with the words and concepts to name and explain phenomena. Together these two powerful senses help us perceive much of what surrounds us. The five senses are the portals through which the raw materials for learning enter our bodies.

 The more of the learner's senses we engage in organized and meaningful ways, the more easily learning can occur.

A note of caution, however. Numerous advocates of multimedia instruction aimed at targeting multiple senses hype systems and methods that use combinations of media and assert that these are highly effective for learning. This type of oversimplified and wholesale advocacy is *not* supported by research. While the notion of multisensory instruction may please learners initially, especially the combination of auditory plus visual presentation, research evidence suggests that this may, in fact, overwhelm learners' information-processing capabilities. Use of attractive, "seductive" elements often does nothing more than add irrelevant noise to the learner's information-processing system.[3] There is a major distinction between spatially and temporally *integrated* multisensory input versus mixtures of not-well-connected audiovisual (and even other) sensory messages. The evidence indicates that the former has a beneficial effect whereas the latter tends to produce a decremental (negative) effect on learning.[4]

Filtering the Stimuli: The Brain Stem, the Autonomic Nervous System, and the Endocrine System

Information is constantly bombarding our senses. Do we perceive all of it?

☐ **Yes**   ☐ **No**

Test yourself. Before we asked this question, were you even aware of the sensations your blouse or shirt was creating on your body? Did you hear every sound around you? When you were concentrating, did noises seem to fade out? Our human makeup is such that we selectively perceive environmental stimuli. We only notice what appears to be relevant. In your opinion, is that good?

☐ **Yes** ☐ **No**

From a survival perspective, the answer is a resounding yes. If we perceived everything around us, we would not be able to eliminate the irrelevant. That lion bearing down on us should command all of our attention, and the pretty blue flower nearby should not distract us.

As an information-processing organism, we are hardwired with an automatic ability to filter out perceptual irrelevancies. It is part of the role three key systems in the human body—the brain stem, the autonomic nervous system,[5] and the endocrine system—play. These automatically adjust our awareness to environmental stimuli. They create what is scientifically referred to as "arousal," which triggers the release of adrenaline to increase heart rate and thus pump more oxygen to the muscles and brain for fight or flight. In particular, the autonomic nervous system manages respiration. It causes our attention to be alert and aroused by environmental information or to ignore it. Figure 3-1 depicts this gatekeeper function.

Attention, like breathing, tends to be automatically controlled. You can take charge of both for a short time, but as soon as you cease consciously controlling them, they revert to automatic. From a training-learning perspective, that is very important. Whether it be a live trainer, a computer-mediated learning program, or a video clip in a DVD, if the learner unconsciously feels that the information is not

Figure 3-1. The Autonomic Nervous System Filters External Stimuli

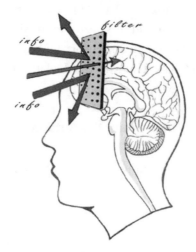

vital to his or her needs, the autonomic system may raise the threshold of sensory input and filter out what is being transmitted. As a result, there is no perception and no learning.

Short-Term Memory: Time and Capacity

Information that passes our perceptual filters enters our short-term memory. That's not a place; it's an information-treatment function. The information is examined and either dropped or passed into long-term memory. How short is short-term memory? Imagine receiving a piece of information in a training session. What would you estimate to be the length of time that short-term memory will hold that piece of information, if left untreated, before it totally disappears?

- ☐ 10 to 15 seconds
- ☐ one to two minutes
- ☐ one to two hours.

If untreated, information in short-term memory begins to disappear almost immediately and is gone in somewhere between 10 and 15 seconds. Short-term memory is like a buffer zone. It fills up rapidly and then quickly empties. This is due to a process known as endocytosis, which causes short-term memory to decay. From a practical perspective, this is also because survival requires you to treat, sort, eliminate, or store information at great speed. Thank those long-gone ancestors whose superior learning capabilities enabled them to live enough years to pass those wonderful characteristics on to us.

How much information can we hold in short-term memory? Not much. For a long time, research suggested that five to nine items (or chunks) of information can be accommodated at a time. The size of a chunk depends on the prior knowledge of the learner. For example, is 213 one item or three? The answer is, "it depends." If those are three individual digits to be retained, they are three items. If you see the three numbers as a Los Angeles telephone area code, you process the code as a single chunk. More recent research suggests that more individual variability exists than previously thought.[6] More than likely, however, for most people, around four "chunks" may be more accurate. Frightening, isn't it?

For training and learning purposes, regardless of capacity, it's important to create meaningful chunks that condense several pieces of information into one. This facilitates perception, learning, and retention. Here's an example:

- ▶ The four cardinal points of a compass are north (N), east (E), west (W), and south (S) *(four items to store in memory)*.
- ▶ Remember this acronym: NEWS *(one item to store in memory)*.

By creating a single chunk, we reduce the short-term memory load. The more naïve the learner is (that is, the less prior knowledge she or he possesses for a given topic), the more rapidly short-term memory fills up. When learners are in information-overload mode, it doesn't matter how much data you transmit. They can no longer efficiently learn and retain.

Long-Term Memory: Time and Capacity

If the learner views the information in short-term memory as important for storage (usually an unconscious decision), then the information enters long-term memory. How long is long-term memory? Think of when you were a child and of a friend or a favorite toy you have not thought about in years. Can you "picture" that friend or toy? Your ability to do so indicates that long-term memory really means l-o-n-g. Depending on how we store information in our long-term memory warehouse, we may retrieve it many years later. If it is not a distinct, highly unique memory, it may become blended and confused with others, but well-organized and stored information can be retrieved throughout your whole lifetime.

For fun, let's test your long-term memory. Fill in the blanks in the following statements. Of course, you will not recall any of these that you didn't originally learn.

1. The first human to set foot on the moon was _____.
2. There are _____ days in September.
3. The square on the _____ of a right-angled triangle is equal to the sum of the squares on the other two sides.
4. $9 \times 9 =$ _____.
5. Einstein's famous formula is E = _____.

That was a fact-recall exercise. Here are the correct answers:

> *Answers:*
> 1. Neil Armstrong
> 2. 30
> 3. hypotenuse
> 4. 81
> 5. mc^2

How well did you do? Most of our test subjects scored four or five out of five even though they had not used these facts for many years. The information was well retained.

With respect to capacity, long-term memory is practically limitless. The human brain has the potential to store huge amounts of information. Never worry about filling it up. The problem is not in the storage but rather in the retrieval.

What Does This Mean for the Learner … and the Trainer?

Learners generally want to learn; trainers want learners to learn. The disconnect arises in the "what" and the "how" of learning. By understanding that learners are information-treating organisms with sensory capacities, information-processing constraints, and memory load limits, and by attending to their information-handling and storage capabilities, we can facilitate what both learners and trainers want— effective learning. Remember these two key points:

- Learning is change. This change begins with receiving information from as many senses as possible in an integrated, reinforcing manner. If the information is transmitted in a meaningful, organized, and relevant way, it will pass through the learner's filters and enter his or her short-term memory.
- Information that is chunked and organized appropriately to the learner's ability and experience level is more easily stored in long-term memory and, most important, more readily retrieved.

Learning is change in mental (cognitive) structures, change in the potential for new behaviors. The learner is transformed. The learner's mind is no longer the same as it was before the learning took place. The transformation provides the learner with the ability to act in new ways.

Remember This

We close this chapter with a brief review challenge. Select the word or phrase in parentheses that best fits each of the following statements:

1. In designing and delivering training, it is more important to focus on the characteristics of the (*learner/trainer*) than of the (*learner/trainer*).
2. Learning means (*memorizing/change*).
3. Humans have a (*small/large*) capacity to learn.
4. Our learning characteristics have been programmed for (*today's environment / an environment that no longer exists*).
5. The purpose of excellent training is (*transformation of the learner / transmission of clear content*).
6. Each of our senses has (*the same/different*) processing capacities.
7. Most of the time, the environmental information we attend to and how much we focus on it are governed by our (*conscious will / unconscious brain and nervous systems*).
8. The short-term memory of a novice learner fills up (*rapidly/slowly*).
9. "Chunking" information required for learning (*facilitates/impedes*) retention and retrieval.
10. The main challenge with information in long-term memory is (*retrieval/storage*).

Here are the answers and comments:

1. In designing and delivering training, it is more important to focus on the characteristics of the learner than of the trainer. As any good salesperson will tell you, start with the customer. Our learners are the starting point. We are merely the means for achieving success that they and the organization value.

2. Learning means change. The change occurs in the learner's cognitive structures, which results in the potential for behavior change.

3. Humans have a large capacity to learn. We have not yet calculated just how great it is and perhaps never will. However, we must respect the information-processing capacities of our human learners.

4. Our learning characteristics have been programmed for an environment that no longer exists. Humans have evolved over millions of years. We are born with an ability to adapt to our environment. The modern classroom and workplace are completely different from the environments of our ancestors. We use our characteristics that favor learning, and we manage those that conflict with it.

5. The purpose of excellent training is transformation of the learner. (Enough said already!)

6. Each of our senses has different processing capacities. Although they vary a great deal, all the senses are important for different learning requirements. Taste, the lowly 1 percent sense, can be critical for survival in dealing with food.

7. Most of the time, the environmental information we attend to and how much we focus on it are governed by our unconscious brain and nervous systems. These non-voluntary mechanisms are critical to survival in a hostile environment.

8. The short-term memory of a novice learner fills up rapidly. Unfamiliarity with new subject matter or skills produces numerous tiny chunks of information bombarding short-term memory. The novice learner is soon in information overload, and the learning system falters. The result is confusion or turn-off.

9. "Chunking" information required for learning facilitates retention and retrieval. Chunking assembles individual items into a single, comprehensible unit. For example, "BMW" (the familiar name of a car manufacturer—one chunk) is also a mnemonic for the order in which you place objects on a table from left to right when doing a "proper" setting: bread (plate), main (course plate), water (glass): BMW. This helps a novice server set a table

correctly and takes up far less space in short-term memory than the full seven words of the sequence.

10. The main challenge with information in long-term memory is retrieval. Putting things into long-term memory is much easier than finding things you stored days, weeks, months, or even decades ago. As trainers, our challenge is to organize for storage/retention and facilitate with practice for retrieval.

Section 2

What You Must Know
to Be a Better Trainer

Chapter 4

Getting Learners to Learn

Chapter highlights:

▶ Differences between how experts and novices process information

▶ Different types of knowledge and how each is processed

▶ The trouble with subject matter experts

▶ The key role of the trainer.

This chapter begins with three common scenes in which we find a knowledgeable person attempting to teach a novice learner. As you read each one, ask yourself the following questions:

▶ Why isn't this working?

▶ Is it anyone's fault?

▶ Have I ever been in a similar situation, either on the giving or the receiving end?

▶ What was the result?

Scene 1: Driven to Distraction

Father: All right, Gail. Now press on the clutch—no, not the brake, the clutch—with your left, not your right, foot.

Gail: Should I do it fast or slow?

Father: Push down fast, but not too fast. Now, move the gearshift into first gear. Then ease up on the clutch as you give it gas.

Gail: Do I move the gearshift fast or slowly? Do I use my left foot for the clutch? And do I push it fast or slowly?

Father: It doesn't matter. For the gearshift, I mean. And what did you ask about the left foot? Of course, the left foot. And do it … no … no … you're giving it too much gas!

Gail: Daddy, the car is bouncing. What do I do now?

Father: Hit the clutch! Stop pressing on the gas! Hit the brake! Oh no! Now look what you've done!

Gail: I hate driving! I hate you! I quit!

Scene 2: As Easy as Cherry Pie

Junior: Grandma, I love your cherry pie. Can you tell me the recipe so I can make one?

Grandma: Well, I'll try. You need lots of flour, some sugar, eggs, and milk.

Junior: Do you need cherries?

Grandma: What a silly question! Why, of course. You can't make cherry pie without cherries.

Junior: How much flour? And sugar? And all the other stuff?

Grandma: Well. I guess you need about three cups of flour … or is it four? And the sugar … let me think … you know, I can't say for sure. Isn't that strange? And I've been baking these pies for more than 60 years.

Junior: You mean you can't tell me how to make a cherry pie, Grandma?

Scene 3: Electrified

Experienced customer agent (CA): Now we come to a really important part of your job—informing customers of a scheduled electrical shutdown.

Novice CA: Do I call them all up?

Experienced CA: No … yes … no. Well, sort of. I mean not you personally. Well, sort of personally. You record a voice message and send it out.

Novice CA: How do I know whom to call?

Experienced CA: By accessing the customer database and matching the affected transmission lines with the appropriate customer electrical address.

Novice CA: And how do I know which transmission lines are affected? Also, where's the database?

Experienced CA: *(losing patience)* From the work orders. And the database is in the computer.

Novice CA: Will I find their street addresses and phone numbers there?

Experienced CA: *(exasperated)* No. Only their electrical addresses. You know, the alphanumeric code related to a transformer or cut-off point!

Novice CA: Huh?

Let's analyze what happened in those three scenes. You can compare your answers to the questions we asked you up front with our answers.

Why isn't this working? In all of the scenes, it is obvious that learning isn't advancing very quickly. In each case, we had a true subject matter expert (commonly known as an SME) and a novice learner. You would think that if these SMEs know so much, they should have no trouble making the other person learn. But it's not happening because experts and novices do not process information in the same way. In fact, the greater the expertise, the less the expert thinks like a novice learner.

Surely, you have had someone give you directions in a town or location that you've never visited before. The dialogue goes something like this:

Direction giver:	You get on Mill Creek Highway and head west for a few miles until you see School Road. Get off and take it north for, oh, a couple of miles to the Fairlane strip mall. Just a block before, you'll turn into a small lane—it's a bit hard to see because of the trees, but there's a Johnny's Pizza just behind it.
Direction taker:	*(head swimming)* Where's Mill Creek Highway?
Direction giver:	You're on Mill Creek Highway.
Direction taker:	But it says Highway 10.
Direction giver:	Yep. That's Mill Creek Highway all right. Just follow my directions, and you can't miss it.

And have you missed it? You can see that how the expert direction giver views his world differs from the way the novice direction taker sees it. Stand by—the problems intensify before we finally navigate our way through them.

Is it anyone's fault? The succinct answer is "no." In each scene, including this last one, both parties desire a successful outcome. Both are fully motivated and actively engaged in the teaching-learning process, but somehow things fall apart.

What was the result? Learning breakdown. We have yet to meet someone who has not participated in one of these frustrating episodes. There is a prevalent belief that the best way to learn something is to ask an expert, despite the fact that research demonstrates, time and again, how differently experts and novices view the world—and, more specifically, how something should be learned.[1]

Here's a good example: In a classic research study, novice and expert chess players were shown chess games in progress, with pieces spread all over the board. The board and pieces were then hidden after several seconds, and both the experts and the novices were asked to set up the chess pieces to reproduce exactly what they had seen. Who do you imagine more accurately placed the chess pieces?

☐ expert chess players
☐ novices.

The experts did far better. They perceived patterns, chunked the information, and didn't clutter their short-term memories with detail. Novices, focusing on individual pieces, fared poorly. The two groups viewed the world in markedly different ways.[2]

Different Types of Knowledge: Declarative and Procedural

Here's a challenge for you. You most likely live in an apartment or house. You're there every day, or at least frequently. To a certain extent, you are an expert on your home. In the box below, write the number of windows in your home. If you are at home, don't go around physically counting. Access this information from your memory. Accuracy is important, so take your time.

Number of windows:

Unless you recently replaced or bought coverings for all of your windows, you probably didn't have the answer instantaneously. In our experiments we find that people come up with the answer the same way you probably did. First, you pictured your home. Then you wandered through it mentally. If there were levels, you went floor by floor. If we were watching you, we probably would have seen your eyes go out of focus and then actually move as you "looked inward" and walked through your home. We might even have seen your lips moving as you counted windows. That is very normal. But why couldn't you simply state the number of windows instantaneously? After all, you're an expert on your home. The answer to that question addresses the core of the major problem in each of the earlier scenes. Keep reading to discover why.

 Become familiar with these two terms: declarative knowledge and procedural knowledge. They are key to unlocking many learning mysteries.[3]

The human brain is amazing. It is an intricate system of millions of individual elements, each doing its own thing. Yet, somehow it all works. The brain is not a coherently designed and engineered organ. We are born with a brain that carries out myriad simultaneous and independent activities. Most parts of the brain are totally oblivious of the activities going on in other parts. Among the activities the brain conducts is the processing of information for learning. That information, which comes from the outside world, is taken in and transformed into knowledge. The knowledge we possess that allows us to name, explain, and talk about matters is called *declarative knowledge*. No other species on earth even vaguely comes close to humans in our ability to learn and use declarative knowledge.

Look at these four items and put a checkmark beside the actions you imagine require declarative knowledge:

☐ 1. Name the capital of France.
☐ 2. Ride a bicycle.
☐ 3. Explain the causes of World War II.
☐ 4. Navigate a database.

Items 1 and 3 are examples of declarative knowledge (name, explain, and/or talk about). Items 2 and 4 are examples of another important category: *procedural knowledge*. That type of knowledge enables us to act and do things, to perform tasks. Unlike declarative knowledge, which is almost exclusively restricted to humans in any sophisticated form, procedural knowledge is readily available to all animals.

So, how related are declarative and procedural knowledge? Let's figure this out for ourselves. Naming the number of windows in your home required declarative knowledge. Although you are an expert about your home, you didn't have the number readily available in declarative form. Instead, your expertise is in walking through your various rooms and locating windows—procedural knowledge. You can "do," but not readily "say." This is because humans process declarative knowledge and procedural knowledge very differently.

Can you ride a bicycle? Can you maintain your balance on the bicycle? Most people answer "yes" to both questions. Now explain exactly what your body does to keep the bicycle from falling down. You might mention pedaling, moving from side to side, holding on to the handlebars, and so forth. When we probe bicycle riders about *exactly* what they do to keep the bike steady, however, they end up saying, "I can't explain it. I just do it."

Most expertise develops that way. The majority of what we have learned to do has been acquired without words. By trial and error over time, we simply have built up the capability to do it. And here's where that presents a problem in training: Organizations commonly approach someone who knows how to do something (an informal definition of an expert) and ask him or her to teach novices how to do it.

Now for a paradox: These experts have acquired their capability over time and with practice. In other words, they possess most of their expertise in the form of *(select one):*

- ☐ declarative knowledge
- ☐ procedural knowledge.

In almost all cases, their expertise is in the form of procedural knowledge. But when asked to train others, usually in a short amount of time, they are expected to transmit their knowledge by explaining, giving examples, and providing contexts and cases. In other words, they teach *(select one):*

- ☐ declaratively
- ☐ procedurally.

The experts deliver declaratively. Then the learners have to convert the declarative knowledge from training back into procedural knowledge to meet the expectation of being able to "do" things in a new way. Simple and vivid examples of this are when a golf pro tells you how to hit a golf ball straight or a skating coach tells you how to make a quick stop when rollerblading. Much easier said (declarative) than done (procedural)!

Research on learning tells us that what we learn declaratively cannot be readily transformed into procedural knowledge unless we already possess similar procedural knowledge. The reverse is also true. Procedural knowledge does not easily convert to declarative knowledge. Therefore, although you know your home well and you mentally walked through it to count the windows, you still may have missed a few.

This conversion difficulty also accounts for the problems in our earlier scenes:

- ▶ Daddy can't convert his car-driving knowledge (acquired procedurally) to the right declarative language. Even if he could, Gail can't readily absorb his declarative explanations and convert them into procedural capabilities.
- ▶ Grandma knows how to bake a cherry pie, but can't recite the recipe.
- ▶ The experienced customer agent can inform customers of electrical shutdowns, but has obviously confused his novice learner.
- ▶ The local resident can't readily speak the clear directions that will help the tourist find his way from Mill Creek Highway.

Here's a fun exercise that demonstrates how expertise that lets us do things (procedural knowledge) simply does not provide all the declarative details. In fact, we often don't even have a (declarative) explanation for how to do it right (procedurally).

Correct the grammar in these two sentences:

When I were in Paris, I ate a croissant with every meal.

_____

If I was in Paris, I would eat a croissant with every meal.

_____

You most likely changed each one correctly. (When I *was* in Paris, I ate a croissant with every meal. If I *were* in Paris, I would eat a croissant with every meal.) Unless you are a grammar specialist and have the declarative knowledge, it is unlikely that you can explain (declaratively) why you corrected each of the above (procedurally).

Here is the declarative explanation: "When I was in Paris..." states a *fact*. This requires use of the *indicative mood* in English grammar. The form "was" is the correct first person singular past perfect indicative form. Yay! However, "If I were..." states a *possibility*, which in formal English grammar requires use of the *subjunctive mood* and "I were" is the correct first person form. You did it (procedurally)! Did you know all of this (declaratively)? Ah well, be that as it may, you probably get the point.[4]

In our testing of this exercise, very few people knew why each form was right. Several knew about the subjunctive or spoke about "conditional" situations, but no one absolutely nailed it despite the high rate of procedural success. (Incidentally, in the United States saying, "If I was..." is informally acceptable in the spoken form—more declarative information.)

With an awareness of the kind of knowledge we want our learners to acquire—declarative or procedural—we can adjust the way we present learning material to them. If it's talk-about knowledge (for example, what or why information, fact recall, or names), we can create activities that provide what must be learned and have our learners practice declaratively. If we want them to acquire do and use types of knowledge, our strategy changes to a more hands-on approach. The bottom line is to match what our learners have to learn with the mode of training/instruction/education we employ. (We'll cover this in a more planned and organized fashion in chapter 6.)

One final note on these two types of knowledge. Gaining procedural knowledge eventually allows us to gain fluency in doing things without having to think about what we are engaged in. Running a photocopier or processing an insurance claim are procedural tasks that we can expertly deal with through practice. However, what if we change the model of photocopier to a more computerized version, with buttons and viewing panels in different places, or what if the insurance claim forms change and the rules governing how they are to be handled alter?

Methods to produce efficient procedural knowledge result in rapid fluency, *so long as the conditions remain the same.* Declarative knowledge allows us to generalize to new circumstances through explanations. It may slow down the performance, but it permits adaptation to new requirements. We may want our soldiers to assemble and disassemble a certain model of firearm they regularly use to the point of *automaticity* (act perfectly without thinking about it). What if they suddenly find themselves on the battlefield with a different firearm? Without some form of declarative, mental rules about how a variety of models work, they may get lost trying to make sure it works, flounder about in confusion, and expose themselves to increased risk.

The bottom line is that while each type of knowledge requires a specific form of instruction for desired performance, often a combination of both—explanation and practice—works to produce a more effective result.[5]

Key Ingredients for Learning

Cognitive psychology research suggests that three major factors influence how much and how well we learn: ability, prior knowledge, and motivation. Let's examine each of these in detail.[6]

Ability

The capacity with which we were born that enables us to acquire new skills and knowledge varies among individuals. Just like height or musculature, we arrive on the scene with a certain mental (or learning) potential. It may be unfair but some of us are born taller, slimmer, more physically attractive, or able to learn more quickly than others.

This general learning ability is the intellectual capacity with which we are genetically endowed. It strongly influences our overall capability to learn. Note the word "general." Those who have greater general ability grasp more quickly, comprehend more easily, and recall more efficiently than others do. They seem to get it faster and play it back or even enhance it better than those not as intellectually able.

Recently, many nuances have been added to the construct *ability* and its almost synonymous cousin, intelligence (usually defined as the ability to think about ideas, analyze situations, and solve problems, which is measured through various types of intelligence tests). While general ability is usually broken down into nonverbal ability, concrete reasoning ability, and abstract reasoning ability, researchers have stretched further into "multiple intelligences."[7] Educational psychologists now view individuals as multifaceted and have created tests to measure verbal linguistic, mathematical logical, musical, visual spatial, bodily kinesthetic, interpersonal, naturalistic, and even existential "intelligences." In all cases, these appear to be considered inherent characteristics.

Obviously, like musculature, the way in which ability is fostered and trained can seriously affect how well one's cerebral (and other) capabilities grow and develop. As trainers, it is important for us to note that learners vary in their ability to learn. We have to be aware of the differences in ability and compensate for those who do not learn as rapidly as others. We also have to keep the more generally able learners constantly stimulated and challenged to maintain their focus.

Although we all possess general intellectual ability, we also are endowed with specific abilities at birth. An ear for music, a golden voice, athletic agility, and artistic talent are extremely valuable specific learning abilities that are more important than general intellectual capability in certain instances. The innate, specific abilities of Michael Jordan in basketball, Barbra Streisand in music, and Pablo Picasso in art have played enormous roles in allowing those "learners" to achieve far beyond others who may have received the same "training."[8]

Prior Knowledge

General and specific abilities greatly influence learning, but how much a person already knows about what he or she is being taught also strongly affects learning.[9] A brilliant philosopher or mathematician may not learn as well as a less intellectually gifted carpenter when receiving some new piece of instruction about carpentry. Prior knowledge helps the learner acquire additional knowledge or skills more rapidly.

Let's test that assertion. Below are two French verbs—one a regular verb, the other irregular. Which one is the irregular verb?

☐ *danser*
☐ *tenir.*

In chapter 2, you learned that French regular verbs end in "er." If you picked that up then, you probably correctly selected *tenir* as the irregular verb above. Your prior knowledge helped here. If you missed it, that's OK. You didn't possess the prior knowledge, and you had to work harder. So, the more you know about something, the easier it is to acquire additional knowledge and skills in that subject.

Motivation

We all have seen the power of high motivation—the desire to achieve something. We also have seen the reverse: Those who don't care, have no drive, or seem to lack interest in learning rarely achieve proficiency in new knowledge and skills. We often talk about motivation and its importance, but what is it? Motivation appears to be affected by three major factors: value, confidence, and mood.

Value. The more we value something, the more motivated we are about it. In figure 4-1, we have placed *motivation* on the vertical axis and *value* on the horizontal. Notice that as the learner attributes a greater value to what is to be learned, motivation increases. If you value being seen as someone who knows opera or football, you will become more inspired (that is, motivated) to learn about it. The higher the value attributed to what is to be learned, the greater the motivation.

Figure 4-1. Motivation Increases With Value

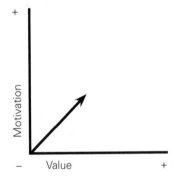

Confidence. If you feel totally inept in your ability to learn something, how motivated are you to try?

- ☐ highly motivated
- ☐ unmotivated.

The answer, of course, is unmotivated. Low confidence in learning is strongly correlated with low motivation. As the confidence of the learner increases, so does the motivation, as illustrated in figure 4-2.

Overconfidence, however, leads to a decline in motivation. If the learner feels that "this is so easy, I don't even need to try," motivation plummets, as shown in figure 4-3.

The optimal point of motivation is where the learner has enough confidence to feel she or he can succeed, but not so much that the desire to learn declines. This

Figure 4-2. Motivation Increases With Confidence

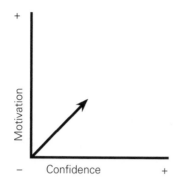

Figure 4-3. Overconfidence Reduces Motivation

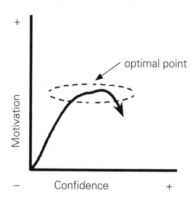

high point of motivation is one of challenge ("I have to work at it to succeed") and security ("if I do work at it, I know I can succeed").

Mood. We all know that if we're not in the mood, our motivation to learn goes down. Personal feelings affect our mood as does the atmosphere of the learning and working environment. A positive learning-working environment tends to improve a person's mood and, hence, his or her motivation as illustrated in figure 4-4. But a frivolous or manic mood might have bizarre and unpredictable effects on motivation. A positive mood is one in which you are open and optimistic without being flighty or euphoric.[10]

To summarize this section on the three key factors that affect learning—ability, prior knowledge, and motivation—trainers are generally content people placed in the role of helping people acquire sufficient knowledge and skills to perform something they don't know how to do. Asking them to step outside of their area of

Figure 4-4. Motivation Increases With Mood

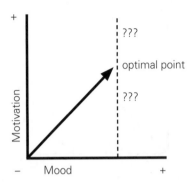

expertise and become totally "customer focused," that is, *learner centered,* is a challenge. However, trainers can derive enormous satisfaction when they see that their charges "get it." By watching learners and sizing up how well they can absorb what the trainer provides, by acknowledging and shoring up prior knowledge, and by exemplifying how worthwhile it is to achieve what the trainer is helping them to attain he or she will experience the high that comes from their successes. If training were just a telling task, everyone would excel at everything.[11]

 ## Adapting for Differences in Ability, Prior Knowledge, and Motivation

Ability, prior knowledge, and motivation strongly affect learning. Can we, as trainers, instructors, educators, or managers of learning influence all of these? Fortunately, the answer is "yes."

Ability

Although we can't alter a person's ability, we can observe and detect his or her strengths and weaknesses. As a result, we can adapt the learning system by taking the following measures:

- ▶ adjusting the amount of time for learning
- ▶ providing more practice for those who require it
- ▶ simplifying and breaking learning into smaller chunks for those who are experiencing learning difficulties
- ▶ providing additional support for those who need it
- ▶ including activities with greater challenge for those who learn more quickly
- ▶ providing alternative learning paths.

Computerized testing and assessment capabilities built into modern learning management systems, which are now very present in medium and large organizations, make determining the ability levels of learners somewhat easier. Performance tests can be created and deployed. Time to acquire skills can be tracked. Study of a learner's learning choices and paths can also provide clues. The purpose of all of this, of course, is to better determine learner ability and provide necessary and sufficient instructional support.

Those are only a few ways of compensating for differences in learning ability. The key is to observe and acknowledge such variations and make suitable modifications to the instruction, whether through live interaction with trainers and/or peers, online, from a book, or through practical experiences on the job.

Prior Knowledge

If learners are missing prerequisite knowledge and skills, we can make adjustments to these gaps by

- ▶ creating pre-learning session materials to close the gaps
- ▶ building special supplementary learning events prior to or concurrent with the learning sessions
- ▶ creating peer tutoring pairs and teams to provide mutual support for overcoming gaps
- ▶ providing overviews and summaries of prerequisite content in outline or summary form
- ▶ directing learners to online sites that can fill knowledge or skill gaps
- ▶ assigning tasks and experiences that fill in missing background and knowledge.

That's only a starter list. Offering sources of knowledge or resources for acquiring prerequisite skills can help bring learners up to speed quickly.

Motivation

Based on the three major factors that affect motivation, we can overcome deficiencies in the following ways:

- ▶ Enhancing the value of what is to be learned. Show the learners what's in it for them. Provide examples of benefits. Show them admired role models valuing what is to be learned. The more the learners perceive personal value in what they are learning, the more motivated they will become.
- ▶ Adjusting the learners' confidence levels with respect to the learning content. Be supportive to build their confidence that they can learn but provide sufficient challenge so that they don't become overconfident about it.

▶ Creating a positive learning atmosphere and work climate. The more open and optimistic the context you build, the more open and positive the learners will be, and that leads to greater motivation and to learning. Watch out for threat levels during training. Stress that breeds anxiety and fear of failure severely dampens learning.

Keep in mind that all learners are different. Whether as a group in a classroom, as a team at the worksite, or individually through a manual or via computer in real time or asynchronously, they come to us with widely differing characteristics. Training, in its broadest sense, is a compensation for what each of our learners lack.[12] Just imagine what our job would be if all of our learners came to us with elevated general and specific learning abilities, vast prior knowledge, and tremendous motivation. Would we *(check one)*:

☐ teach until they learned what we provided them?
☐ give them the learning resources and then get out of their way, providing only feedback and reinforcement as they progressed?

If you checked off the second box, you're right. Talented, knowledgeable, motivated learners only require learning resources and useful feedback that is corrective to get them back on track when they have erred and confirming to let them know when they got it right. The less they possess of ability, prior knowledge, and motivation, the more we trainers have to work to compensate for what they lack.

Yes, that's our job—compensating for what learners don't have, managing the learning context, and providing feedback and rewards for success.

Remember This

Let's close this chapter with a summary of the main points. Of course you will have to do most of the work. Select what you believe to be the best word to fit each sentence below. Cross out the inappropriate options. Our role will be to offer feedback and provide a reward. We're just getting out of your way.

1. Experts and novices treat the same content information (*similarly/differently*).
2. The size of a chunk of information is (*larger/smaller*) for a novice than for an expert.
3. An expert mechanic has acquired most of her expertise (*declaratively/procedurally*).
4. The same mechanic, when assigned to instruct a group, usually transmits her expertise (*declaratively/procedurally*).
5. The mechanic-instructor's learners are then expected to go back to the job and apply the new knowledge (*declaratively/procedurally*).

6. Often a combination of both declarative and procedural instruction—explanation and practice—works to produce a (*more/less*) effective result.
7. Three key ingredients for learning are ability, prior knowledge, and (*motivation/information*).
8. The (*more/less*) a learner values what is to be learned, the higher his or her motivation.
9. Highly motivated, able learners with excellent prior knowledge require (*more/less*) teaching.
10. Training activities are a compensation for what the learner (*possesses/lacks*).

Now here's our feedback:

1. Experts and novices treat the same content information differently. Novices' short-term memories rapidly fill with new content, and they easily plunge into information overload.
2. The size of a chunk of information is smaller for a novice than for an expert. An expert's chunk may contain a great deal of condensed information. For novices, each detail frequently becomes an individual chunk.
3. An expert mechanic has acquired most of her expertise procedurally—by doing rather than by naming and talking about what she has done.
4. The same mechanic, when assigned to instruct a group, usually transmits her expertise declaratively. She talks about, describes, and explains what she thinks she does in her work—and that may not be fully accurate or complete.
5. The mechanic-instructor's learners are then expected to go back to the job and apply the new knowledge procedurally. The aim is to get them to do the job. What a paradox!
6. Often a combination of both declarative and procedural instruction—explanation and practice—works to produce a more effective result. The declarative portion provides a framework for the application. It can help learners deal with new situations, adapting procedural knowledge they have acquired.
7. Three key ingredients for learning are ability, prior knowledge, and motivation. At this point, you've got it. You require no further explanation.
8. The more a learner values what is to be learned, the higher his or her motivation. There is a straight-line relationship between perceived value and motivation.
9. Highly motivated, able learners with excellent prior knowledge require less teaching. Our instruction should provide only what the learner is lacking.
10. Training activities are a compensation for what the learner lacks. The greater the abilities, prior knowledge, and motivation the learners possess, the less they require of us. We increase our support appropriately.

Organizations generally select trainers on the basis of subject matter expertise, and in this chapter we have seen how that leads to instructional problems. Content is not enough.

We are dealing with adult learners. Their success is our success. So let's proceed to the next chapter to discover how we can get into our learners' heads and hearts to help them learn.

Chapter 5

Adult Learning Principles

Chapter highlights:

▶ Four key adult learning principles
▶ Several sample situations
▶ The Training Golden Rule.

Have you ever completed a course of study that truly inspired you? One in which you really got a lot out of the learning experience? You left feeling more competent—at least understanding how you could become more competent—and confident that you could do it! We hate to interrupt this pleasant reminiscence, but instruction also has a darker side.

Have you ever taken a course or participated in a learning session that left you disappointed? Did you tune out and turn off early in the session? Although you had some interest to learn and grow in whatever was being presented when you arrived, you left with a negative attitude and with little you could use.

Let's look at what turns adult learners on or off, and what helps or disrupts their willingness to learn.

Good Classes and Bad Classes

What makes a great learning experience? We have posed this question to thousands of working adults, from managers operating in executive offices to workers out on the front line, from highly sophisticated knowledge professionals to routine-task physical workers. We've been repeatedly amazed by the similarity of responses across all work levels and types and all worker groups. Let's see how your responses match. Here is the specific question we always ask: Think of a great course, class, or learning session you attended. What made it great for you?

Examine table 5-1. Those are some of the most common responses we've heard in the past. Check off those that apply in your case. We've left a few blanks for you to add your own.

Now, over to the flip side. We posed the following question to our adult groups: Think of a rotten course, class, or learning session you attended. For you, what made it rotten?

Table 5-1. Examples of What Makes Great Training

☐ It responded to my needs.
☐ I could see how it applied to me.
☐ There was a lot of participation.
☐ I was drawn in quickly.
☐ The explanations were clear and concise.
☐ I could relate to the examples.
☐ It applied to my job.
☐ I could ask questions at any time.
☐ I didn't feel stupid.
☐ I understood where I was going.
☐ There were lots of takeaways I could use.
☐ It helped me do my work better.
☐ The session was interactive.
☐ I could try out what was taught.
☐ I got feedback on how I did.
☐ There was warmth and humor.
☐ I learned a lot from the other participants.
☐ The materials were clear and useful.
☐ I felt respected.
☐ There was lots of two-way communication.
☐ There wasn't a lot of time wasted.
☐ The instructor "spoke my language."
☐ I felt I added value to the session.
☐ I learned a lot of useful stuff for me.
☐ _____
☐ _____
☐ _____

In table 5-2, check off the items that you feel apply to your negative experiences. Adult learners we questioned generated the items in table 5-2.

Table 5-2. Examples of What Makes Training Poor

☐ It was too far removed from my interests.
☐ I couldn't see how I would use it.
☐ It was a one-way transmission of information.
☐ I soon was in information overload.
☐ There was little to no discussion.
☐ There was little to no practice.
☐ There was little to no feedback to me personally on what I did.
☐ The materials were poorly designed.
☐ A lot of time was wasted.
☐ There was very little I could take back to my job.
☐ The content was OK but the methods for communicating were poor.
☐ I was a passive listener most of the time.
☐ I couldn't understand what was being taught.
☐ The language and/or jargon lost me.
☐ There were few, if any, examples that I understood.
☐ It was dull, monotonous, and boring.
☐ There was little or no class interaction with other participants.
☐ I was just another body in the course.
☐ I contributed nothing or little to the session.
☐ I didn't learn much.
☐ I couldn't ask questions when I wanted.
☐ _____
☐ _____
☐ _____

Let's perform a little analysis on your responses. We can't see them but if they are in the typical range, we generally discover the following:

Good class: Somebody—the instructor, a course designer, or a decision maker of some sort—made an effort to create a learning experience that was relevant to you from a personal perspective (work and/or life); structured it so that you knew where you were going; provided the content in a way that was meaningful to you; gave you opportunities to get involved meaningfully; and provided you with tools and/or a sense of direction for applying what you learned to your work, your life, or both. Bravo! Kudos to the person who made this happen.

Bad class: Somebody, perhaps even the instructor, decided this was useful for you; figured out not only what you needed, but at what level and in what format and sequence it made sense to deliver it; made sure that it was full of the right content that he or she believed you should have; and dumped it into you. You were an empty vessel into which the instructor or the instructional materials poured the contents.

Perhaps we have set up a straw man and your experience wasn't quite that simple or that bad. Nevertheless, in our many years of research and observation we have found few instructional programs—live, computer-based, print-based, or video-based—that truly focus on the needs and characteristics of the adult learner.

The proper care and handling of adult learners is extremely important when building terrific training sessions, regardless of the means of delivery—live or otherwise. Most of the training we have witnessed (confirmed by our research with many adult learners) is reminiscent of our school and college days. Although we were bored or confused by our teachers and professors when we were students, as instructors and trainers we tend to repeat the practices we hated in others.

How can we break out of this pattern? The cues and clues are the items in tables 5-1 and 5-2 that describe good and bad training. We can break away from boring, unproductive practices by focusing on our learners as adults with the same sorts of needs, concerns, desires, fears, frustrations, quirks, ambitions, capabilities, and personal priorities that we have.

Our job, as trainers, instructors, and educators, is to help our adult learners learn. Their success is our success. That sounds simple, but it's challenging. We can do it by understanding how adult learners learn and by applying that insight to our practices. What's great about this is that it all makes sense, is not that hard to do, and is incredibly rewarding. ("Wow! They learned from me, and they can all do it!") In addition, you can test this on yourself. By leaving the trainer role and assuming a learner's position, you get to see that what you are attempting really will work. Be your own guinea pig.

Four Key Adult Learning Principles[1]

Considerable research has been done on adult learning.[2] So much research, in fact, that this chapter could easily expand to become a whole book.[3] For our purposes, however, we focus on four key findings from all that research. These findings were generated by Malcolm Knowles, a leader in the field of adult education (also called "andragogy"), as well as others, and we believe they are the most applicable and meaningful principles for adult learning in the work setting.[4] These four key principles are

- ▶ readiness
- ▶ experience
- ▶ autonomy
- ▶ action.

What follows is a brief review of each of those principles. A concluding section of this chapter will show you how to use the principles effectively to become a star trainer.

Readiness

Imagine the following scene. In one hand I have a pitcher filled with water. In the other I have a glass with a lid. What happens when I try to pour water into the glass? Obviously, it spills over the glass and my hand because the inside of the glass is closed off.

This physical example of wasted effort is analogous to a trainer trying to pour content into a closed adult learner's mind. Not much enters. So what to do? How can we open the mind? The answer is simple and straightforward. Adults come to a learning situation with their own priorities and attitudes. They are ready to learn when they decide to open their minds and spirits to it. How can you get them to do this, especially if they are determined not to do so? There is one truly effective way: Show them in a believable manner that what you have to offer

- ▶ solves a problem or avoids one for them
- ▶ provides an opportunity or increased status
- ▶ includes professional or personal growth.

It must be clear that it is for *them*, not for you or the organization. You can't fill a glass with water if the glass has no opening. You can't fill a learner with skills, knowledge, or new values and attitudes if his or her mind is blocked.

The *readiness* principle is simple: Always focus training on your learners' needs. Make your training session respond to the learner's question: "What's in it for me?" When you can structure your training—whether live, online, or at a distance—so that meaningful benefits are reinforced constantly, both explicitly and implicitly, your learners will open themselves to what you are sharing with them. The following sample situation illustrates that fact.

Sample Situation: Protect Yourself. A group of MBA graduates recruited from the top 10 percent of their classes was in the second week of a training program at the bank. The instructor, a seasoned credit manager, is scratching his head and wondering how to start the afternoon session. According to the training timetable, the subject is the C-549 overdraft protection form. This group of learners is sharp and demanding. They quickly lose interest if the content appears boring. Several instructors have already been crushed by the coldness and lack of interest of the group when it sensed that the topic was boring, not challenging, and not personally valuable. So how will the credit manager teach this priority population for the bank about the important but not exciting C-549 form? He faces his bright, upwardly destined class of young adults and launches into a story:

"Imagine that you've been dreaming for years of owning a Porsche sports car. You really want it. By saving and working extra hours, you finally pull together a decent-size down payment so that you can just make the monthly payments on what you're earning. Finally, you've done it! You go to pick up the car, but suddenly realize you don't have enough cash to get the insurance. It's OK. You'll pick it up, drive it home, and then figure out the insurance.

"Driving back from the dealership, you gaze around, proud of your new wheels. You hope someone you know will spot you. Your eyes wander. Too late you see the garbage truck just ahead of you. You slam on the brakes. There's a screech, followed by a loud bang. Collision!

"As you examine the wreckage, you wonder if you really were lucky not to have been killed. What will you do now, with no insurance, no car, and no money?

"What if you could have had some free insurance that fully protected you from personal financial disaster? An insurance that helps you avoid personal and career disaster? Would you have taken it? Would you like me to hand it to you right now? For free?

"Then, let's meet the C-549, a simple form that protects you, not from an auto wreck, but from a career disaster in the form of a loan you issued that you thought was great, but which suddenly becomes vulnerable. You could be in hot water, but here's C-549! It's your insurance policy, which removes your personal responsibility once it's filled out. Let's examine it closely together. Just imagine. This form can help you protect your Porsche."

If you were one of the young MBA graduates in that training, would you have been caught up in the story? Would you want that free insurance policy? What would you see the instructor offering to do for you? *(Check off all that apply.)*

☐ Solve a problem.
☐ Avoid a problem.
☐ Provide an opportunity.
☐ Provide status or growth.

In this case, he is offering a means to avoid a problem. By presenting any or all of these in a way the learner values, you enhance the learner's readiness and increase the probability of learning and retention.[5]

Experience

Here's a question for you: *Combien font cinq fois soixante-douze?* The answer isn't difficult. It's *trois cent soixante* (360). Of course, you have to know some French to respond.

This leads us right to something we encountered in chapter 4: the effect of prior knowledge on learning. Adult learners come to each learning event with their unique former knowledge. This is what we may term as their *experience*. Adult learners possess a great deal more experience than do children. Some of it facilitates learning, but it also may act as an inhibitor. Adult learners learn if the training is pitched at their level and type of experience. If the training goes over their heads or is outside of their experience base (as in the case of our French math question above, which really asked, "How much is 5×72?"), then you lose them. Once lost, they are difficult to find again.

Treat adult learners as if they have little or no experience when they do, and you insult them and lose them. It is critical to effective training that you acknowledge the rich store of experience your learners possess—perhaps different from what you are training them on, but no less valuable—and exploit it. Help them to contribute to their own and other people's learning. And be aware that some of their previous experience can create resistance to new knowledge.

Here's a sample situation to illustrate our point:

Sample Situation: You Want Customer What? The public transit company for the city decided to do something about the rising number of ridership complaints and declining revenues. After much investigation, it decided to send every one of its 4,000 bus drivers to a course on customer service. The well-intentioned instructor had just opened the session with an overview of what the course was to accomplish when an irate participant shouted, "You want me to improve my customer service?

"Last week I did just that. I helped a nice old lady who could hardly walk get off the bus. She could barely get down the steps. I stopped the bus and slowly, carefully helped her off. Just as I got her steady on the sidewalk, an inspector pulls up, tells me I'm late. Complains that I left my seat. Writes me up and hands me a disciplinary warning. Customer service? No thanks!"

The experience principle suggests that the more you factor the experience of your learners into the design and delivery of your training, the more effective the learning outcome. Here are some basic rules for doing so:

- ▶ Check the backgrounds of your learners (aptitudes, prior knowledge, attitudes, learning and language preferences, prerequisite skills, culture, and relevant strengths or deficiencies). Don't lose them by aiming your training session too high or too low or by presenting it in a personally or organizationally unacceptable manner.
- ▶ Use vocabulary, language style, examples, and references that are familiar without being patronizing.
- ▶ Draw examples and experiences from the group to enrich the session and build bridges from the familiar to the new.
- ▶ "Inoculate" your learners. When there have been bad experiences, warn them that you are moving into negative territory. Diffuse resistance by demonstrating sympathetic awareness of past problems. To illustrate, let's return to our bus drivers and start the training session over again.

Sample Situation: You Want Customer What? [Take Two]. Being aware of the work realities his learners have faced on the job, the instructor began the session by acknowledging his participants' experiences and urging them to share with the group:

"When we talk about customer service on the bus, we often get heated discussions about the positives and negatives as we do our job of transporting our riders to their destinations safely and on time. Can anyone give me an example from his or her work in which customer service paid off for both you and the customer?

"Now, can anyone give me an example where trying to deliver customer service backfired?

"Great. These positive and negative experiences you have had show us that a simple view of customer service—be nice, polite, friendly, helpful—is too naïve for our kind of work. Let's examine some statistics and examples of what is happening in our transit company and others. Let's look at some trends occurring outside of our industry that may affect us. Then let's put our heads together to analyze the information and figure out what's really right for our customers, our company, our community, and, also important, ourselves. We are responsible for our customers' transportation and safety regardless of the traffic, weather, road conditions, and crazy drivers out there. Let's see what we can do about serving our customers despite all these obstacles."

Obviously, this approach is based on respect for the bus drivers' backgrounds and experiences. It acknowledges that the subject is tough. It also treats the drivers as adults and asks that they help figure out what is right by weighing the numerous variables and ultimately deriving intelligent and workable customer service guidelines with which they can live. It avoids any impression of arbitrarily imposing a set of preestablished rules on them.

Does Tapping Into Experience Really Facilitate Learning?

As early as the 1870s, Hermann Ebbinghaus, a German psychologist, began measuring the relationship between experience and the rapidity of learning (the velocity of the learning curve). By the mid-1930s, the U.S. Air Force had developed mathematical models and formulas for calculating the precise effect of previous experience on speed of learning. Limited as these formulas may have been, they did quantitatively demonstrate a relationship between experience and learning efficiency.

Recently, neuroscientists discovered through experimentation, specifically on observed effects of experience on learning, how impactful, neurologically, prior experience can be on new learning.[6] In a quote from one of the experimenters, "[the study findings] suggest that information on [an] experience is kept for a long time…this finding indicates the way in which new neurons in the adult brain could contribute to learning and long-term memory by storing the information of one's previous experiences." By drawing from and speaking to our learners' experience, we definitely can increase the impact and effectiveness of learning.

Autonomy

How much freedom of choice (that is, *autonomy*) does a young child have? Does she or he decide what to wear, what to eat, how to get to school, how to organize his or her day, or where to have dinner? The answer is typically "no." Adults largely manage children's activities—especially at school where administrators generate class schedules. Subject matter and content flow are the realms of the department of education and the teachers. Homework is meted out by the teacher-authority. None of that is necessarily bad, but it does contrast strongly with most modern workplace environments. Although people still must work within guidelines, increasingly more autonomy—or self-directedness, to use an adult learning term—is being handed to workers in setting goals, making work and resource priority decisions, handling customers, cutting deals, and creating organizational strategic plans.

When we enter the learning arena, particularly in formal classes, we often see a return to traditional, school-based, teacher-centered models of instruction. Training, in its broadest sense, requires a dynamic climate for adult learners to grow and develop. Adult learners understand best if they take charge of their learning. After all, their value in the organization and the marketplace depends on what they know and are able to do. They own their personal human capital, which they invest in their jobs. It is in their best interest to build their human capital accounts. The more they take charge, the greater the value they—and their organizations—acquire.

Adult learners like to participate actively and contribute toward their learning. Re-examine the examples of good training in table 5-1 and notice how many address the issues of participation and contribution. The more the learner does and contributes, the more the learner learns.

Adult learners want to make their own decisions. Decision making is a major characteristic of adulthood. There are two values in this for learning. The first value is that decision making requires gathering information, analyzing that information, generating alternative decisions, weighing the consequences of each alternative, and, finally, sorting through and selecting what appears to be the optimal decision. All this mental engagement strongly contributes to learning and retention and to increasing the future application to the job of what has been decided. The second value to decision making is that the more the learner participates in the decision, the higher the probability that the participant will consider the decision credible and therefore will commit to it. This contribution has a powerful impact on comprehension, retention, and application posttraining.

Adult learners want to be treated as independent, capable people. They require respect, even when they make mistakes. Respect is an essential aspect of autonomy, especially in a learning context. It enables the learner to try and to err without feeling threatened or put down. In many ways, adult learners are more fragile and vulnerable than children. The fear of failure and accompanying loss of face can be high.

The balance between being challenging—"go ahead and take charge"—but supportive—"Don't worry if you don't succeed; it's all right"—is a delicate one for the trainer, instructor, educator, or instructional designer.

 To operationalize the autonomy principle, we suggest you take the following actions:

▶ Create lots of opportunities for learners to participate in your training sessions. Build in exercises, hands-on practice, cases, simulations, games, and discussion opportunities. (In later chapters we'll describe how to create these—especially in chapter 8.) Testing, but not necessarily with exams, offers a great opportunity for learners to participate. (We devote chapter 9 to the subject of testing.)

▶ Build in numerous opportunities for learners to contribute their unique ideas, suggestions, solutions, information, and examples. The more they contribute, the more they'll feel they own the learning and commit to making it useful.

▶ Reinforce independent and innovative ideas. By rewarding such ideas, you encourage learners to adapt the learning in ways that enhance their own performance potential.

On a final note concerning self-directedness, we are not suggesting that adult learners simply take total control of their learning in initial stages of acquiring new competencies and knowledge. Prior knowledge of a content area and prior experience in "taking charge" of one's own learning affect the degree of control the adult learner can effectively handle. Autonomy exists on a continuum from a nearly completely controlled environment to increased loosening of constraints. As the competence and confidence of the adult learner increases, so, too, does his or her autonomy. Nevertheless, within even the most structured learning program, providing opportunities for participation and contribution should be maximized.[7]

Action

If the proof of the pudding is in the eating, then the proof of the training is in its successful on-the-job application. Have you ever gone to some form of training or instruction, found it wonderful, rated it highly, and then never used it?

Here is a list of some courses we've taken in person, online, from a DVD, or from a hardcopy manual. We enjoyed them, thought they were great, but somehow they didn't have staying power. Check off any that sound familiar to you. Add a couple of your own at the end.

☐ Spanish ☐ first aid
☐ painting on silk ☐ flattening your stomach
☐ touch typing ☐ table decorations
☐ project management ☐ Chinese cooking
☐ a programming language ☐ bread baking
☐ running meetings ☐ calculating with the abacus
☐ time management ☐ _____
☐ scientific investment ☐ _____ .

Don't get us wrong. We do bits and pieces of many of these topics—we conduct meetings, we try to manage our time, and we even exercise a little. While we were in the learning mode, we were inspired, motivated, and found that what we were learning made excellent sense. The problem was in the follow-through. Here's an interesting question: What percentage of people who go on a diet program and lose weight maintain their weight loss 12 months later?

☐ 10%   ☐ 20%   ☐ 30%   ☐ 40%   ☐ 50%
☐ 60%   ☐ 70%   ☐ 80%   ☐ 90%   ☐ 100%.

The dreadful but correct answer is 50 percent.[8] About half of dieters who actually lose their targeted weight, regain much of it within 12 months. Within two years, the result is even worse—and this is even with diets that included exercise. These findings fit in well with the action principle.

Adult learners in the work setting participate in training to learn how to improve or alter their performance on the job. To ensure buy-in from the learners, their attention must be focused on immediate application of what they are supposed to learn. If they can't see how they can put it into *action* as soon as they return to the job, their interest and learning decrease. And if they don't receive any form of posttraining support to help them sustain application of what they are learning, they may find the training entertaining and enlightening, but they won't apply it back on the job. As with weight loss programs, dramatic change can occur during the learning period. But off the program and back in one's normal environment or with no food and exercise plan or support systems, old habits soon reassert themselves. Without an action orientation back to the job, learning dissipates quickly. This is an enormous challenge for trainers and training managers.

 To develop an action mindset in our learners, we must design training that will do these things:

▶ Point out how learners can apply their learning immediately and provide them with on-the-job support mechanisms.
▶ Provide opportunities within the training sessions to practice new learning in an environment that is as close to the learners' work setting as possible. Practice increases competence and confidence, both highly correlated with motivation to transfer learning to the job.
▶ Ensure that the new learning can be applied on the job. Work with the operational environment to align policies, procedures, feedback systems, incentives, resources, and rewards with the new learning. That requires

the trainer to assist learners' supervisors in encouraging and supporting application of the new learning.

▶ If the learning is used only occasionally (for example, in emergencies, or twice a year when the auditors arrive), create job aids and refresher opportunities that keep the learning accessible.

The bottom line in the action principle is, "If you don't use it, you lose it." Adult learners have to be action driven because they face so many competing priorities in the workplace. Successful adult training must factor in the action orientation.

Sample Situation: Adult Learning Principles in Action. Your company has experienced some unpleasant occurrences over the past year. It's been tough in the global marketplace. There has been tremendous pressure to improve output and to extract increased productivity from each employee, from the president to the most-recent hire. Competition is fierce, and the economy is uncertain.

Alarmingly, the human resources department and line management have noticed the following internal problems:

▶ increased rates of absenteeism

▶ increased requests for sick leave

▶ people suddenly quitting

▶ greater tension in the workplace, including open arguments and even some physical attacks

▶ higher rates of depression, breakdowns, divorces, and substance abuse.

An HR study has determined that the major cause of these negative factors appears to be stress. The company has decided that although the competitive environment isn't going to decrease pressure, it can implement programs to alleviate some of the negative effects. It has given HR adequate funds to launch a stress management program.

You have been selected to be part of the "Coping with Stress" team. There will be a number of initiatives, from redesigning work environments and building new exercise facilities to creating greater job flexibility and job sharing arrangements, and so forth. As part of the learning initiative group, you have been tasked with developing a training program on "Stress and Stress Management" for all employees, from seasoned executives to entry-level new hires. The program is to be delivered live in groups of 12 to 20. The training session will be one day long (7.5 hours). A generous budget has been promised, but you will have to make a strong case to obtain your funds.

You've been studying stress and stress management with expert consultants for the past six weeks. During that time you and they have identified this program content:

- ▶ What is stress? Its psychological and physiological symptoms.
- ▶ Evaluating your own stress level.
- ▶ Your stress profile.
- ▶ Sources of stress at work.
- ▶ Sources of stress outside the workplace.
- ▶ Effective responses to stress.
- ▶ Ineffective responses to stress.
- ▶ Ways to manage stress.

Your immediate mission is to take a first pass at the content and come up with an initial plan for the training. You decide to approach this task by applying the four adult learning principles to the one-day course. Let's see what happens.

Readiness

How do you open the learners' minds and spirits to the content? How do you show the value of the learning for them? Take a moment to consider this. What would you do to get them ready?

Pause. Reflect. Jot down some readiness ideas.

_____

_____

 Here are some of our suggestions, and we don't claim that ours are the best. Consider them in addition to the ones you wrote.

- ▶ Before the program invitations go out, send information about stress via email or with pay notices or checks to all employees.
- ▶ Provide eye-catching information on the effect of stress in the workplace and in our personal lives.
- ▶ Break down the silence barrier by letting people know that stress is a common concern that leads to undesirable but normal feelings and behaviors.
- ▶ With the invitations to the stress sessions include a list of benefits to the individual, team, organization, family, and friends.
- ▶ Prior to the session, send out a simple, easy-to-respond-to stress assessment. Offer to provide an explanation and interpretation of scores during the session.
- ▶ Create a welcoming, low-stress environment for the session.

▶ Open the session with a dramatic, personal, stress-related anecdote that is a bit shocking, but also one with which participants can empathize. Draw them into a dialogue early.

▶ As you open each new part of the session, begin with a discussion or activities that emphasize the session's personal benefits to participants.

Experience

How do you speak the learners' language and build from their experience at the right level? How do you acknowledge and exploit positive and negative experiences?

Pause. Reflect. Jot down some ideas of how to ensure that you deal with and draw from participants' experiences.

_____

_____

 Here are some of our ideas:

▶ Interview employees at various levels prior to developing your training session. Collect war stories about stress occurrences. Find out what sorts of stress people experience that cut across all employee groups, and what sorts of stress are more specific to certain populations.

▶ Convert those stories and the information you gather into examples, role plays, and anecdotes (even videotape vignettes, if funds are available) for use during the session.

▶ Collect research data on how people experience and deal with stress in organizations similar to yours.

▶ In your interviews or focus groups with employees, find out how they deal with stress at work and at home. Integrate their solutions into session activities and materials.

▶ During the session, ask participants to define stress in their own words and to share experiences, sources of stress, and solutions to eliminate it.

▶ Provide case examples and let participants form self-selected teams to solve them.

▶ Press the participants to explain the rationales for their solutions based on experiences, both personal and from observation.

Autonomy

How do you get participants to take charge of their own learning? What must you do to get them to participate and contribute?

Pause. Reflect. Generate some ideas for making the participant-learners as autonomous as possible.

_____

_____

The key in this case is to build numerous exercises that require participation and contribution. Develop scenarios, role plays, cases, brainstorming, and practice activities that require learner involvement. Examples of those activities are shown in table 5-3.

Table 5-3. Examples of Participatory Learning Activities

Activity	Example
Scenario	• Show a video vignette from a known film or popular television show or play an audio-recorded scene that is dramatic and stressful. Open the discussion. • Have two or three participants read roles for various characters in a stressful situation. Stop at a dramatic moment and draw reactions, solutions, and so on from the participants. (Draw from your earlier interviews to build scenarios.)
Role play	• Based on your research, develop a role-play setting with a stressful theme (for example, aging parents with health problems coupled with high work demands and inadequate resources). Have participants play out the roles to increase or reduce stress.
Cases	• Provide reality-based cases dealing with different stress themes. Have participants select the cases they wish to work on in teams. Have teams identify key stress elements, symptoms, causes, solutions, and so forth. Debrief with the teams. Draw from the solutions to generate lists of principles for coping with stress.
Brainstorming	• Select some of the stress examples from the focus groups you conducted during your research and brainstorm ways of dealing with them.
Practice activities	• Demonstrate stress identification or stress reduction exercises. Have participants practice, for example, relaxation techniques, self-massage, and partner massage. (Note: These activities are only for those who are comfortable doing them. You don't want the activity to create more stress.) • Provide a menu of materials, artifacts, and techniques. Have participants select these and try them out.

Action

How do you make sure adult learners see that they can apply what they are learning to their jobs and lives immediately? How can you maximize transfer from the learning context to the real world?

Once more, pause. Reflect. Come up with suggestions for making the stress and stress management content something the participants see they can use right away and with success. Action!

_____

_____

 This is the toughest of the learning principles, but being aware of that prepares you to do many things to operationalize learning. Consider the following means:

▶ Create a blank personal action plan for use throughout the entire session. As participants go through each activity, they make notes or check off items in various sections of the action plan that they can apply immediately following the training.

▶ Provide company materials and lists of resources and community services with contact information that apply to the different topics in the session (for example, a company employee assistance program and a list of support groups, financial assistance agencies, substance abuse programs, and career assistance programs).

▶ Distribute audio and video materials that provide information participants can share on or off the job, or ones that help reduce stress at the office, at home, or in the car.

▶ Create a buddy system among participants and establish regular contact times.

▶ Develop an automated stress-o-meter that pops up on a person's computer screen back on the job. He or she responds to questions weekly and obtains feedback on stress level and stress reduction progress. The individual can compare himself or herself with self-selected groups by choosing among different ages, genders, types of work, or other descriptors.

The possibilities for developing and delivering learner-centered educational opportunities based on sound adult learning principles are endless. This sample situation asked you to reflect on how you might apply the four adult learning principles to a stress and stress management learning session. With this approach, are you focusing more on the

☐ learner?

☐ content?

We're certain that you checked off learner. The content only comes alive when you focus on the key adult learning principles. Can you name them?

1. _____

2. _____

3. _____

4. _____

Check your responses against column A in table 5-4. Then match the four items in column A with the appropriate statements in column B.

Table 5-4. Four Principles of Adult Learning

Column A	Column B
Readiness	1. Adult learners must participate in and contribute to their learning.
Experience	2. Adult learners must see how they can credibly apply what they have learned immediately.
Autonomy	3. Adult learners see the benefits to themselves of what they are learning and thus open their minds to it.
Action	4. Adult learners are not empty vessels. They learn best when the learning content and activities integrate with what they already know and are aimed at the right level.

You've got it if you matched the following items: readiness—3; experience—4; autonomy—1; and action—2.

The Bottom Line on Adult Learning Principles

Training is a waste of time—yours, your participants', and your organization's—if it doesn't work. By focusing on adult learners and their needs and characteristics, your (and their) probability of success skyrockets. You, we, and our learners are so much alike. What works for us, by and large, also works for them. The golden rule in all of this is, "Train others as you would have them train you." Keep this in mind when you move to the next chapter where we derive a model and create a plan for building effective learning sessions based on that golden rule.

Remember This

Many important points were raised in this chapter about adult learning. We close this chapter with a brief review quiz. Complete each of these statements by crossing out the less appropriate option.

1. A "good" class is characterized by an instructor, a course designer, or a decision maker who makes the effort to create a learning experience relevant to (*you from a personal / the organization from a business*) perspective.
2. In "bad" classes, the instructor treats you as an (*individual driven by your personal needs / empty vessel into which knowledge can be poured*).
3. Given that we were frequently bored or confused by our teachers or professors, observation of trainers shows that we tend to (*focus on our learners' needs, concerns, and issues / repeat the practices we often hated as learners*).
4. Our success as trainers, instructors, and educators comes from (*the excellence of our presentations / learner success in applying what we taught*).
5. "Andragogy" is the field of study dealing with (*adult/child*) teaching-learning.
6. The most effective way to build readiness in adult learners is to (*show them what's in it for them / demonstrate how what they are learning benefits the organization*).
7. Treating adults as if they have no experience when they do generally (*insults them and you lose them / relaxes them and opens them more fully to your instruction*).
8. In general, adults like to (*participate actively and contribute to their learning / absorb what you tell them during instruction so they can reflect before trying things out later*).
9. To ensure attention and buy-in from adult learners, focus on (*immediate/ eventual*) application.
10. Training should be considered a (*valiant effort / waste of time*) if it doesn't get applied back on the job.
11. Train others (*to be like you / as you would have them train you*).

Here is what we would have chosen with a brief rationale for each choice.

1. A "good" class is characterized by an instructor, a course designer, or a decision maker who makes the effort to create a learning experience relevant to you from a personal perspective. The learner is the center of attention. That's why we insist on all of our training being "learner centered." It's all about the learner, your customer. If learners don't "get it," neither they nor the organization will benefit.

2. In "bad" classes, the instructor treats you as an empty vessel into which knowledge can be poured. No need to dwell on this one. Learners are not inert, passive vessels. They are driven by their individual requirements and interests. Attaching your instruction to these will open them up to what you offer.

3. Given that we were frequently bored or confused by our teachers or professors, observation of trainers shows that we tend to repeat the practices we often hated as learners. Alas, so true! We are imitators. We may have hated what we experienced, but then, lo and behold, there we are doing it to others. Ingrained models of behavior are hard to shed. Fight it.

4. Our success as trainers, instructors, and educators comes from learner success in applying what we taught. Simply put, their success is our success. We do not train to impress or be great presenters. That is another occupation. There is nothing wrong with presenting well except when it gets in the way of learners doing more. The keys to excellent instruction are practice and feedback. Emphasize what they do.

5. "Andragogy" is the field of study dealing with adult teaching-learning. Pedagogy is the teaching of children.

6. The most effective way to build readiness in adult learners is to show them what's in it for them. As any good salesperson will explain, the benefit sell is the most effective. The expression "What's in it for me?" (WIIFM) applies well to our learners.

7. Treating adults as if they have no experience when they do generally insults them and you lose them. Rather than ignore what your adult learners have experienced over time, exploit it. Even if the experiences have been negative, bring these out and deal with them. Demonstrate that what you are providing are means for overcoming previous negative experiences or enhancing and building upon what they already possess.

8. In general, adults like to participate actively and contribute to their learning. The principle of autonomy in adult learning centers on the fact that adults actively engage in their day-to-day decision making. They engage and contribute in their work. So should they in their learning. The more they contribute

the more ownership they create for themselves. Probability of use back on the job increases.

9. To ensure attention and buy-in from adult learners, focus on immediate application. If you don't use it, you lose it. Eventual use rarely happens. Proximity between learning and application strengthens connections in the brain and increases ease of retrieval.

10. Training should be considered a waste of time if it doesn't get applied back on the job. Sorry. No one can afford valiant efforts, as noble as they may be. Training is costly, resource demanding, and time consuming. If it didn't work, we lost valuable resources. The most valuable of those is time.

11. Train others as you would have them train you. You may be a paragon of every virtue—no offense meant—but the bottom line is like the golden rule: Train as you would like to be trained.

To summarize this chapter:

> ▶ Our job as trainers, instructors, and educators is to help adult learners learn. Their success is our success.

> ▶ By applying the four key adult learning principles—readiness, experience, autonomy, and action—you open your learners' minds, connect with what they already know, get them involved, and lead them to successful on-the-job application.

> ▶ The golden rule of training is, "Train others as you would have them train you."

What a great segue to the next chapter.

Chapter 6

A Five-Step Model for Creating Terrific Training Sessions

Chapter highlights:

▶ Six universal principles from learning research
▶ Model for structuring training
▶ Worksheets to guide and support application
▶ Means to retrofit existing training to the model.

What if we offered you a simple, easy-to-use training tool that significantly increased the probability of learning success with any group, of any size, on any topic? Would you want it? In this chapter, that's exactly what we present to you. No strings attached, no caveats, no maybes or sometimes. In a way, this chapter is the heart and soul of *Telling Ain't Training: Updated, Expanded, and Enhanced*. We're not diminishing the importance of the other chapters, but things do come together here. So, prepare yourself.

First, here's a brief review. In chapter 1, we set up some challenges to establish the central theme of this book: Telling ain't training. We also wanted you to immediately experience the style of this volume: fun, challenging, participative, and conversational.

Chapter 2 provided you with some basic vocabulary—training, instruction, education, and learning—and presented a focus, a mantra: "learner centered, performance based." It also stressed that the medium isn't the message and that the content of this book applies to all forms of instruction, regardless of the delivery vehicle. In chapter 3, we visited the senses, the brain, and memory to acquire an understanding of the learning characteristics and limitations of our learners.

Chapter 4 focused on why we often have difficulty communicating our knowledge to our learners, even though we know a lot. It emphasized how differently experts and novices process information and described the fundamental distinctions between declarative and procedural knowledge with all of the inherent implications. Finally, chapter 5 provided a structured overview of adult learning and exemplified four key adult learning principles.

The stage now is set for building effective learning sessions. You have had enough information and argumentation to convince you that we require a structuring mechanism that differs from the one we observe in most work settings. Where do we turn for this? Once again, research on learning helps direct us.

Six Universal Principles From Research on Learning

How would you classify yourself as a learner?

- ☐ more auditory
- ☐ more focused on details
- ☐ more visual
- ☐ more focused on the whole
- ☐ more social
- ☐ more right brain
- ☐ more independent
- ☐ more left brain.

When we observe individuals at work and play, we notice differences among them. Each person appears to possess a unique set of capabilities and traits that sets him or her apart. We naturally assume that they have their own *style of learning*. Also, our observations suggest that, ideally, we should tailor our learning sessions to each learner. Obviously, this is an awesome challenge and most likely not feasible, especially with so many learners and so few resources.

What then can we do? Must we compromise? Must we accept less?

We have good news and bad news to share with you, depending on your point of view. We have boxed each of them below so that you can self-select the one you prefer.

The Bad News	The Good News
Sorry. We humans are not as unique as we like to think we are. Research in learning indicates that there are significant differences in the way individual learners are affected by different types of instructional approaches. However, the detectable differences in the research findings do not translate into a major overall impact on learning. We are alike in more ways than we are different.[1]	The good news is akin to the bad. As much as we would like to believe that each of us is incredibly unique, unless we have some form of perceptual or cognitive disability, we are all very much alike in how we perceive, process, store, and retrieve information. Well-designed and well-delivered instruction seems to have a broadly similar impact. This allows us to design sound instruction based on a universal set of principles and to achieve a high degree of effectiveness with a wide variety of learners.[2]

Now that we have given you both the good and bad news, we arrive at a single conclusion: If we can derive some overall, "universal" principles from research on learning, we can mold them into a model for teaching most learners most subjects with a relatively high success rate. What are those universals? They make such good sense that they are almost embarrassing to share.

Here are six words that sum up a lot of findings from research on learning: why, what, structure, response, feedback, and reward. Let's examine each of them.

Why

As reasonable as it may seem, if the learner knows "why" he or she is supposed to learn something and the reason makes sense to—is valued by—the learner, the probability of learning increases. This sounds similar to the readiness principle from the previous chapter. Readiness suggests that the adult learner learns more easily if his or her mind is open and ready to take in new information. The key is to show what's in it for the learner.[3]

Research in which different learner groups received instruction with and without a meaningful "why" produced different learning results. In the research studies, "why" is frequently represented by the terms "expectancy value" or "task value," referring to what the learners perceive investing in the learning effort offers them. Groups with strong rationales that convincingly explained how the learners would benefit from the instruction paid closer attention and retained what they had learned more accurately. This appeared to be true regardless of the type of learner. The clearer and more meaningful the "why" offered, the better and more long lasting the learning.[4]

What

There's an old saying, "If you don't know where you're going, you'll probably end up someplace else." This is true also of learning. Have you ever been in a class in which the instructor/teacher/professor wandered aimlessly through the course material? You sat there trying to figure out where this person was heading, and you felt lost. Research on learning demonstrates the value of clarifying to the learners what it is they will be able to do by the end of the lesson, module, or course. Such early information acts as a set of guideposts or a map. The clearer and more meaningful it is for the learners, the higher the probability they will learn it.

However, this should not be confused with provision of specific instructional objectives at the front end of a course when the objectives may be meaningless to the learners. Studies done on "specific instructional objectives," their use, and their placement in instruction had confusing and contradictory results.[5]

Structure

Examine the array of symbols below for 15 seconds. Ready? Go!

$?$*#*$?£*£##?$?*££?*#£#$

Stop! Cover the array with a piece of paper.

Now reproduce the array in the same order in the box.

Done all you can? Compare the two arrays and give yourself one point for each symbol you placed in the correct sequence. The maximum number of points is 25.

Jot your score down here.

Now, repeat the exercise using the array below. Once again, you will have 15 seconds to "learn" it. Ready? Go!

$$$$$????? ***** £££££ #####

Cover the array and reproduce what you remember in the space below.

Then score yourself again. As before, you get one point for each symbol placed in the correct sequence.

Compare arrays. Enter your score in the box.

Let's examine the results. Did you do better in the first or the second trial? When we try this out with adult learners, we rarely discover scores above four or five in the case where the symbols are all jumbled up.

However, when these same symbols are placed in an easy-to-understand, structured order, most people score a perfect 25. Amazing! Same symbols (or content) and different structures produce dramatically different results.

Humans seek order. Where there is none, they will create it artificially. Think about gazing at clouds. Don't you see shapes in what are really random patterns? And what about the man in the moon? The research tells us that the clearer the structure of the content is for the learners, the more easily they will grasp and retain it.[6]

Here's one more example of this all-important structure issue. Imagine that we offered you $10,000 to name all the states of the United States without using any references or getting any assistance. One error, and you receive nothing. What would you do to be 100 percent sure you get all the states right? Check off the most probable strategy for you. If none fit, add your own.

- ☐ Just randomly name them as they pop into my mind.
- ☐ Use the alphabet as a guide and name them alphabetically.
- ☐ Break up the United States into regions and name states by region.
- ☐ Start on the east (or west) coast and name all the states in order down the seaboard and along the southern and northern borders. Then fill in spiraling toward the center.
- ☐ Use a rhyme, song, or other memory device to organize my recollection of all the states.
- ☐ My method:_____.

We have asked this of hundreds of adult learners. Every one of them selects some structured and systematically organized method. Not one person chooses to name them randomly. The need to bring order or structure to what we deliberately try to learn and recall is universal among all types of learners, although the nature of the structure can vary.

Response

The more learners actively respond to learning the content, the better they learn and retain it. Response can take the form of answering a question, filling in a blank, labeling something, solving a problem, making a decision, or even discussing and arguing. It can take any form that elicits an active response to learning the content. Before we share a little more about the research on active responding, here's a quick challenge. Check off your choice below.

- ☐ Learners learn better if the response they emit is out loud or written down—an overt response.
- ☐ Learners learn better if the response they emit is in their heads—a silent or covert response.
- ☐ Learners learn better if they respond. There is no significant difference between overt or covert responding.

Ready for what may appear to be the surprising answer? The correct one is the second choice. Almost everyone selects the first choice, but what the research shows is that active responding is the critical ingredient. What is also important is that the response be a meaningful one. We have seen so-called interactive e-learning in which learners move objects; click on items; and enter numbers, letters, and even words that have no meaning with respect to what they are supposed to be mastering. This is empty responding. It has some limited value in that it may maintain the learners' attention for a while, but it does little to clarify meaning or assist retention.

Examples of this, both live and mediated, are learning games in which the gaming aspect becomes so dominant that the learning content fades out. The response is about the game, not the content, and it ceases to be relevant or meaningful.

Here is a note on the research concerning active responding and covert versus overt responses. Most of the studies were conducted in the 1960s and 1970s. We decided to delve back into these to reassure ourselves about what we were affirming. Sure enough, the preponderance of research findings supports covert responding, mostly because the mental engagement compared favorably with some empty types of overt responding (for example, raising hands, clicking on something, or repeating text). Two conclusions emerge here. First, response must be meaningful. Second, there must be an element of reflection before deciding on a response.[7]

Concerning meaningfulness and its importance, think of yourself performing routine tasks in which you are responding but are no longer mentally engaged. Have any of the following ever happened to you? Check off those that you have experienced.

☐ You've driven for several minutes and then suddenly realized you were on "automatic" and can't remember what you've done or how you ended up on a frequently traveled route you didn't intend to take.

☐ You performed your morning routine (shower, shave/make-up, hair, and so forth), and then had to check whether or not you had put on deodorant.

☐ You studied for an exam and read several paragraphs or pages only to realize you can't recall a thing about what you've just read.

☐ You've been introduced to new people at a social event, smiled, shaken hands, and then noticed that you couldn't remember the names of the people you had just met.

☐ You finished your meal then couldn't remember what you just ate.

Both of us checked off *all* the items, so don't worry if you felt that you were beginning to lose your mind. You were simply on automatic, a normal mechanism that allows you to perform unconsciously. The problem is that during these periods you are not mentally engaged in your responses. No new learning occurs. Even with a gun to your head, you cannot recall what you did although you responded appropriately. Active, conscious response during initial learning—overt or covert—is essential for comprehension and recall, but the learner must be completely mentally engaged.

Feedback

Feedback is one of the most powerful mechanisms for learning.[8] The problem is that a lot of myths are associated with feedback. Feedback is information that learners receive about how on or off target they are (for example, in identifying a component of a system, describing a process, solving a problem, or throwing a curve ball). The learner responds in some way to a critical part of the learning or to all of the learning elements that lead to objective attainment. Feedback comes to the learners from an instructor or from the environment that informs them how on or off target their responses have been. This helps the learners to adjust or continue the responding. From an instructional perspective, feedback should be either corrective (to let the learner alter responses) or confirming (to let the learner know that he or she has attained the partial or complete objective).

 Here's what research tells us about feedback:

▶ Feedback that the learner perceives as directed toward the task helps improve performance.

▶ Feedback that the learner perceives as a criticism of himself or herself tends to hinder or reduce performance.

- ▶ Immediate feedback helps improve performance on simple tasks.
- ▶ Delayed feedback seems to be more effective on what learners perceive as complex tasks (feedback given too soon can confuse learners by overloading short-term memory).
- ▶ Frequent and specific feedback helps improve performance. However, if the feedback is too detailed or specific (for example, "In your golf swing, alter the angle of your elbow by 11 degrees, turn your left foot out by four degrees and advance it two inches, adjust the angle of the front surface of your club 2 degrees…"), it confuses the learner and may have an adverse effect on performance.

Reward

If you put on a new article of clothing and receive compliments about your appearance, what is the likelihood you will wear it again in the future? It's relatively high if you conform to what the research tells us.[9] In learning, if we achieve an objective—master a piece of learning—and are rewarded for our success, the probability of retaining that learning increases. Recognized success encourages most people to learn and retain. When behaviorism was in its heyday, from the mid 1950s to the mid 1970s, the value and impact of reward was almost a sacred law.

Cognitive research tends to temper some of the extreme enthusiasm for the power of reward, but almost all learning researchers still acknowledge the value of reinforcement. There is a major distinction between intrinsic rewards—those that emerge from the sense of accomplishment when you succeed at learning something—and extrinsic rewards that are associated with something tangible that you are given for learning (for example, a gold star, food, money, or removal of something unpleasant). The more one can include and build in intrinsic rewards, the joy that springs from the learning itself, the better it is for the learner. With certain learners, however, extrinsic rewards in the form of tokens, points, privileges, and removal of unpleasant chores, such as washing dishes, can help associate learning with pleasant experiences.

Taken together, those six universals drawn from research on learning lay the foundation for a powerful instructional model. When supported by what we have learned about how people process information and adult learning principles, we discover the following essential ingredients for creating effective and efficient learning:

- ▶ letting the learners know why the learning is beneficial to them
- ▶ helping the learners clearly understand in a meaningful way what it is they will be learning

▶ creating structured activities and information that facilitate acquisition of targeted skills and knowledge

▶ building into the learning some opportunities for frequent and meaningful responses

▶ providing appropriate, corrective, and confirming feedback with respect to learner responses

▶ including appropriate intrinsic and extrinsic rewards, which each learner values, to enhance the pleasure of the learning process and its successful outcomes.

A Universal Model for Structuring Any Learning Session

Based on the preceding essential ingredients, we now introduce you to a user-friendly, easy-to-apply model for developing any learning session. It allows for all sorts of variations. In this part of the chapter, we present examples of its use with different content, contexts, and target audiences. Applying this model can provide you with an instantly successful learning session. As you become more familiar and comfortable with its use, you can incorporate other elements into it from this volume and from your own experiences and observations. The model has been tested and used in hundreds of organizations with demonstrable success.

As you will discover, it is easy to use and makes good sense for creating learner-centered, performance-based instruction.

Figure 6-1 presents, in overview, our five-step model for structuring training. Here are some details about the elements of the model.

Rationale

Provide a rationale. Explain why learners should learn whatever you are presenting to them. Early on in any learning session, the learners require an explanation of why they should attend the session, whether live, e-learning, video-based, or in print. If the learner knows why she or he should learn something and values it, the research suggests that learners have a higher probability of learning it. This is directly tied to the readiness principle—the opening of the mind and spirit—described in chapter 5. In the rationale, the instructor or the instruction informs the learners about what is in it for them and for others (for example, peers, customers, and the company's shareholders). The rationale either can provide an explanation or can lead the learners to discover on their own why they should learn this.

Let's work with an example using somewhat familiar content, performance objectives. Imagine that the audience consists of internal subject matter experts (SMEs)

Figure 6-1. Five-Step Model for Structuring Training

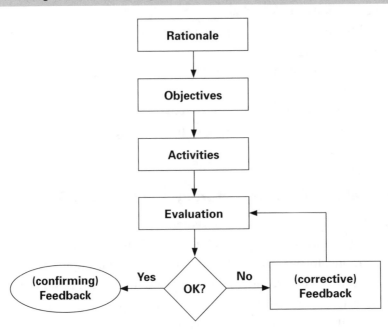

who have been tasked with developing and delivering training sessions to customer organizations and third-party vendors who will be selling your products and services. What might we include in a rationale for acquiring skills in developing performance objectives?

Rationale:
- As trainers, your success is measured by the success of your learners.
- The more concrete and verifiable what you want your learners to be able to do and say, the more easily you can identify their successes or shortcomings.
- Learning objectives are the targets toward which all of your instruction and all of the learners' learning are aimed. They provide concrete goals for everyone to attain.
- The more easily you can create these objectives, the more readily and smoothly all the other parts of your instruction will fall into place. It will make your lesson planning much easier.
- If your learners know where they are going, the probability that they will get there becomes higher.
- In the rationale, you provide a form of overview of where you are heading in the session. You also build a desire to learn by underscoring how useful, interesting, and exciting this session will be to the learners.

Performance Objective

State the performance objective to the learners. Tell them clearly what they will be able to do by the end of the session. If the learners know what they are supposed to learn, research suggests that there's a better chance that they will learn it. The instructor or, if self-paced, the instructional material states the objectives meaningfully in terms of the learner and not in terms of the trainer or training system.

Which of these statements is more appropriate as an objective?

- ☐ You will be able to convert a service call to a sales call.
- ☐ I will show you how to convert a service call to a sales call.

The first statement is more appropriate because it is expressed in terms of the learner. The second states what the trainer will do and as such is not a suitable learner-centered, performance-based objective.

The instructor or instructional material also states the objective in concretely verifiable (measurable or observable) terms. Select the item from these two options that you believe is a better performance objective:

- ☐ You will state the four steps for transforming a service call to a sales call.
- ☐ You will know the steps for converting a service call to a sales call.

The first objective is better because it uses a more verifiable verb, "state," and names a specific number of steps. The more concretely verifiable the objective is (without it becoming obsessive or trivial), the better the performance objective.

Continuing our example of the content SMEs learning to become trainers, here is how the performance objective might be phrased:

Performance objective: Participants will be able to create for their training sessions performance objectives that are stated in terms of the learner and that contain verifiable verbs and specific performance standards.

Activities

Create learning activities that lead to attaining the performance objectives. If learners do things that lead directly to meeting the objectives, there's a better chance that they will attain those objectives. This means that the trainer (or training designer) creates or selects only those activities that lead the learner directly to meeting each objective.

Here is one of the key benefits of this model: It is lean and focused. The rationale provides benefits for the learner. The performance objectives state the contract between the training and the learners—what they will be able to do and how well. Now, the activities cut out the extraneous and frequently disruptive noise. They focus sharply on objective attainment, nothing more or less. The activities are designed to encourage—even require—learner participation plus more. The activities also should stimulate the learners to contribute their own experiences, imagination, and judgment. After all, these people are adults!

Important to successful learning activities is that they be inherently interesting, even fun. This means that the trainer or training designer should build in elements of challenge, curiosity, and fantasy. For challenge, the activities present difficulties that, with effort, can be overcome to achieve hard-won success. Curiosity means not telling the learners everything at once. The activities have the learners wondering what will happen next. They're curious but not confused.

Finally, fantasy acts like spice. It piques interest and is imaginative. It provokes creative participation. This makes the activities fun and interesting and helps promote a broader type of transfer to the job (encourages visualizing a wider range of application than if all the activities are narrowly focused on the immediate job). Chapter 8 contains 25 examples of interesting learning activities, many of which contain all of these elements.

In our example on performance objectives, possible activities might include these ones:

Activities:
- For rationale, start with examples of vague statements and clear performance objectives. Have participants select those they prefer and articulate why.
- State benefits of performance objectives for training sessions with job-related examples.
- State the performance objective of this session and analyze and discuss with participants their expectations and the value of this objective.
- Conduct an exercise that has participants identify examples of good performance objectives compared with non-examples, and have them give reasons for their selection. Summarize by highlighting critical characteristics of excellent performance objectives.
- Conduct an exercise in which participants first edit poorly constructed performance objectives, then create objectives from given content, and finally share and correct them in teams. Provide some fantasy content (for example, butter a bagel, pilot a flying saucer). Provide a checklist for verifying objectives.

- Based on their self-selected content, participants generate performance objectives, edit their own, and then edit others' objectives.
- Conclude with a wrap-up discussion on benefits and techniques for generating performance objectives. Participants review all objectives of this session and critique, edit, or approve them.

Evaluation

Evaluate learner performance. Check to see whether learners have learned. If the learners are assessed on what they are supposed to learn, they have a better chance of learning it. It is important, however, to evaluate in terms of the performance objective and not the person. The trainer or the training system verifies the degree to which each learner has met each objective for the desired level of performance. In self-paced, computerized training, this can be automated and the results recorded for remediation, prescription, or later review. Learning management systems (LMSs) have become very advanced in helping you do all of this.

However, we caution that the results will only be as good as what you programmed the LMS to perform. In live settings, the trainer does what is feasible. This can include asking questions; requesting real or simulated demonstrations; having learners do exercises and then self-evaluate, peer correct, or evaluate in teams; and providing problems and cases and verifying both process and outcome.

The most common tools for checking attainment of performance objectives are performance and written or oral tests, observation checklists, and performance results. (In chapter 9, we go into much more detail on tests and testing.)

Returning to our example, we might handle evaluation in this way:

Evaluation:
- For the exercise on identifying examples and non-examples of good objectives, use an answer key. Include discussion to justify responses.
- Have participants derive and state critical characteristics of excellent performance objectives.
- Check all edited and generated objectives using the performance objectives checklist.
- Check all participant-generated objectives for their own content using the performance objectives checklist.

Feedback

Provide feedback in terms of the performance objectives. Let learners know if they've got it right. Correct them when they go astray.

If learners receive information on how well they are learning, they tend to learn better. For this reason, learners must receive feedback throughout the training session. As mentioned earlier with respect to research on feedback, always give feedback in terms of the performance objective and not the person. Generally, the best time to provide feedback is directly after the evaluation. For difficult or complex tasks, however, feedback can be effective if it comes just prior to the next attempt or practice. This acts as a refresher in terms of learning and a just-in-time prompt. If evaluation causes anxiety, which is frequently the case with adult learners, don't keep them guessing. Provide sufficient, immediate feedback to reduce stress and encourage learning.[10]

Most important, feedback comes in two forms: corrective, which explains to the learners how they can attain the objective, and confirming, which informs the learners that they have attained the objective. Corrective feedback always must be stated positively and encouragingly.

Feedback is not always something one can specifically plan for. Nevertheless, the feedback component is essential and omnipresent in training. In our example, we might offer this feedback

Feedback:
- As learners acquire skills and knowledge about performance objectives, provide corrective and confirming feedback on a continual basis.
- Following each exercise, provide specific information on how to improve performance or confirm the correctness of the response in relation to the performance objective.

Figure 6-2 presents the five-step model for structuring training annotated with a summary of the main points made in this section of the text. This model, as simple as it appears, incorporates significant findings from research on learning that help learners acquire new learning efficiently and effectively.[11] In the next section, we transform the model into operational worksheets and try them out with content.

The Training Session Planning Session

Examine figure 6-3 and note how we have transformed the five-step model into a planning sheet. The planning sheet enables you to take a first cut at creating your training session. Also note two of its key characteristics. First, it is not content centered. Rather, it forces you to think about the learners. It begins with the requirement for a rationale that provides meaningful benefits to the learners. It also requires learner-centered, performance-based objectives that are meaningful to and valued by the learner. It specifies the activities that will lead the learners to objective attainment.

Figure 6-2. Annotated Five-Step Model for Structuring Training

1. Rationale	Explain why learners should learn this and how it applies to their work.
2. Objectives	Inform learners of what they will be able to do.

Give learners things to do. Make these interesting and don't bore them.

3. Activities

Check to see if they have learned.

4. Evaluation

5a. (confirming) Feedback ◄ Yes — **OK?** — No ► **5b. (corrective) Feedback**

Inform them they have got it right.   Check learning.   Correct them when they have gone astray.

Activities must maintain at least a 50-50 balance between learner and instructor or instructional content in self-paced mode. It then asks how learner attainment of the objectives will be evaluated. (In chapter 9, we'll spend a considerable amount of time on appropriate evaluation methods and tools.) The final step, corrective and confirming feedback, should be a natural outgrowth of the evaluation and spontaneously adapted to how each learner performs. It may be useful, however, to anticipate where difficulties will occur and how these can best be addressed if the learner needs to be brought back on track.

Second, note the brevity and simplicity of the planning sheet. You are asked to think about each session and then write your plan in bulleted format. Remember, as we discussed in chapter 2, our natural tendency as content specialists or SMEs is to fill up a training session plan with content. Here, instead, we are asking you to focus first on the customer. When you have planned your training-learning strategy, you can go for the necessary, relevant content that the learners can absorb and retain.

Now let's proceed to an example that enables us to try out this training session plan. Ready for your first test flight? We'll start with a fantasy setting to keep things simple.

Figure 6-3. Training Session Planning Sheet

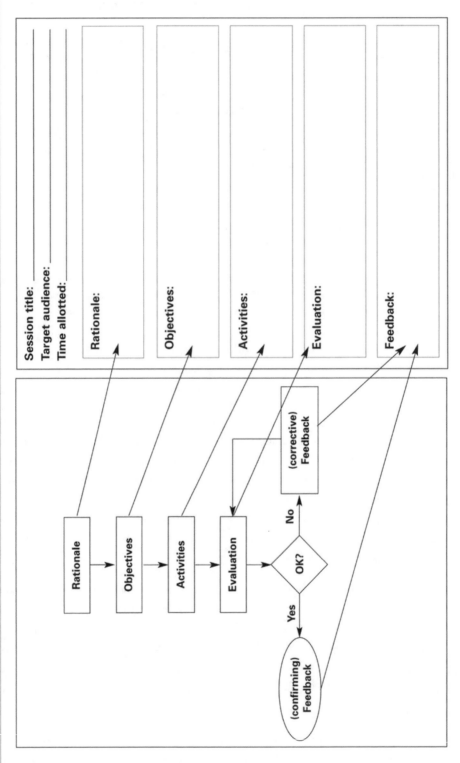

Session title: _____
Target audience: _____
Time allotted: _____

Rationale:

Objectives:

Activities:

Evaluation:

Feedback:

Rationale → Objectives → Activities → Evaluation → OK?

No → (corrective) Feedback

Yes → (confirming) Feedback

Sample Planning Scenario: A Ticket to the Fair

Background: Once a year, the state holds a large-scale fair. For one week, hundreds of thousands of paying visitors flock to it. Each year, the State Fair Commission hires temporary workers for various jobs. You are responsible for training 45 ticket sellers. They have to be accurate and fast because lines can get long and paying visitors impatient. Accuracy and speed are the two key success criteria. The system is totally manual. All of the potential ticket sellers are novices, have gone through background checks, and are bonded.

Target audience: Part-time ticket sellers with education levels ranging from grade 10 to some college. All are over 18; some are as old as 70. About two-thirds are women. None have dexterity problems or significant hearing or vision impairments.

Session subject: Calculating admission costs, taking money, issuing tickets, and giving change.

Time allotment: Two hours, 30 minutes.

Training context: Classroom and crudely simulated ticket booths.

Given the details of the scenario, we developed the training session plan depicted in figure 6-4. We detailed this training session plan a little more fully than we might normally. As a first example, however, we felt that a little extra information would help you visualize the training session more clearly. Once you have read it, assess the plan using checklist 6-1.

You may have had to do some guessing to complete checklist 6-1, but overall a "yes" should be checked off for each item. If not, determine what we could have done to obtain checkmarks in all of the "yes" boxes. Improve our session, please.

The Training Session Scripting Sheet

The training session planning sheet simply was a first attempt at organizing a learner-centered, performance-based learning experience. In many instances, that may be sufficient. All you would have to do is add the timing, plan your resources, and then collect and prepare your materials for tryout. Here is a simple rule of thumb for planning learner-centered, performance-based training sessions:

 The more content expertise the trainer possesses, the less content information you require in your plan. The more training capability and experience the trainer possesses, the less instructional detail you require in your plan. This is mainly true for live, synchronous training. For self-paced learning of any nature, the final plan must contain more details for both content and instructional methods.

Figure 6-4. Sample Planning Sheet

Training Session Planning Sheet

Session title: Selling tickets, collecting money, and giving change

Target audience: State fair ticket sellers (15 participants per session)

Allotted time: Two hours, 30 minutes

Rationale:

- The most important and trickiest part of the job is selling tickets and making correct change.
- Despite background noise, if you've got the knack, you won't have problems.
- You are responsible for your errors up to $100. Learn the job right, and you will be error free.
- Every day we have a bonus for the quickest and most accurate ticket seller.
- Some people get hostile when you are slow or make errors. This session will help you avoid the pain.

Objectives:

Overall objective:
Participants will be able to sell the exact number and type of tickets, collect the exact amount of money, and give the correct change for any customer without error and at an average time of 20 seconds per transaction (maximum group of eight people per transaction).

Specific objectives:

- Identify the exact numbers and types of admission tickets the customer requests.
- Calculate the exact total cost in 10 seconds with no errors.
- Collect the correct total amount with no errors.
- Give the customer the exact change with no errors.

Activities:

- Draw from participants what concerns them most about their new job.
- Show how this session helps decrease or eliminate those concerns.
- Present key points of rationale and discuss each one.
- Show ticket price / customer job aids and demonstrate use.
- Using different voices and admission requests, have participants determine exact request and cost.
- After several examples, time the exercise.
- Using play money and coins, have participants practice collecting money, issuing tickets, and giving change. This is a peer-pair activity.
- In simulated ticket booths, create a practice session putting all parts together. Loudly play audiotape of background noise.

Evaluation:

- Practice exercises with timing toward the end for each activity.
- Final evaluation: In the simulated ticket booths, each learner services 10 peer customers, each with different characteristics and requirements. An audiotape plays loud background noise. Peers talk.

Feedback:

- Provide participants with feedback on how they are doing and how they can improve through self-assessment, peer assessment, and trainer verification.
- Provide timing and accuracy information following final evaluations. Suggest ways to improve, as necessary.

Checklist 6-1. Training Session Planning Sheet Assessment

Criterion	Yes	No
The rationale is presented in terms of the learners.	☐	☐
The learners participate and contribute in building the rationale.	☐	☐
The performance objectives are stated in terms of the learners.	☐	☐
The performance objectives are verifiable.	☐	☐
The performance objectives are appropriate to the learners and the content.	☐	☐
The activities are appropriate to the performance objectives (they lead the learners to attain the objectives).	☐	☐
The activities require learner participation at least 50 percent of the time.	☐	☐
Learners can participate and contribute during the activities.	☐	☐
Evaluation is appropriate to the performance objectives.	☐	☐
Feedback is appropriate.	☐	☐
The session can be conducted within the allotted time.	☐	☐

When greater elaboration of the training plan is called for, the five-step model can be expanded to accommodate more scripting. In this book we provide a set of training session scripting sheets only for live, instructor-led training because every other type of delivery method has its own unique set of detailed requirements. Linear video scripting differs from random-access, learner-controlled video scripting, and both are dissimilar to all of the endless varieties of e-learning formats.

We have found the training session scripting sheets depicted in worksheet 6-1 and figures 6-5 and 6-6 to be helpful when circumstances warrant their use. These are a few of such circumstances:

- ▶ When you have relatively inexperienced trainers: It gives them a script to follow and increases their probability of success.
- ▶ When your trainers are insecure about the session: The scripting sheet becomes a "security blanket" for them.
- ▶ If you have several trainers running the same session (some of whom like to do their own thing): It provides uniformity of approach.
- ▶ In situations with a high requirement for consistency across trainers and locations: Scripting sheets lay out a common approach that facilitates monitoring of consistency.
- ▶ Where there is frequent turnover of trainers: New trainers have a ready-to-run session already prepared for them.

Worksheet 6-1. Training Session Scripting Sheet

Session Title: _____

Target audience: _____

Time allotted: _____

Objectives:

Do	Say	Resources	Time

Figure 6-5. Contents of the Training Session Scripting Sheet

Session Title: _____ Taken from the session planning sheet

Target audience: _____ Taken from the session planning sheet

Time allotted: _____ Taken from the session planning sheet

Objectives: Taken from the session planning sheet. If there is an overall objective, state it first. Then include the specific objectives.

Do	Say	Resources	Time
This resembles stage directions in a play. List in order what both trainer and learners actually do—what can be observed.	This is like the script of a play. You provide the trainer with actual words or speaking suggestions. If the trainer requires content help, detail content points. If the trainer requires instructional methods guidance, detail instructional messages he or she is to state.	This is like the prop specifications for a play. For each instructional activity or event, list the media or resource requirements.	For each instructional activity or event, list the exact time allotment.

Figure 6-6. Sample Training Session Scripting Sheet

Session Title: Selling tickets, collecting money, and giving change

Target audience: *State fair ticket sellers (15 participants per session)*

Time allotted: *Two hours, 30 minutes*

Objectives: *Overall objective:*
Participants will be able to sell the exact number and type of tickets, collect the exact amount of money, and give the correct change for any customer without error and at an average time of 20 seconds per transaction (maximum eight people per transaction).

Specific objectives:
- Identify the exact numbers and types of admission tickets the customer requests.
- Calculate the exact total cost in 10 seconds with no errors.
- Collect the correct total amount with no errors.
- Give the customer the exact change with no errors.

Do	Say	Resources	Time
• Smile warmly. Pose questions to group.	• Ask: "As you face this new job as ticket sellers, what concerns, even fears, do you have right now?"		• Eight minutes
• Write responses on flipchart (F/C).	• Ask: "As I point to each item you have given me, raise your hand if you feel this. I'll write down the numbers."	• F/C and felt-tip markers.	
• Point to each item on the F/C, count raised hands, and jot down number.		• F/C and felt-tip markers.	

• Show key points from rationale.	• State: "As you can see, quite a few of you share the same fears and concerns. Let me assure you that this is normal. Everyone is a bit scared of the unknown. What is great for you is that this session will lay a lot of those concerns and fears to rest. Let's see why." • Explain how this session prepares the learners to serve the customers, despite all the noise and pressures. • Stress the benefits and fun the learners will derive from the practice exercises in this session and note that they may win prizes.	• Prepared F/C sheet with session benefits for learners.	
• Show prepared F/C with objectives. • Read, explain, and discuss overall specific objectives. Move briskly. If there are concerns, put those on a separate sheet for handling later.	• State: "Here are the objectives for this session. Let's read the overall one first and discuss it. Then I'll briefly explain each of the specific objectives you will achieve by the end of this session."	• Prepared F/C sheet with objectives.	• Three minutes

Using the Five-Step Model to Retrofit Existing Training Sessions

Suppose you have inherited someone else's existing course materials and plans. You examine them and discover that they are not much more than large data dumps. They are rich in content but essentially involve telling/one-way transmission. They may even include a vast number of slides with scripted text. What can you do to increase their effectiveness without starting from scratch? (This equally applies to a great deal of print and computer-based courses.)

Here is our suggestion for retrofitting existing training to the five-step model: Take one existing, content-heavy course. Examine it to determine its overall reason for existence. Derive from all of this material what people exposed to it are supposed to be able to do with the content. For example, suppose the course is about a new line of products, and it is aimed at the sales force. By reviewing all the course materials, you derive the following rationale and objectives:

Rationale: The market has been crying out for a new line of sewing needles. With the population aging and sight declining, people are finding it harder to thread needles. They also are looking for needles that are better and more versatile. Coinciding with this is an upsurge in sewing hobbyists as people retire and have more leisure time. Interest in needlepoint, fashion design, dressmaking, quiltmaking, and even sailmaking has grown. Our new needles have attractive features and benefits for wholesalers, retailers, hobby clubs, and end users that knock the socks off the competition. They offer you incredible opportunities to corner the market, increase sales, and significantly improve your earnings. Not only that, they are entirely innovative products.... (We think you get the idea.)

Overall objectives: By the end of this session, you will be able to identify innovative sales opportunities for the new product line, favorably position it against all of your competitors, and present the novel products in a way that increases customer profit margins by 20 percent to 30 percent and your commissions and volume by at least 20 percent to 40 percent.

Specific objectives:

▶ Name and describe the unique features and benefits of the new needle product line and each of the products.
▶ Precision target wholesale, retail, and hobby club customers for the product line and/or specific products.

Notice how you are taking an existing, content-based course and transforming it into a more learner-centered program?

Break the existing course into its individual components. Reorganize it, if necessary, to create a logical learning sequence, one based on the logic of learning, not the logic of the content. Eliminate unnecessary components or place them in a reference manual if management won't let go of them.

▶ For each retained component, create a rationale and objective.

▶ For each component, create interactive, participative activities that involve the learners.

In our example, have the learners play games to match features and benefits to products. Instead of telling them about the appropriate products for specific customer groups, provide customer cases and, in teams, have the learners examine the product documentation and recommend suitable matches. Build a full menu of engaging, learner-centered, performance-based simulations and exercises.

To evaluate, create challenging quizzes; tests; competitions (after all, these are sales representatives); and especially cases for individuals, peer pairs, and teams to solve. Provide tools and checklists for peer and self-evaluations. Develop an evaluation activity for each performance objective.

Make sure that throughout the revamped session there is room for a lot of dialogue and feedback that confirm and correct as appropriate.

Voila! The five-step model can become a retrofit recipe for converting dull, telling sessions into highly motivating and effective learning events.

Final Review of the Five-Step Model

This has been your longest chapter so far. It requires pulling together some key content. Figure 6-7 is a blank chart for the five-step model coupled with some key points about each part of it. To help you retain the model, fill in the blanks beside each number. Then, in the circles place the letter of the correct key point that relates to each element. To check your responses, turn back to figure 6-2.

Remember This

Once again, we have a quick, closing quiz. Just cross out the incorrect option in parentheses to make each sentence come out right. Then we'll give you our take on how we would answer.

1. We are all (*alike / very different*) when it comes to how we perceive, process, store, and retrieve information for learning.
2. Expectancy value helps learners determine the (*why/structure*) of a learning session.

Figure 6-7. Five-Step Model for Structuring Training

a. Inform them what they will be able to do.

b. Inform them they have got it right.

c. Check to see if they have learned.

d. Correct them when they have gone astray.

e. Give them things to do. Make these interesting and don't bore them.

f. Explain why they should learn this and how it applies to their work.

g. Check learning.

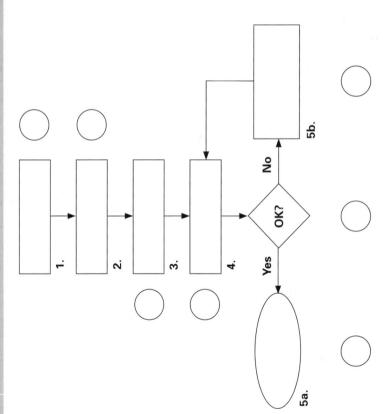

3. If you don't know where you're going in a learning session, you'll probably (*soon figure it out / end up someplace else*).
4. Humans seek order and structure in instruction. If there is none, (*they will create it artificially / accept this state and be with it*).
5. Meaningful covert and overt responding (*slow down a learning session / increase the probability of learning*).
6. Essential for initial learning is (*active, conscious engagement / an automatic, unconscious mental state*).
7. Feedback should be (*positive or negative / corrective or confirming*) following evaluation of learning.
8. A feeling of accomplishment based on something you value is an (*intrinsic/extrinsic*) reward.
9. In the five-step model, "rationale" is related to the adult learning principle of (*autonomy/readiness*).
10. Sophisticated LMSs provide (*meaningful, usable diagnostic, instructional and learner data automatically / learner data that is only as good as what you program it for*).

Here is our feedback:

1. We are all alike when it comes to how we perceive, process, store, and retrieve information for learning. Unless there is some physiological or pathological issue, humans treat information using the same biological mechanisms. As a species, most of how we deal with new learning is generalized across all of us.
2. Expectancy value helps learners determine the why of a learning session. Expectancy value can be colloquially stated as WIIFM—What's in it for me?
3. If you don't know where you're going in a learning session, you'll probably end up someplace else. An old, but all-too-true saying. Without a clear sense of where the instruction is headed, learners become easily lost and soon flounder or make incorrect assumptions about the learning message. Training must provide learners with clear objectives that are meaningful to them.
4. Humans seek order and structure in instruction. If none exists, they will create it artificially. We seek to make order out of chaos. New skills and knowledge are more easily stored in long-term memory if they are logical and organized for connection to prior knowledge. Then, through practice, the learning becomes progressively easier to retrieve.
5. Meaningful covert and overt responding increase the probability of learning. There is no research evidence to suggest that active learner responding affects the length of a learning session. However, there is massive evidence that such response engagement produces more effective learning and retention.

6. Essential for initial learning is active, conscious engagement. An unconscious state of mind does not allow us to register what is being taught. When we "zone out," we are no longer aware of what is happening. Learning goes practically nowhere. Active mental engagement, however, increases the probability of learning, especially during initial stages when we are still seeking to make sense of new material.

7. Feedback should be corrective or confirming following evaluation of learning. Positive and negative feedback have connotations that are incompatible with supporting learning. Feedback should be focused on task, not person, and either provide the right dose of information to place the learner back on track—corrective—or let the learner know that she or he has met the desired goal—confirming.

8. A feeling of accomplishment based on something you value is an intrinsic reward. Intrinsic rewards are internally generated based on personally meaningful success. Extrinsic rewards originate outside of the learner. These are valued more than accomplishment of the learning task itself and compensate for the lack of internal interest in goal accomplishment.

9. In the five-step model, "rationale" is related to the adult learning principle of readiness. The rationale gives the learner a valued reason for learning. It helps open the mind to the learning session and is therefore most related to the readiness principle.

10. Sophisticated LMSs provide learner data that is only as good as what you program it for. While LMSs can do wonderful things, particularly those that have been around for a while and have versatile capabilities, what you ask it to do gets you what it gives back to you. You must configure your LMS to produce the right types of data in the most usable, comprehensible formats. How you program it determines what you will obtain from it.

To close out on this central chapter, bear in mind that although we are attracted to the notion of how unique each of us is, when it comes to learning we are far more similar than we are different.

If adult learners know why they should learn, what they will be able to do as a result of learning, see how all the learning pieces fit together, practice, get feedback, and are rewarded for their learning … they learn.

By applying the five-step model—rationale, objectives, activities, evaluation, and corrective and confirming feedback—you increase the probability of learning.

Now we can turn to how we can help make learning stick, the subject of the next chapter.

Chapter 7

Getting Learners to Remember

Chapter highlights:

▶ Critical differences between so-called good learners and poor ones

▶ Five metacognitive skills

▶ Six sets of cognitive strategies to facilitate learning and retention.

Careful structuring of training sessions, captivating content, and attention to adult learning principles—taken together, those elements should result in superior training. But despite the care with which we attend to all of them, we sometimes don't achieve the learner transformation we (and often the learners) desire. We can lead the learners to training but we cannot make them learn. How well learners acquire the declarative or procedural knowledge we package for them largely depends on what they do if and when they receive it.

Enter chapter 7. First, we'll consider key differences between "good" and "poor" learners; that is, those who "get" what we are training them on, retain it longer, and use it more appropriately, and those who don't. That leads to a discussion of an important subject in cognitive psychology and practical learning application—metacognition.[1] Don't be alarmed; we'll make this impressive-sounding term approachable shortly. When we've dealt with metacognition, its importance for learning, and what we can do to help learners with less developed metacognitive skills, we'll drill down further.

This chapter introduces six sets of cognitive (mental or information-processing) strategies that you can exploit to facilitate learning. Overall, you will take away from this chapter clear explanations of why some learners learn better than others; of things you can do about that disparity; and of how you can help all of your learners learn better, faster, and with long-lasting results.

Metacognition: The Executive Learning Controls

In chapter 4, we described three major influences on learning: ability, prior knowledge, and motivation. We now add to our list a fourth influence that is critical for successful learning: *metacognition*—the set of higher-level (meta = above, beyond) control processes that guide our deliberate information-processing activities. These executive-level processes come into play anytime we set mental or cognitive goals for ourselves, such as learning or solving a problem, and then attempt to meet them in an efficient way. We develop skill in using these higher-level processes at a young age and continue to improve them as we learn how to learn. Think of metacognition and the metacognitive skills as the mind's operating system (a concept borrowed from R.C. Clark, 2008)[2] in charge of high-level supervisory processes. We engage these skills every time we learn something new.

Why Metacognitive Skills Are Important

Picture yourself wandering in a forest, alone and starving. You're desperate to eat. As you enter a clearing, you spot a chunk of food. Your mouth waters. But before you can make a move, a tall, muscular, mean-looking person steps into the clearing, growls, and hungrily lunges for the food. Cooperation obviously won't work here. It's survival of the fittest. Who will be the survivor? The rough and tough big brute or you?

Nature has dealt you and "Brutus" different physiques. He is genetically gifted with great size, powerful musculature, and raw force. You aren't. Who do you think is most likely to win? Place your bets on the outcome:

☐ Brutus wins. He eats. You starve.
☐ You win. Delicious!

Hold it! What if you are smaller and less muscled but have tremendous skill in the martial arts? Does that change the probability of your success? Will you consider changing your bet?

Although not exactly perfect, the analogy of raw ability to learn and well-developed metacognitive skills to size/musculature and martial arts skills illustrates the importance of highly developed executive-level thinking and planning capabilities. Studies conducted to examine the major differences between excellent and poor learners have highlighted the importance of metacognitive skills to establish learning goals, plan for them, execute them, and achieve positive results. The more unfamiliar the learning or problem to solve, the more beneficial well-developed metacognitive skills become. Research has demonstrated that, despite equal intelligence of subjects, variations in metacognitive skills lead to greater or lesser success in learning.[3] This has tremendous implications for training. By helping adult learners strengthen their metacognitive skills we can enhance learning and retention, even for those who may not be as intellectually endowed as their colleagues.

What are these metacognitive skills? Researchers and authors describe them in different ways. We are comfortable with the descriptions of five such skills that are frequently mentioned in the literature in one form or another and how they operate to a greater or lesser degree in good and poor learners. Their descriptions are paraphrased and summarized in table 7-1.

Why are these skills important to us as trainers, instructors, educators, or learning managers? They're significant because we are only as successful as our learners. As hard as we may work to structure learner-centered, performance-based training sessions, if the learners lack the metacognitive skills—the ability to skillfully and strategically handle what we provide—our effectiveness—our success—decreases.

So what can we do? First, remember that our instruction is a compensation for what the learner lacks. Examine the information in table 7-2, which suggests remedial actions for learners who lack any or all of the primary learning influences.

 With respect to metacognitive skills, conduct a learner analysis prior to planning your training. Identify beforehand how well prospective learners have performed or learned in the past. Examine learner records to identify where problems have occurred in previous training. Observe on the job what types of problems performers experience. Question supervisors. As you begin to train, watch for metacognitive weaknesses.

Table 7-3 suggests ways you can compensate for such weaknesses.

This section was not meant to turn you into a learning therapist. It is to inform you of some important learner characteristics that can facilitate or inhibit learning by taking into account the state of your learners' metacognitive skill levels as a group or when you encounter an individual learner you want to assist. To help you see if you've acquired the essential points about metacognition, turn to exercise 7-1 and match a few learning situations that have metacognitive problems with their possible interventions. If you match most or all of them correctly, pat yourself on the back. If you miss any, we suggest going back over the explanations

Table 7-1. Metacognitive Skills in Good and Poor Learners

Metacognitive Skill	Good Learner	Poor Learner
Planning	Faced with new learning, reasons out what must be done, creates a plan to accomplish the learning, and organizes time and resources appropriately.	Faced with new learning, doesn't know what to do. Randomly tries various approaches without prior planning. Uses whatever comes to mind and muddles through. Applies what has been used before, whether or not it worked or even fits the new learning challenge.
Selecting	Looks, listens, studies, analyzes, and sifts through the chaos to identify critical and focal elements of the new material. Separates the wheat from the chaff.	Doesn't know where to turn. Everything is important; everything has to be learned. Is soon overwhelmed by the flood of new information and is drowned in the details. May make inappropriate or trivial selections.
Connecting	Continually seeks to build linkages with prior knowledge. Attempts to understand the new content and link it with what is already known. Creates personally meaningful analogies and mnemonics.	Views the new content as a mass to be digested and attempts to memorize it without linkages to known skills and knowledge. Isolates the new learning from previous experience and does not make useful connections with what has been mastered previously. May create erroneous or false analogies.
Tuning	As new information is received and the learner practices with it, he or she brings the new knowledge into sharper and clearer focus. Adjusts analogies and mental images to coincide more accurately with new learning. Discards erroneous assumptions or early helpful learning crutches that are no longer required.	Obtains a fuzzy understanding of the new learning, but cannot bring it into focus. Continues to add more information rather than to test, adjust, and eliminate. Cannot create a clear picture of the new knowledge and skills and thus makes errors or applies the new learning in an overgeneralized manner.
Monitoring	During learning, replaces unproductive or insufficient strategies with more likely-to-be successful ones. In applying new learning, makes adaptations to conceptual models and identifies limitations and the extent to which new learning can be applied. Constantly verifies understanding and application and adjusts accordingly.	During learning, uses known strategies whether they work or not. Applies more effort instead of taking a different learning tack. In practice, applies new learning in a rigid fashion, forcing what has been learned to fit each case. Practices with few or erroneous modifications. Does not monitor impact and make necessary changes conceptually or operationally.

Table 7-2. Remediating Learner Deficiencies

Deficient Factor Affecting Learning	Remedial Actions
Ability	• Break the learning into smaller chunks. • Simplify. • Use lots of concrete examples. • Eliminate nonessential content. • Provide sufficient practice for each smaller chunk of learning to ensure mastery. • Build slowly from the simple to the complex. • Illustrate.
Prior knowledge	• Create special learning sessions that focus on prerequisite skills and knowledge. • Build connections with familiar past experience. • Distribute materials that provide essential prerequisite material with practice exercises as needed. • Create tutorials and remedial sessions. • Pair individuals who have prior knowledge gaps with those who can help them out; share knowledge. • Create study teams with mixed levels of knowledge and make them responsible for helping each other.
Motivation	• Demonstrate the value and benefits of the learning to the learners personally and to others. • Show admired role models buying into the learning content. • Build confidence by providing guided and supported practice; reward success. • Include sufficient challenge to stimulate involvement. • Provide success stories. • Maintain an upbeat, positive atmosphere. Make learning fun and rewarding.

and suggested interventions on the previous few pages and try again. Metacognition is still relatively unknown among training practitioners, and your knowledge of this important aspect of learning puts you a step ahead of the pack.

One last note on metacognitive skills: We tend to develop them over time, starting early in our childhood (as early as infancy).[4] You may have noticed that some people you didn't consider especially gifted did better in school than others who were supposedly bright.

Metacognitive skills may have played a strong role there. In your training of adult learners, remember that you can help those whose skills[5] have not been well developed by doing what we have suggested. They will acquire proficiency with your content. Research suggests that if learners are guided to apply metacognitive skills

Table 7-3. Remediating Metacognitive Skill Deficiencies

Metacognitive Skill Deficiency	Remedial Actions
Planning	<ul><li>Inform the learner of what it will take to succeed.</li><li>Provide checklists of required materials and resources.</li><li>Provide guidelines for preparing to learn, creating the right physical and mental environment, and budgeting adequate learning. Include a suggested learning/study timetable.</li><li>Review with the learners how to plan for learning success. Answer questions. Monitor performance.</li></ul>
Selecting	<ul><li>Clearly indicate what is important in your instruction and all related materials.</li><li>Tell the learners where to focus their attention and energy.</li><li>Review important points with learners.</li><li>Provide cues to help select focal points. These cues may include bold headings and subheadings, underlined words and terms, tabs, page inserts with boxed key information, and reviews of important items.</li><li>Prepare learners to listen/read and select key points. Provide information as learners take notes. Review and verify what they have selected. Provide both confirming and corrective feedback.</li><li>Provide notetaking guides or blank figures and diagrams that cue and guide selection of priority information.</li><li>Create frequent exercises and tests that emphasize key learning elements.</li></ul>
Connecting	<ul><li>Have learners recall relevant prior knowledge and link new learning directly to it.</li><li>Use familiar or easy-to-relate-to examples that render concrete novel or abstract concepts, processes, principles, and procedures.</li><li>Include analogies, metaphors, and other types of comparisons that build bridges between known and unknown knowledge and skills.</li><li>Draw on the learners' backgrounds or observations to create connections between what they have seen or felt and what they are learning now.</li></ul>
Tuning	<ul><li>Provide practice, examples, and cases that require learners to apply learning immediately.</li><li>Create practice that focuses on large, obvious differences with the familiar. Gradually include exercises and application activities that require increasing amounts of subtle discriminations and fine-tuning.</li><li>Vary practice activities that require different learning and problem-solving approaches.</li><li>Evaluate and provide confirming and corrective feedback frequently through self-tests, checklists, or observation and live intervention.</li></ul>
Monitoring	<ul><li>Provide simulation experiences that require application of new learning in realistic contexts. Vary the nature of the experiences. Increase levels of difficulties.</li><li>Have peers monitor and observe each other during learning application. Use observation instruments and checklists to record application. Have peer learners debrief each other.</li><li>Observe live or videotaped application on the job. Question learners and debrief them.</li><li>Place learners in on-the-job learning/practice situations. Have them self-assess using structured assessment tools. Have experienced workers observe application of learning with structured feedback.</li><li>Question learners about their learning. Ask where they are having difficulties and jointly select different learning techniques.</li></ul>

Exercise 7-1. Remediating Metacognitive Deficiencies

Learning Situation	Metacognitive Problem and Possible Intervention
☐ 1. "Boy, am I confused. All these words—so many details. Everything looks important. What a lot to study and learn!"	a. Connecting problem—Build a bridge to what the learner already knows. Use analogies and vivid examples. Show how this relates to familiar content.
☐ 2. "I can't quite get it. Sometimes I'm right on. Then the next time I'm a bit off. I'm somewhat lost. I feel like I'm close, but not right on target."	b. Selecting problem—Explicitly point out what is essential to learn. Provide cues and highlight key content. Provide a study map or guide.
☐ 3. "Everything seems so new. All these strange ideas and words. New concepts and new procedures. Nothing feels familiar. It's really abstract."	c. Planning problem—Point out what it takes to organize for success in the course. Provide suggested amounts of learning and study time. Hand out a recommended study schedule with suggestions for gathering resources and/or preparing a personal learning environment.
☐ 4. "Well, this is going to be a heavy course from what I can see of the outline. I'll just do what I've always done. Just plunge in and play it by ear."	d. Monitoring problem—Suggest alternative learning techniques. Provide simple application practice in low-fidelity simulations. Give feedback on performance. Increase variations and complexity with comprehensible feedback. Confirm appropriate behaviors and results.
☐ 5. "I dunno. I keep on doing the same thing. Why can't I learn it? Sometimes I seem to get it right. Then they tell me I'm not going about it correctly or you can't apply it in this case. I'm just not getting better."	e. Tuning problem—Clarify subtle distinctions. Provide more practice and specific feedback to bring concepts, principles, and procedures into clearer focus. Probe for gaps and misunderstandings and clarify as needed.

Answers: 1-b; 2-e; 3-a; 4-c; 5-d.

and think about what they are doing, not only does learning of the content improve but so do their metacognitive skills. This is called *reciprocal teaching*.[6] Imagine! By doing the right things by our learners in our subject-matter fields, we also strengthen and arm them for future learning adventures.

Cognitive Strategies: How to Build Learning Faster, Better, Cheaper

When creating products and services for an organization, there is a saying: "Good, fast, cheap—choose two." In other words, if you want it fast and good, it will cost you a lot. Is it fast and cheap you desire? Then the quality of the result will suffer. Are good and cheap your choices? Sorry, but you won't get it quickly; we'll do it when we can. In this section, we offer all three. We introduce you to six cognitive strategy groupings that you and your learners can apply. These strategies have been shown to help speed up learning, make it stick more powerfully and longer, and actually cost less in time and energy for both teaching and learning. You will be able to develop learning activities that take advantage of all of these benefits.

First, what are cognitive strategies? We borrow both definitions and much of what follows from three author-researchers at the university of Illinois: Charles K. West, James A. Farmer, and Phillip M. Wolff (1991).[7] *Cognitive strategies* are the mental methods we use as we study and learn. Unlike metacognitive skills, which are higher-level, executive skills we deploy for any learning, cognitive strategies form a database of thinking and learning packages that we can apply to specific learning situations. They enable us to organize a piece of learning so we can internalize and recall it more easily. Let's apply a simple example right now. We'll come back to its underlying foundation later. Examine the two Lincoln pennies depicted below.

In the coin on the left, Lincoln is facing right. In the coin on the right, he is facing left. Without peeking at a real Lincoln penny, which depiction is correct, A or B?

Your answer:

The correct answer is A. We've tried this test with thousands of American adult learners and, amazingly, 60 to 70 percent of them select B although they have seen the coin numerous times. They just weren't paying attention. When we ask our audiences if they would bet $10,000 on their selection before we reveal the correct answer, we find few takers.

So how do we ensure that we remember which direction Lincoln faces? Here's a statement to help: "Our great president, Lincoln, always did right by the people." Will you remember now? Probably. But what about the nickel, dime, and quarter? Which way do the presidents on those coins face? Here's a cue: "All the other presidents were left behind." Yes, they face left (except for the new Jefferson nickel that faces three quarters right in relief).

What's the point of this coin discussion? It's simple. You now probably will remember this set of not very useful facts for the rest of your life. Associating some arbitrary (hence hard to retain) facts with a mnemonic device that's easy and familiar ("… did *right* by the people … were *left* behind") is a powerful means for grasping and retaining information. It is part of a cognitive strategy that is good (learn and retain well), fast (you learned it quickly, didn't you?), and cheap (two simple sentences—not much mental storage and retrieval cost).

Now that you have been introduced to cognitive strategy, let's continue tuning your understanding. Cognitive strategies are collections of methods that help people learn. Good learners have a larger repertoire of these strategies and use them more naturally, frequently, and appropriately than do poor learners. They also obtain better results. Although there are many ways to organize and discuss cognitive strategies, we will adapt and present highlights to help you integrate cognitive strategy use for transforming your learners.

Six Types of Cognitive Strategies

▶ **Clustering:** Different ways to arrange information for easier perception, understanding, retention, and recall.

▶ **Spatial:** Visual displays of information that lay out a large number of elements in a manner that is easy to comprehend and to retain or recall.

▶ **Advance organizers:** Organized, short introductory information packages that set an expectation or build a vision. They help the learner picture what's to come and how it relates to prior knowledge or to content that has come before.

▶ **Image-rich comparisons:** Analogies, metaphors, and literal comparisons that build bridges between what the learner already knows and the new learning.

▶ **Repetition:** Activities that allow learners to rehearse content they have encountered and practice it in organized ways until it sticks in the mind.

▶ **Memory aids:** Groups of easy-to-remember letters, words, or images that help store and retrieve more complex material.

What follows are more detailed discussions of those six cognitive strategies, with examples and suggestions for use.

Clustering Strategies—Organizing Information

Here are 20 words for you to remember. As usual, we give you only a limited time to do it—30 seconds. Ready? Go!

tennis, leopard, checkers, Australia, rice, tag, pasta, turkey, dog, Holland, orange, hopscotch, iguana, popcorn, billiards, ostrich, Denmark, bear, China, bagel

Now cover those words with a piece of paper. In the space below, write as many of the words as you remember.

Uncover the word list and enter the number of words you got correct in the box below:

Your score:

Now study the next set of 20 words for 30 seconds. Ready? Go!

Animals	Games	Countries	Food
giraffe	hockey	Fiji	egg
salamander	chess	Russia	pretzel
goose	skipping	Belgium	cherry
wolf	ping-pong	Norway	chocolate
mouse	handball	Japan	peanut

As before, cover that list and write the words you remember in the space below. Check your answers and record the number of words you correctly recalled.

Your score:

Was there a difference in your two scores? Most likely your score was higher with the second set of words because the words were clustered by headings. Any form of logical grouping facilitates perception, comprehension, storage, and retrieval. Clustering strategies can take many forms: classifying (as we did here), listing a procedure logically in a recipe, sequencing events on a timeline, organizing objects in a logical arrangement like describing a house room by room, and even inventing a code from a logical set of numbers as we did at the outset of this book (pp. 3 and 4).

Anytime you cluster declarative or procedural knowledge into logical, easy-to-understand groupings, you employ a highly successful cognitive strategy.

Spatial Strategies—Visually Displaying Information. Laying out information to be learned in some kind of visual manner often helps learners see how things relate. This form of spatial organization is another way to trigger and foster successful learning. Figure 7-1 depicts one type of spatial representation. Notice how all the subtasks for packing a suitcase are laid out. With that form of map, learners can see at a glance all the necessary and sufficient things they have to do. It facilitates learning, monitoring, and remembering.

Another common spatial organizer is a flowchart, which is excellent for helping learners visualize a sequence of steps and practice and retain the steps. In the sample flowchart depicted in figure 7-2, notice the diamond-shaped boxes (discriminators) that trigger a decision. Flow diagrams can become much more complex, but when working with novice learners, a simple representation with limited explanation helps the learner *see* what is involved in an entire procedure.

One other common spatial organizer is the matrix. We're going to teach you a little more French using a matrix to assist. Here is how to conjugate a regular French verb:

1. Take the infinitive (example: *donner* = to give).
2. For the present tense, drop the "er" (donn) and add the endings listed below.
3. For the future and conditional tenses, add the endings below to the infinitive (donner).

Person	Present	Future (will)	Conditional (would)
Je (I)	-e	-ai	-ais
Tu (you, singular)	-es	-as	-ais
Il, elle (he, she)	-e	-a	-ait
Nous (we)	-ons	-ons	-ions
Vous (you, plural or formal)	-ez	-ez	-iez
Ils, elles (they)	-ent	-ont	-aient

Example: Je donne (I give); *tu donneras* (you will give); *elles donneraient* (they [all females] would give).

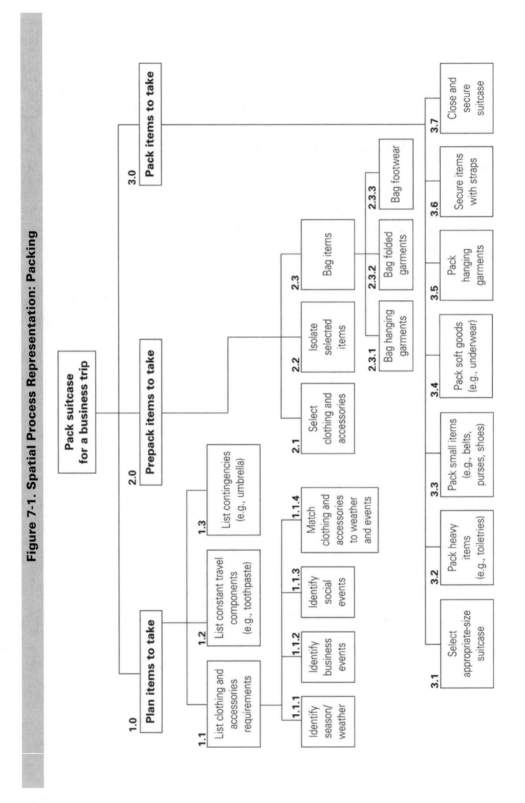

Figure 7-1. Spatial Process Representation: Packing

Figure 7-2. Sample Flowchart: Checking Voicemail

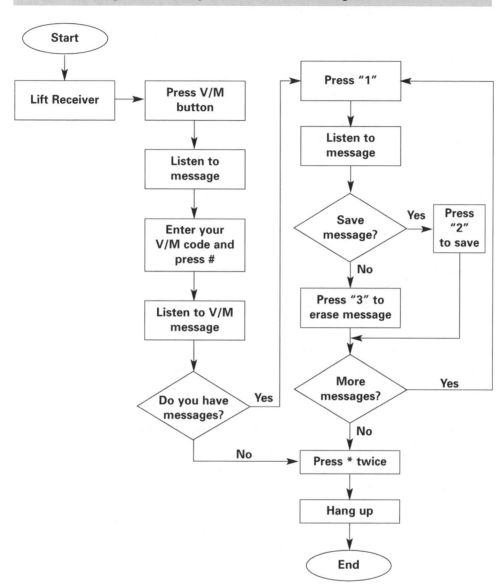

Does the information organized in a matrix format work? Try it for yourself.

*Il parl*_____. (He speaks.)
*Nous march*_____. (We will walk.)
*Vous dans*_____. (You [plural] would dance.)

The correct answers are *il parle, nous marcherons,* and *vous danseriez.* Bravo if you got them right. If not, review the matrix. It should be a big help for learning, application, recall, and self-evaluation.

By the way, in that example we actually combined both a logical procedure and a matrix. Combining cognitive strategies is itself an excellent strategy.

A matrix also can be used as a central focus for a lesson. Learners can participate in constructing it and then use it for studying, for recall purposes, and even for application. For example, an instructor or an e-learning lesson may be used to introduce new bank branch personnel to the four major accounts that new customers are offered. As each account type is presented, it can be placed in a matrix such as the one shown below, with key information filled in by the instructor/ instruction and the learners as the lesson progresses.

Account	Key Features	Key Benefits	Limitations
Current			
Money market			
Savings and checking			
Bonus savings			

The matrix organizes essential information and helps learners make logical comparisons and discriminations. It can be used to teach; as a gameboard for recall; or as a job aid, first with simulated cases and later with real ones back on the job.

Advance Organizers—Looking Ahead to Future Information. A lot of research has been conducted on the use of advance organizers for facilitating understanding, learning, recall, and even transfer to the job.[8] All in all, the results of appropriate use of this type of cognitive strategy can be powerful. An advance organizer is usually a brief introduction made prior to getting into a new topic or set of skills that gives the learner a heads-up about what's coming. It is almost always short. Most times it links prior knowledge to new material and makes comparisons and logical linkages. It may outline the new content and prepare the learner mentally to approach it with the proper mindset.

Chapter 1 of this book is something an advance organizer for what has followed, albeit an unusual and lengthy one. Each chapter of this book has a form of advance organizer in the introductory bullet points that enumerate the chapter highlights. Below is an example of a more typical advance organizer for a new unit of learning. Ideally, it would also include a rationale for the learner to increase learning readiness.

Advance organizer example for a chapter on procedural knowledge

You've had the opportunity to play with different aspects of declarative or "talk about" knowledge in the last chapter. You saw that this type of knowledge is largely treated and stored in the neocortical areas of the brain. It is our newest form of knowledge. You also practiced techniques for recognizing and recalling declarative content. This chapter introduces you to our "do" knowledge. It's called procedural knowledge. Unlike declarative knowledge, we share the ability to acquire this form of knowledge in large measure with all other animals.

Basically, just like an abstract for an article, an advance organizer situates the learners immediately and gets them thinking about what is up next. You can use it at the front end of a course, module, lesson, or unit. By building the link between known and new, setting out key highlights of what's to come, and packaging it in a clear and enticing manner, advance organizers prepare learners, increase understanding, and enhance application to the job.

Image-Rich Comparisons—Analogies, Metaphors, and Comparisons. As children we were introduced to stories such as Aesop's fables or the biblical tales about the loaves and the fishes or the prodigal child. Plato taught us the allegory of the cave to describe the relationship between the real and the ideal worlds. Throughout our lives we have been taught with image-rich comparisons. We use metaphors in our daily speech: "She's a peach!" or "He's a skunk!" Our computer interfaces are built on metaphors. We have a "desktop" on our screen along with menus and icons.[9]

Image-rich comparisons are extremely powerful for learning and retention. If you just remember that "a stitch in time saves nine," you will know that preventive maintenance saves us dollars, time, and resources while it helps us avoid personal disasters.

The strength of this cognitive strategy lies in the bridge (connection) that is established between what the learner already knows—the familiar—and what is yet to be learned. Table 7-4 is a list of performance objectives for various modules or lessons and a few possible metaphors to help facilitate learning that new content. There also are some blanks for you to test your imagination. Try your hand at coming up with a metaphor for each blank. There are no right answers. We'll share our suggestions for the last three objectives after you've given it a try. Go ahead now.

After much discussion, for the last three objectives we settled on the following metaphors: design a course—building a house, organize files—spring cleaning,

Table 7-4. Making Metaphors

Performance Objectives	Metaphor
• Access a database	• Smart yellow pages; library
• Service a piece of equipment	• Medical diagnosis
• Sell luxury items	• Fine restaurant
• Select a vacation	• Exploration/adventure
• Provide effective customer service	• Receiving guests at home
• Design a course	• _____
• Organize files	• _____
• Create and manage teams	• _____

and create and manage teams—sports or theater production. There are many possibilities. Ours are feasible. Most likely, so are yours.

Drawing once again from research and experience, the point is that image-rich comparisons fire the imagination and facilitate learning. They are fun to use, enjoyable to generate (to involve the learners in creating image-rich bridges between prior knowledge and new material), and incredibly effective as cognitive strategies for learning.

Repetition—Practice, Practice, Practice. This catchall collection of cognitive strategies doesn't sound glamorous. Nonetheless, repetition and rehearsal in their various forms can be immensely effective, especially for long-term, hard-wired learning. Do you remember how long ago you learned to recite the alphabet? All these years later, do you ever get the sequence wrong? Do you ever forget a letter? What about the multiplication tables? Here are four examples. Can you complete these in less than 10 seconds? Go!

$7 \times 5 =$ _____ $6 \times 6 =$ _____ $9 \times 9 =$ _____ $8 \times 6 =$ _____

When we try these with adults who say they haven't done multiplication for several years, many spout all four responses in less than five seconds! Whether declarative (capitals of Europe, parts of an engine, or steps in a process) or procedural (run an air-brake test on a locomotive, dance a tango, or verify an audit report), learning is involved and organized for repeating/rehearsing to store and recall. Table 7-5 presents some suggested repetition techniques with examples of their application.

Table 7-5. Repetition Techniques

Technique	Application Examples
Repeat the words or steps. Give it a rhyme or a beat. Rap it.	• Classes of hazardous goods • Procedure for disassembling and assembling a piece of equipment
Read/listen to content. Take notes. Convert each point to a question. Keep on asking the questions until you get them all right. (Can be done in teams.)	• Policies that must be internalized • Product features and benefits • Emergency shut-down procedures
Make up test questions (or have learners make up test questions) for a body of material. Test until perfect.	• Professional body of content for certification (e.g., law, accounting, network engineering) • Security measures for various contexts (e.g., physical, intellectual property, antiterrorist)
Create notetaking guides. These can be lists with keywords that require explanations or elaborations, unlabeled diagrams or matrixes or flow diagrams with empty boxes. Learners fill in as content is provided, then compare with models. Study. Repeat until perfect.	• Technical course with lots of processes and new vocabulary • Course on body language with illustrations of postures and meanings • Actions to take for different types of fires

One of the tried-and-true methods of studying for comprehension and retention is the SQ3R: Survey, Question, Read, Review, Recite method. Recently we visited a famous university where we observed a study course for freshmen. The students were practicing SQ3R with a variety of content and were delighted with the results. Although developed in the late 1930s and early 1940s, SQ3R was miraculously new to those freshmen.

 Study, memorization, practice, rehearsal, self-test, and test all have demonstrated the power to assist learning. The keys to all of these are organization, meaningfulness, and systematic application. Over time, content acquisition improves, as does efficiency in learning.

Memory Aids—Tools for Retention.[10] We saved the best for last. This cognitive strategy, also known as *mnemonics,* is a favorite for remembering. It is so powerful that students in technical programs, the military, law, and medicine memorize hundreds of mnemonics in their studies. Essentially, a mnemonic is a memory crutch—a group of easy-to-remember letters, words, or images that help learners store and retrieve more complex material. We'll examine four kinds of mnemonics here, all of which you can use to help your learners retain key information. You can also encourage them to create their own.

▶ **Acronyms:** This is everyone's favorite. You take the first letter of each item to be remembered and create a meaningful word or phrase. One of the most common is HOMES for remembering the five Great Lakes of North America: Huron, Ontario, Michigan, Erie, and Superior. We've created one for the six cognitive strategies: I SCRAM (image-rich comparisons, spatial, clustering, repetition, advance organizer, and memory aid). It may not be great, but because we created it we remember the strategies more readily.

▶ **Acrostics:** Acrostics involve creating a meaningful phrase to represent something to be memorized. A common one is, "Every good boy deserves fudge." The first letter of each word represents the names of the lines on the musical staff:

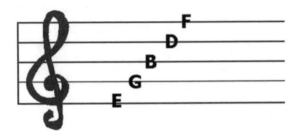

▶ **Rhymes:** People have developed numerous little rhymes to retain hard-to-remember facts. A well-known example in the English language is "30 days hath September, April, June, and November. All the rest have 31...." Few people remember the rest of the rhyme, but that's enough for most people to work with.

▶ **Key words:** These are important words embedded in phrases or sentences that are easy to recall. We demonstrated this with the Lincoln penny ("... right by the people") and the other coins ("... were left behind").

There are many other mnemonic techniques and a large variety of books on how to create and use them to improve memory. Several of those resources are provided in the end notes.[11] Remember that you can help your learners by creating mnemonics, encouraging them to generate their own memory aids, and then having them practice them to strengthen both declarative and procedural learning and recall.

Cognitive Strategies—A Final Word

All the cognitive strategies presented in this chapter are packages of thinking modes that we can deploy whenever we wish to learn something. As trainers/instructors/educators, our mission is to create learning success. It would be wonderful if all of our learners were endowed with high ability, deep prior knowledge, and powerful motivation to learn, and all possessed well-developed metacognitive skills along with a large repertoire of oiled and efficient cognitive strategies to cover every specific learning situation. We simply could lay out the learning goals, provide the resources, and stand back. But that's not reality. Our learners come to each learning event with a broad range of strengths and deficiencies, and our job is to structure learning for successful transformation. To do that, we use the five-step model, compensate for metacognitive skill needs by attending to each of its components—planning, selecting, connecting, tuning, monitoring—and apply a wide variety of cognitive strategies to strengthen learning.

Remember This

Let's end this chapter with a final repetition of some key points. Please correctly complete the statements that follow by crossing out the inaccurate word or phrase in parentheses.

1. Well-developed metacognitive skills (*can/cannot*) overcome ability deficiencies.
2. We are (*born / not born*) with our metacognitive skills fully developed.
3. Clustering, memory aids, and repetition (*are / are not*) metacognitive skills.
4. Planning, selecting, and connecting (*are / are not*) metacognitive skills.
5. As trainers, we (*can/cannot*) compensate for metacognitive weaknesses in our learners.
6. President Franklin Roosevelt faces (*right/left*) on the U.S. dime.
7. As trainers, we (*can/cannot*) use cognitive strategies to help our learners acquire, store, and recall required skills and knowledge.
8. Learners (*can/cannot*) develop their own cognitive strategies.

Here are the answers:

1. Well-developed metacognitive skills can overcome ability deficiencies. They can help learners make maximum use of their innate abilities to learn and remember.
2. We are not born with our metacognitive skills fully developed. We begin in infancy to develop them and continue to hone them as we learn.
3. Clustering, memory aids, and repetition are not metacognitive skills. They are cognitive strategies.
4. Planning, selecting, and connecting are metacognitive skills along with tuning and monitoring.
5. As trainers, we can compensate for metacognitive weaknesses in our learners. This is a major part of our job. Information transmission is not.
6. President Franklin Roosevelt faces left on the U.S. dime. We threw this one in for fun.

7. As trainers, we can use cognitive strategies to help our learners acquire, store, and recall required skills and knowledge. We exploit these strategies and strengthen them in our learners through the activities and materials we provide.

8. Learners can develop their own cognitive strategies. Assisting them through use of these strategies is called reciprocal teaching. They learn our content and strengthen their ability to learn other content by acquiring the cognitive strategies we employ.

This chapter focused on the mental skills and strategies our learners need to learn effectively and how we can create our instruction to help them in that task.[12] The next chapter presents four overall approaches to training and includes a cornucopia of learning activities you can build into your training sessions. Take a break here. We'll meet you again in chapter 8.

Section 3

Applying What You Have Learned—Making Learning Research Work

Chapter 8

Training Approaches and a Cornucopia of Learning Activities

Chapter highlights:

▶ Four major types of training

▶ Twenty-five learning activities

▶ Templates for creating active training

▶ A simple formula for effective training: teach-prompt-release

▶ Online resources for learning activities.

This chapter has two main themes. The first deals with the various ways we train in the workplace. We present four types of training that cover most approaches employed in formal workplace learning settings, describing each of them for you with examples and suggesting how you might use them alone or in combination. This will broaden your vision of how to approach your training missions and assist you to decide consciously what you should do and why you should do it.

The second part of the chapter focuses on a wide variety of activity templates you can use to spice up learning, integrate cognitive strategies in a natural way, and maximize learner involvement. Keep in mind that the more the learners do—especially if it is meaningful to them—the more the learners learn. Active learners, engaged in meaningful and stimulating activities that are clearly tied to desired performance objectives, learn the best and retain the longest.

Four Major Types of Training

We've often heard the expression, "different strokes for different folks." In a broad sense, the four major types of training we describe here are for different types of learners. Let us caution you right away. The same learner may be an excellent candidate for all the types of training, but at different stages of her or his learning with respect to a specific skill or knowledge area. We'll examine each of the types and determine how you can use them appropriately.

The four types of training are *receptive, directive, guided discovery,* and *exploratory.* Various learning researchers and professionals use other classification systems and names. We find these four, which Ruth Clark, in her book on *Building Expertise* (2008) employs, to be convenient and useful.[1]

Receptive Training

This type of training falls into the "telling" mode. Essentially, the view of the learner is that of a vessel into which good, wholesome, nutritional information is poured. The danger in using this type of training lies in the expectation that learners will be able to convert what they hear and see into usable skills and knowledge.

The receptive mode does, however, have some limited value. Basically, it makes learners "aware." Well done and presented in an interesting manner, it can demonstrate value to the learners and build their motivation to accept, learn, support, and desire to discover more. For highly knowledgeable learners, it may be sufficient for them to make connections with and adapt prior knowledge to new circumstances. The training content is frequently transmitted in one direction. Learners have little or no control, except to tune out, turn off, or daydream.

Sadly, much of what is called training in the workplace is of a receptive nature. Here is a true case we experienced in a progressive, world-renowned high-tech company:

> A team of highly qualified software engineers (PhDs) had just completed a major overhaul of an operating system (O/S). They were tasked with going out to train the worldwide group of engineers who would support and troubleshoot the new, improved O/S. Their approach to the training was to bring the support/troubleshooting engineers together for five days; hand them each a manual (approximately 1,200 pages); and tell them about the new and upgraded O/S, how it was developed, how it differed from its forerunner, what their challenges had been, how they had overcome them, what they had had to leave out, and so forth. When we asked if they were going to have participants engage in troubleshooting practice, they were taken aback. They hadn't planned on it.

Given their target audience of system troubleshooters, is that how you would have gone about the training? The receptive type of training *can* have a limited role in introducing something new, adding additional nuances to content that is already well known to the learners, presenting fascinating anecdotes, and building awareness and enthusiasm, but it soon wears thin with any audience. Our bottom-line advice with respect to receptive-type learning is to use it sparingly. Always seek an alternative, except in the case of short, consciousness-raising sessions.

Here is a note on awareness, consciousness-raising, or so-called training sessions. Our bias, based on experience and what research indicates works (or does not work) to build long-term learning and retention, is to avoid these. Awareness or consciousness is an initial stage in the learning process. Unless consequences are dramatic (knowing that there is a 10-foot drop ahead), awareness does little to change behavior. Are smokers aware of the dangers of smoking? Does that strongly influence their smoking choices? Are we aware of world hunger? If so, what behaviors have we altered? Awareness, without a specific behavior change, generally goes nowhere. Our concern is that having conducted an awareness session, an organization may conclude that it has achieved something of value. Little evidence supports the idea that being aware that a crossroad is a dangerous spot for accidents reduces risky behaviors and accident rates. Awareness of safety hazards is insufficient to eliminate safety violations. These sessions generally fall within the category of receptive training and provide little to no value other than creating an illusory sense of having done something worthwhile.[2]

Directive Training

This approach to training is akin to the U.S. Army infantry slogan: "Follow me." As its name suggests, this method directs. In this approach, you analyze the knowledge and skills required to lead learners from where they are to where you want them to be. You create clear performance objectives and matching test items (more on this in chapter 9). Then you organize and sequence learning blocks or units that direct the learners from their starting positions to defined intermediate and final finishing lines. There's little learner control, but, unlike in the receptive type of training, learners are actively and meaningfully engaged as they progress along predetermined paths.

The directive approach is particularly well suited for learners who have little experience with the learning content, require support to build competence and confidence, and will later perform on the job in ways that are identical or similar to what they learn in the training. Here is a list of tasks to be mastered by a group of learners. The learners are relative novices with respect to the implied content.

Put a checkmark in the boxes before those tasks you feel qualify for the directive approach to training.

☐ 1. Start up a piece of new equipment.
☐ 2. Troubleshoot a piece of complex equipment.
☐ 3. Perform an accounting calculation.
☐ 4. Audit a small business.
☐ 5. Determine if a customer meets predetermined criteria for a loan.
☐ 6. Based on customer characteristics, suggest a type of account.
☐ 7. Counter a variety of customer objections.
☐ 8. Create a basic webpage in HTML.

Before we provide our responses, one can make arguments for and against directive training for each of those tasks, depending on the nature of the learners and the depth of the learning. Assuming the learners are relative novices, we chose tasks 1, 3, 5, 6, and 8 as possible candidates for a directive approach, especially for initial learning. Our rationale: Narrow range of options in performing the task; close to on-the-job requirements with little variation; and relatively straightforward content. We decided that tasks 2 and 4 require broader vision and greater depth than a directive type of training might provide (except for some initial steps, perhaps). For task 7, we felt that answers would be too mechanical for dealing with the spectrum of possible customer objections. We believe that other options are available. Let's turn to these.

Guided Discovery

In this type of training, control is shared between the learner and the trainer or training program. Guided discovery is generally case based. Learners immediately plunge into cases, scenarios, or problems. They may require some initial input, but mostly they take the initiative. The learners may reach out to a variety of information sources or support tools, either physically material or electronic, to deal with the situation. The learners themselves have to discover what to do and when to do it. They seek and identify appropriate information and tools to proceed. The instructor or instructional program offers assistance in the forms of cues, prompts, suggestions, and corrective feedback along the way or redirection, consulting services, and debriefings.

The amount of guidance or support and its nature depend on the skill and knowledge level of the learners. For less knowledgeable, less independent, or less confident learners, the training may include a great deal of guidance. The more capable and knowledgeable (or skilled) the learner is, the more independently he or she can function. In that case, the role of the trainer or training is to confirm, debrief, add editorial nuances, proffer variations, and, of course, reward. When learners achieve high degrees of competence and confidence, they are ready for the next type of training.

Exploratory Learning

Here we build and organize a rich learning and informational environment for the learners and then truly get out of the way. The learners are in control. They know what is required and set out to search for whatever exists to resolve the issue and help them progress to the next level. Usually, only general goals are set (often by the learners). Large databases of information integrated into a knowledge management system provide an ideal environment for exploratory learning. At a less sophisticated level, a workshop with all the tools, materials, and manuals does the same thing. Learning is usually individualized. The trainer can monitor and provide feedback or support and debrief as required. In exploratory learning, the trainer is essentially a resource for the learners.

With what the Internet offers today, independent, well-informed learners can generally engage in remarkable exploratory learning. As an example, we encourage you to select something you would like to learn (for example, how to play cricket, soapstone carving, or how to make a soufflé) and explore the web. Note how quickly you discover learning resources that actually help you acquire new skills and knowledge. We selected these topics at random and were overwhelmed with the rich resources available, from step-by-step instructions, videos, and coaching tips to people all over the world ready to help out and chat with you. This is both extraordinary and exciting for trainers who access these resources to create a variety of training session types.[3]

Pulling the Four Types of Training Together

There is a natural progression among the four types of training with respect to learner control and sophistication. Table 8-1 summarizes some key points about the training approaches.

 To conclude the discussion of these types of training, here are some summary points:

▶ All of the types are different ways of approaching training.
▶ All of the types have a place in training, but the receptive approach is the most frequently used method—and it should be the least often employed. Essentially, it's just telling, and *telling ain't training*.

▶ Directive learning provides the trainer and the organization with the greatest control. The side effect is decreased learner initiative and more narrow, nearer transfer-of-learning potential.

▶ Guided discovery is an excellent, balanced training approach to encouraging learner initiative under safe conditions. Learning results are usually stronger and more fluid (for example, transfer to a broader range of situations). Learning results are less predictable, and learning time may increase.

▶ Exploratory learning is powerful for sophisticated, capable learners. It allows for greater individualization and personalization of learning. However, it requires sufficient resources, decreases trainer control, and is unpredictable in terms of specific outcomes.

Our recommendation is to use the receptive type very seldom. Focus on the other three. Mix and match your approaches to fit the needs of both the learners and learning. Above all, keep the training *active*.

In support of that last note, the next section of this chapter presents a plethora of training-learning activities that can be built into all courses, modules, or instructional units and lessons. They are particularly suited to replacing receptive training, but they can be integrated into all four approaches.

25 Training Activities You Can Use

This part of the chapter requires a little stage setting. So far we have explored how learners process information to learn, what to consider when training adults, how to structure training sessions (the five-step model), the mental skills and cognitive strategies required for effective and efficient learning, and four major types of training. All of that information helps us better understand our learners and guides us in planning and organizing our training, whether live and face-to-face or not, but we are still lacking concrete training activities that can be immediately applied—today—to make the content of this book spring to life. We believe that you can use some down-to-earth, practical activities that engage learners and dramatically transform telling into training.

What follows in alphabetical order are 25 training activities that you can use in a variety of learning contexts with a nearly limitless menu of content. We provide descriptions and examples. Your job is to supply the imagination. After we describe each activity and exemplify its application, there is a block of space for you to suggest some way you or a colleague might use the activity. At the end of the chapter you'll find a summary table (table 8-2) indicating the training circumstances for which each activity is particularly well suited.

Table 8-1. Four Approaches to Training

Type of Training	Main Uses	Amount of Learner Control	Assumed Learner Characteristics	Dangers
Receptive	• Build awareness • Inform • Motivate	• Practically none, except for questions and answers if permitted • Learner can choose to tune in or out	• Learner is self-motivated • If content is new, complex, or abstract, assumes learner has sufficient prior knowledge • Telling is enough for transmitted information to stick	• With no control, learners feel like targets • If not self-motivated or if content is not perceived as important, learners tune out • Little sticks to the learner's brain • Belief that telling is training
Directive	• Provide a strong, rational path and sufficient feedback for effective initial learning • Quickly build basic required skills and knowledge • Create initial competence and confidence • Predict learning outcomes	• Little; learning path is prescribed, although alternative paths based on learner progress may be offered	• Learner is not necessarily self-motivated • Little prior knowledge • Perhaps has weaknesses in metacognitive skills • Lack of initiative or confidence to assume control • Learners know they will apply learned skills and knowledge in ways that are similar to training	• May turn off more independent learners • May imply one way (or a narrow range) of doing things • Does not encourage exploration or creativity • Limits more advanced learners

(continued on next page)

Table 8-1. Four Approaches to Training (continued)

Type of Training	Main Uses	Amount of Learner Control	Assumed Learner Characteristics	Dangers
Guided discovery	• Encourage learner initiative in a safe learning environment • Case-based to involve learner in analysis and problem solving of increasingly realistic issues • Build wider transfer of learned skills and knowledge • Build independence in learning while providing a safety net • Next steps after directive training	• Moderate to relatively high, depending on degree of guidance	• Confidence to engage in discovery • Some prior knowledge in the content • Good metacognitive skills • Self-motivated to learn, but appreciates guidance and feedback	• For the less confident learner, possible stress or confusion • For the independent learner, still too much outside control—too limiting • Learner can require more time to learn than from receptive or directive training • Outcomes are less predictable than with directive training
Exploratory	• Create an environment for self-initiated learning • Provide maximum freedom for learner to take control of learning • Respond to variety of learning needs that are highly individualized	• The learning goal, the resources, and the paths to explore are at a maximum	• Highly self-motivated to learn • Strong prior knowledge in content and/or self-initiated learning • Well-developed metacognitive skills • Knows what is needed and knows how to find it	• Learner can get lost • Learner may waste time • Not suited to learners lacking the appropriate characteristics • Learner may not learn what is necessary or may draw inappropriate conclusions • Low control and predictability of results

Better Me

This simple activity works well for on-the-job learning. A job tutor or peer tutor has explained how to perform a task or apply a procedure (for example, light and adjust a welding torch flame, access a file in a customer database, or fill in a form based on a work order). After initial guided practice, the tutor offers a challenge: Better me! This means given the same information or task, both novice and tutor race to complete the procedural task. The race can be between tutor and novice (with some form of handicap for the tutor) against the clock or some other standard (for example, accuracy or completeness). By adding a challenge, the learning takes on a gaming dimension and builds motivation. Novices can even compete against their own previous records.

> **Example:** On the job, José was learning about hazardous materials and how to handle them. Shirley showed José how to use the *Handbook of Hazardous Goods*. After explaining how to find information in the handbook and having José practice identifying two items with it, she set the challenge: "Here are five materials. When I say 'Go,' you find the right page that tells you what to do with them. I want all five pages perfect. I'll do it, too, with my handbook. Let's see if I can do it in half your time. You win if I can't do it. Ready? Go."

> *How I think this activity could be used in my organization:*

Concentration

Based on the classic game of "Concentration," a term or picture is placed on one card and its definition or name on another. A deck generally consists of 15 to 25 card pairs. Cards are shuffled and distributed face down in columns and rows. Players, in pairs, take turns turning over two cards hunting for pairs. If a matching pair (term definition or picture name) is turned face up, the player collects the pair and plays again. If not a pair, the turn is passed to the next player. The game ends when no more cards remain on the table. The winner is the player with the most cards. This is a great peer learning activity.

Example: Fred and Alphonse are taking a meteorology course for their navigation qualifications as part of their job. They have to learn all the different cloud formations (12) and be able to name them accurately. They've been given two decks of cards, one with 24 pictures of clouds, and the other 24 containing cloud formation names. Using the rules of "Concentration" they may have learned as children, they are now playing the "Bring in the Clouds" game, memorizing the shape of clouds and their card positions and the cloud names. Because all the cards have numbers, they can check a master sheet to verify if each pair they pick up is correct. They lose points for making errors.

> *How I think this activity could be used in my organization:*

Confrontation

This is a role-play activity that is conducted in rounds. The group is divided into teams of three. Players each receive a card that describes a confrontational situation and are assigned roles (for example, sales consultant, client, and observer). Two players are in a confrontational situation, and the third acts as an observer. Adversary players choose one of five positions they are given to resolve the issue. They compare their choices and then attempt to come to an agreement before time runs out. The sales consultant, for example, works with the customer to achieve common ground. After each timed round, the observer provides feedback. Roles rotate each round. At the end of several rounds, the instructor draws from the group the lessons learned.

Example: The class of supervisors has been learning about mediating disputes in work groups. Now the trainer, Elisa, introduces the participants to the Confrontation activity so that they can put the theory they have been discussing into practice. She creates six teams of three participants each. She distributes a first set of Confrontation cards to the teams. All teams have the same scenario: An experienced worker and a relative newcomer are in a confrontation. The experienced worker wants the "newbie" to keep her fingers off his manuals and reference guides. She complains that he's hoarding them so that she can't do her job properly. Each chooses from five possible choices how he or she wishes the issue to be resolved. They compare their selections. The supervisor has to mediate. An observer with an observation checklist watches and notes what the supervisor does to bring about agreement. There are six scenarios. Each lasts five minutes and is followed by a structured debriefing. Roles rotate.

> *How I think this activity could be used in my organization:*

Critical List

Following instruction on a large amount of content, the instructor divides the group into four or five teams and asks each team to create a list of the five most important points that have been covered. After five to seven minutes, the instructor asks each team to report its list. As these are announced, the instructor creates a common list on a flipchart. After merging redundancies, the common list should contain 10 to 15 items. The instructor asks each team to select the "most important" item. He or she also explains that teams will receive one point for their choice plus one point for each other team that selects the same item. If there is a tie, all tied items become number one. The instructor has teams play two more rounds to identify the next most important items. The scores are based on how many teams make the same choices they do. This encourages consensus thinking. After three rounds, scores are totaled. The instructor debriefs the activity highlighting the top choices and drawing from other key points on the common list.

> **Example:** In a class on customer service, bus driver participants have spent three hours on facts, problems, opportunities, policies, and other content matters that have an impact on ridership, public support, and job security. These issues also affect image and other critical factors. Now the trainer asks participants to create a list of actions that bus drivers can take to improve customer service. After breaking into five teams, each team generates five actions. These are brought together in a common list of 10 to 12. Through consensus scoring and three rounds of activity, participants select three top items and commit to implementing them at the start of the next shift.

How I think this activity could be used in my organization:

Crypto Cluster

The instructor presents a puzzle to the class with encrypted items that are related to a specific theme (for example, benefits of a particular car model, features of automotive technology, and common misconceptions about specific technologies). The items are encrypted using a simple letter substitution system: Some other letter of the alphabet consistently replaces each letter in the item (for example, every "e" in the item may be replaced with a "j" and every "t" may be replaced with an "n"). The challenge for the participants is to decipher the items in the list by using a combination of general cryptographic principles and knowledge of the subject-matter area. This activity can be performed individually or in teams.

> **Example:** The plant is readying itself for installation of new automated equipment. All affected plant personnel have been taking an online set of courses on the new generation of machinery and technology. To help learners attend closely to the new features, benefits, and misconceptions related to the $200 million revamping, the training designers have created a computer-based industrial espionage scenario with encoded information. The learner has to decipher, memorize, and get back to company headquarters after destroying the encoded document. By doing this and answering company questions, the learner saves the company and defeats the competition.

How I think this activity could be used in my organization:

Domino Effect

This game consists of a stack of 20 to 30 domino-type cards. The instructor creates cards that have a term on one end and the definition for another term on the other end. The game is played using rules for "Dominos," except that a player must lay a term against its definition or vice versa.

> **Example:** The auto plant workers have been going through a series of training sessions aimed at upgrading their technical knowledge and skills in electronics, pneumatics, hydraulics, and robotics. What makes the learning difficult is all the new vocabulary. Fortunately, the training group has created some attractive and fun domino games for each of these areas. One half of the card has a term, the other a definition. Playing in teams and pairs, the workers are finding it easier to learn the large number of novel terms and their meanings. And, hey, it's also fun! Incidentally, the training team has just released a computer-based version with which you can play against the computer or another person.

> *How I think this activity could be used in my organization:*

Exam Cram

The instructor divides the class into study groups or pairs and distributes a test to each team. The instructor tells participants that they will be tested on the content. Participants have 20 minutes to cram for the exam, using any resources they have available. The instructor then administers the test or not, his or her choice since the purpose is to get participants to review the content.

> **Example:** The class of sales representatives has spent most of the morning being updated on the new auto technologies for the models they will be selling. Chassis, drive train, electronics, hydraulics, braking, suspension, aerodynamics…. There has been a lot to learn and remember. There's also the stress of the final test. The trainer now surprises everyone. She hands out the 10-question exam and announces that the class can divide up into the teams they had formed earlier and take 30 minutes to cram for the exam using any materials and methods they choose. At the end of 30 minutes, she will remove all training materials, hand out the same exam, and give them 20 minutes to complete it individually. Their scores will be recorded.

> *How I think this activity could be used in my organization:*

Facts-in-Five

Participants receive a card with a five-by-five matrix that has different categories along the columns and different letters of the alphabet along the rows. Players fill each cell of the matrix with a key word beginning with the specified letter that fits the appropriate category. Players' words score extra points for originality. The activity is typically used with a specific content area (for example, computer technology, sales terminology) that limits the types of key words that may be used.

> **Example:** Store management trainees have been learning a great deal about the products the retail hardware chain sells. It's been an amazing eye-opener for many of these fresh-from-college recruits. More than half the names of the products have been new to most trainees. Now the trainer divides the class into four teams and distributes a Facts-in-Five matrix. Along the vertical axis are five letters. Along the top horizontal axis are the names of five store departments. Trainees have five minutes to complete the matrix, placing a product name starting with the assigned row letter under the store department column. Trainees get one point for a product that more than one other person names, two points if only one other names it, five points for every unique product named, and 10 points if no one else is able to put any product in that cell. Teams circulate the cards clockwise after each round of activity. There is a prize for each of the top three overall scores. There are also some self-challenge matrixes in their self-study materials.

> *How I think this activity could be used in my organization:*

Great Debate

The instructor selects from a general topic area (for example, automotive technology or car models) and subtopics that are rich with debatable issues (for example, the efficacy of front-wheel drive and price as the key selling factor). Depending on the size of the class, she or he divides participants into six or eight teams. If there are six teams, the instructor distributes three issues as follows: Three teams each receive one of the issues with a "plus" sign; three teams each receive one of the issues with a "minus" sign. The "plus" teams each take 10 minutes to prepare two minutes of debating arguments on the positive side of the issue (for example, why front-wheel drive is not only desirable, but the best way to go). The "minus" teams prepare two minutes of arguments on the negative side of the issue during the 10-minute preparation period. The instructor randomly selects an issue and a plus or minus to determine which team starts. After two minutes of argument, the opposing team gets to argue its points. Each team receives an additional minute for rebuttals. The instructor continues selecting topics until all have been debated and then debriefs the group on how to use the arguments raised to support a sale.

> **Example:** A group of 12 executive-level senior managers have been on a long-weekend retreat discussing numerous issues. This is the afternoon of the third day. The facilitator introduces the Great Debate activity. Six teams are formed randomly. Each team randomly draws a hot topic it has been discussing with either a plus or minus on it. The topics are flexible standards of business ethics in international dealings, the public right to know about corporate interests, and business unit competition. Each team prepares either pro or con arguments, as indicated, for its assigned topic and then formally debates these. The facilitator, the CEO, and the president observe and assign points. The facilitator debriefs the activity, occasionally soliciting comments from the CEO and the president. The facilitator helps the group draw conclusions on key hot issues.

How I think this activity could be used in my organization:

Hit-or-Myth

Participants receive a list of 10 topic-related statements that are either true (hit) or false (myth). After participants decide individually if each one is true or false, the instructor reviews each statement and discusses it. Statements generally include commonly accepted myths that are false. Participants receive one point for a correct answer plus a one-point bonus for each participant that got it wrong. This scoring system rewards participants who respond correctly to tougher statements.

> **Example:** Because of negative ratings on the ferry corporation's review by government inspectors, all personnel aboard ferries have been ordered to go through intensive training on policies, procedures, and actions for emergency situations. The trainer has created a 20-item hit-or-myth challenge and has distributed it to the participants at the start of the training session. Each participant makes his or her hit/myth (true/false) choices. The trainer records, through a show of hands, the choices of the participants. Then he begins the session using the 20 items as a structuring device. At the end of the session, participants redo the challenge to see if they have "learned." The trainer again reviews the items rapidly and debriefs.

How I think this activity could be used in my organization:

Jeopardy

Just as in the television game, learners are presented with answers, solutions, or even output (both good and bad), and they have to come up with the appropriate questions. This activity can be timed, can have increasing levels of difficulty, or can be scored.

> **Example:** For their peer-assisted learning (PAL) program, Bytecom has created a set of "Jeopardy"-type questions (answers, actually) to use on the job with newly hired technicians. Peer-tutors receive a sheet in their PAL kits that contains these items. The new-hire technician, who has received training and is now going through on-the-job coaching from his PAL peer-tutor, has to make up a question to match the output or breakdown that the

136

PAL peer-tutor selects (for example, PAL peer-tutor: "The keyboard makes a noticeable clicking sound when you type, but there's no output." New hire question: "What are 'sticky keys?'"). The peer-tutor uses this activity as a wrap-up after going through a series of related work activities or intermittently as appropriate.

> *How I think this activity could be used in my organization:*

Jigsaw

The instructor divides the class into teams and assigns team leaders. He or she provides teams with documentation, each dealing with one part of a topic, and asks the teams to prepare presentations about their specific parts. Each team decides on the presentation style and the means for making its assigned content interesting to the group. Team leaders chain the brief presentations into a complete "lecture." The instructor administers a brief quiz at the end and debriefs the group.

Example: The medical workers are at a weekend training session as part of their regular recertification requirements. Recently, the laws affecting their work have undergone a large number of changes. Those changes mostly affect disclosure of patient information, prescription of certain medications and treatments, malpractice, and financial records. Because of the active nature of this group and to create greater involvement, the instructor has broken the participants into four teams. He has handed each team a variety of prepared materials on one of the four topics and assigned them the task of preparing 20-minute presentations to be given to the entire group. Teams have 90 minutes to prepare their individual parts for "Legal Changes Affecting Your Practice." The participants are warned there they will be tested on all parts at the end. Using notes, newspaper articles, prepared overhead transparencies, and their specific materials, each team crafts its 20-minute presentation. Teams deliver their information to the group. The instructor adds editorial comments to each presentation and hands out a test on all the parts to verify learning, provide feedback and additional details, and clear up any misconceptions.

> *How I think this activity could be used in my organization:*

Lecture Team Quiz

The instructor divides the class into four teams and announces that she or he will lecture for 10 minutes on a content area. After 10 minutes, each team must create one question based on the content and be prepared to answer a question on the same content. Teams have five minutes to create a question and prepare potential responses. Team One poses its question to Team Two. Members of Team Two who believe they have the answer raise their hands. Team One's team leader picks a respondent. If the answer is correct, Team Two gains five points. If not, Team Three members consult and provide a team answer. If correct, they receive two points. If incorrect, no points are awarded. Team Two then questions Team One. Once the round is complete, the instructor continues with the lecture and team quizzes through two more rounds. Teams total their scores to determine how well they have retained the lecture information.

> **Example:** Company policy requires that maintenance personnel (those who maintain the track) must attend monthly training sessions. This session is on railway safety. Attention spans can be short, but consequences for unsafe practices can be deadly. The trainer decides to break his session into five-minute clips of information with illustrations and examples. He divides the group into four teams. Each team listens for five minutes, creates one related question, and then poses the question to the team on its right. If a member of that team knows the answer, he or she raises a hand. The questioning team's leader selects the respondent and verifies the answer. If the answer is wrong, the next team to the right is queried. After each five-minute training clip, another team makes up the question. During this question prep time, the other teams share what they learned among their own participants and prepare for the question. Scores are recorded and the top team is rewarded.

> *How I think this activity could be used in my organization:*

Letter Game

The group is divided into four or five teams. Each team receives an envelope with a problem to solve written on it. Each team also receives one fewer index card than there are envelopes. Each team creates a secret team logo or symbol and draws it on each index card. Teams have two to three minutes to read the problem, decide on a solution, write it on one of the index cards, and slip the card into the envelope. Envelopes are passed clockwise to the neighboring team. Once again, the team reads the new problem, creates a solution, and slips it into the envelope. This procedure is repeated until each team receives an envelope but has no more index cards (for example, if there are five teams, each team completes four solution index cards. On the fifth round, there are no more cards). The teams then individually open the envelopes, read and evaluate the solutions, and rank-order them. If there are four solutions, the top-ranked one gets four points, the second gets three, the third gets two, and the fourth-ranked solution gets one. Each team reads its problem and the top-ranked solution and gives an explanation for its choice. Finally, all solution cards are collected and distributed to the teams by logo or symbol. Teams add up their points to determine how well they solved the problems.

Example: A group of systems engineers are in a training session focused on troubleshooting. The instructor hands out an envelope containing four index cards to each of the five teams. Each team creates a team symbol, removes the cards, and draws the symbol on each card. Team A chooses the symbol for an atom, B selects the dollar sign, C writes 777, D draws a tulip on each card, and Team E writes the Greek letter chi on its index cards. Team A passes its empty envelope to Team B, B to C, C to D, D to E, and E passes its envelope to Team A. Each team reads the system problem case written on the front of the envelope, comes up with its solution, writes it on one of its cards, and slips it into the envelope. Teams shift envelopes to their right and repeat the sequence: read, analyze, solve the case on the envelope, write the answer on an index card, and slip it into the envelope. (No peeking at the other cards inside.) This continues until teams receive their original envelope. They pull out the troubleshooting solutions, evaluate them, rank order them from best = 4 points to least worthy = 1 point, and write the rank on the back of the card. Each team reviews its case for the group and provides a rationale for its best solution selection. At the end, the cards are tossed in a pile. Each team finds its cards by symbol and totals its score.

> *How I think this activity could be used in my organization:*

Listening Teams

The instructor divides the group into four or five teams and makes each team responsible for listening and recording key information on a specific topic. The instructor then asks the teams to report the key information in sequence to the whole group in the form of summaries.

Example: The company has mandated that all operations personnel will participate in a one-hour training/information session on modifications to a series of procedures that will come into effect next month. The modifications are a result of new reporting requirements. There are fines for companies that don't comply. The trainer breaks up each group into four listening teams as she presents the changes, and she has participants apply the changes to examples. After each of the four major changes, she turns to the designated listening team for a summary of key points. At the end of the session, she gives the listening team five minutes to present what they consider to be the three key takeaways for their parts. She summarizes and adds any important takeaway points that teams have missed.

> *How I think this activity could be used in my organization:*

Mismatch

This is a simple, fun exercise to verify whether participants have absorbed information about a variety of topics or products presented within a short space of time. The instructor describes four to eight brief scenarios in which someone asks a question and receives an answer. Although they appear reasonable, the questions and answers are mismatched. Participants have to match up the correct question-and-answer pairs.

> **Example:** To conclude the session on handling customer objections, Francine distributes to the participants 10 brief conversation scenarios; in eight of them, the objection and response are mismatched. The group is given five minutes to straighten out the mess. At the end of the five minutes, Francine randomly calls on the 10 participants to read each scenario correctly. The group discusses each response. Francine gives feedback. If the group is a more confident assemblage, she includes a scoring system. She has participants give themselves one point for each right answer and one more point for each other participant who missed the answer to that item. This method rewards getting the answer to the more difficult scenarios.

> *How I think this activity could be used in my organization:*

Ours Versus Theirs

This is a fun, quick, and interactive exercise that focuses on "our" products versus those of the competition. Participants read each of the series (10 to 15) statements (for example, has 10 percent greater fuel efficiency) and select the product to which it applies. Generally, the statements are arranged in a vertical column with our product and one or two competitor's products listed side by side, like this:

	Honda "X"	Toyota "Y"	Ford "Z"
Has 10 percent greater fuel efficiency than the other two.	☐	☐	☐

The statements should create surprise and heighten interest to learn more. This activity is an excellent opener for a content area.

Example: With the company bringing out a new line of printers based on an innovative technology, it is essential that all national sales reps be up to speed on comparing these novel printers against the competition. Gerhard created a new activity called "Beatcha" for both classroom and self-study use. Its purpose is to demonstrate clearly how the Lightning printers beat the competition overall. However, it is critically important that the reps know along which dimensions Lightning products "beatcha" and where they don't. For each of the five new products, he created a list of 10 to 15 statements comparing Lightning with the three top competitors. Participants in teams (class) or individually (self-paced) find the answer by searching specification sheets that have been provided. After all the statements are answered, participants receive feedback and additional information, complete with summary comparison sheets to use during a sales call.

> *How I think this activity could be used in my organization:*

Police Interrogation

The instructor informs the group of the topic to be mastered and announces that there will be a quiz at the end of a specific time period. Learners must question and probe to "force" content out of the instructor. The instructor only answers specific questions raised by participants. The instructor can open the session to individual interrogators or have groups create questions and then interrogate. Prior to the quiz, learners can summarize among themselves what they learned.

Example: Zeta had been training the new "high-potential" management trainees for more than a week. There is still another week to go before they are released for their management internships. She has been enjoying this bright group of ambitious, young people who constantly challenge her. Now it's time to turn the tables. She walks in and announces that in one hour there will be a scored quiz. She announces the topic, Southeast Asian market characteristics and cultural idiosyncrasies, and says trainers can ask her questions to prepare for the test. She will respond honestly but not necessarily completely to all questions. She will give all information except the quiz questions. Trainees may grill her relentlessly on the topic.

At first, the trainees ask a few trial questions. Zeta responds to each one clearly and openly. After a few minutes, everyone is peppering her with probing questions. Some she answers at length, others evasively. For an hour, the interrogation on Southeast Asia runs at a furious pace. When the quiz is finally handed out, none of the trainees experience difficulties answering the questions. They have shown her that they can take charge and get what they need.

> *How I think this activity could be used in my organization:*

Press Conference

The instructor creates a press conference ambiance by organizing participants into teams of reporters charged with drawing out specific information from an "expert." Once the instructor sets the stage and specifies the overall press conference themes (generally three or four), participants create specific questions related to each theme. They write their questions on different colored index cards, one question per card. Card colors are keyed to themes. The instructor collects the cards (into which she or he may seed additional questions). The instructor divides the group into investigative-reporter teams, one team per theme. Teams spend 15 minutes sorting questions and preparing to grill the expert, press-conference style. Each team has seven minutes to question the expert aggressively while its members take notes. Once all teams have quizzed the expert on all the themes, they review their notes for five to seven minutes and list key points that would go into a press release. They report these out loud in turn, accompanied by comments from the instructor. The learners do most of the work and feel that they are controlling the situation; however, the instructor actually gets to present his or her content—plus much more.

Example: In a workshop on games for learning, Hal introduces the topic and the four press conference themes: identifying opportunities to use games, designing learning games, running games, and debriefing learning games. Participants prepare questions for each theme, one per index card (green, yellow, blue, and pink). Hal collects them after five minutes, secretly seeding a dozen questions he has prepared. In four teams, each with a pack of cards for one of the themes, participants sort and organize questions to ask as reporters. Hal then assumes the role of the visiting expert and gives each team seven minutes to ask questions, receive his answers, and make notes. Teams may cut him off and fire another question at will. After all four rounds, teams spend 20 minutes writing up press releases of one page. The teams read out loud their press releases one at a time. Hal editorializes on each. He then collects the four press releases, photocopies them, and hands copies of all four to each participant. The whole press conference activity has taken 90 minutes from start to finish.

> *How I think this activity could be used in my organization:*

Quiz Game

After a half day or full day of instruction, the trainer hands out slips of paper to participants and directs them to review all course notes and materials and individually to identify a single key point worth retaining. The point should be important and specific. This point is the "answer." Each participant privately creates a question to elicit his or her answer and writes it on the slip of paper—question only; no answer and no name. The instructor collects all the questions, shuffles the stack, and passes them out. Participants read the questions on cards they receive and give their answers (open or closed book). Answers are discussed and commented on briefly. If an answer is incomplete or incorrect, the instructor draws the missing information from the group. Participants who miss an answer get a chance to reply or add information to others' incorrect or incomplete answers. This review activity is then debriefed to ensure all key information has been summarized.

Example: To start the afternoon session on a lively note, Ahmed hands out slips of paper to all 12 participants. He asks each one to review all the product class notes he or she has taken in the morning and to find one key point that he or she believes people should remember. Using that point as a desired answer, each trainee should convert it to a question and write only the question, no answer or name, on an index card. As she turns the pages of her notes, Malika spots the following: the RX500 is the only high-speed duplex printer that is PC and Apple compatible with no hardware conversion required. She jots down on her quiz slip, "Which high-speed duplex printer is both PC and Apple compatible? Is any hardware conversion required?" All participants pass in their slips, which Ahmed promptly shuffles together and hands out, one to each person. The participants study the new questions and flip through their notes hunting for the answer. One at a time, Ahmed randomly selects participants to read their questions and give their answers. Ahmed adds details as necessary. All agree that it has been a great review. And although it was just after lunch, no one fell asleep.

How I think this activity could be used in my organization:

Slap Jack

The instructor creates a deck of index cards for a knowledge domain with a term or image on each card. Participants are grouped in teams of three to five players, each with a complete deck. A dealer on each team shuffles and distributes the cards to all members of the team. Players place their cards face down in a single stack in front of them, without looking at them. The instructor calls out a content category within the knowledge domain (for example, mortgages), and each player, clockwise in turn, rapidly draws the top card from his or her stack and tosses it face up on the table. If the card has a term or image related to the selected topic, players slap the card. The first player to slap the card retrieves it and places it face up beside his or her facedown stack. The first player who slaps an incorrect card retrieves it and places it face down. The game proceeds rapidly until all dealt cards are used up. Players count one point for each correct card slapped and subtract one point for each error.

Example: The new-hire employees are learning a lot during their orientation to the supermarket environment. There is so much to learn, but Shakil makes it fun. He pulls out a deck of cards, shuffles it, and deals each of the six trainees 15 cards. On each card is a product the supermarket sells: Granny Smith apple, Campbell's soup, Wonder Bread sandwich loaf,

Dannon yogurt, and so on. Shakil had just taught the trainees about the produce, health and beauty aids, dairy, meat, and deli departments. Now he explains the game: "I'll call out a department, such as 'Dairy.' Starting with Isaac, you each toss a card face up in the center. If someone throws in a dairy product card with 'butter' or '2% milk' on it, you all try to slap it. The first person to get it wins the card. Pick it up and place it face up in front of you. It's worth one point. If you slap the wrong card, you also keep it but place it face down in front of you. You lose a point. I'll keep switching categories of products on you with no warning, so be fast. Highest score wins."

How I think this activity could be used in my organization:

Techno Challenge

The instructor divides the class into two-member teams. Team members alternate between the role of the customer and the role of sales consultant. In timed rounds of 99 seconds, customers ask consultants questions about technology or products. Sales consultants answer as many questions about the technology or product as possible within the allotted timeframe. The customer notes answers on a question list. At the end of the round, players switch roles and repeat the process for different technologies or products. This activity is an excellent review for a content area.

> **Example:** The inbound sales associates are back from training. As team lead, Doris wants to make sure they have learned well and can answer a variety of questions about catalog items, pricing, payments, handling, shipping, and service issues. She sits down beside Jeremy, a recent hire. Using a list of common questions asked by customers, she gives Jeremy 99 seconds to answer as many questions as he can. Then she switches roles and has him play the customer questioning her. They compare how many questions each has answered and which answers are better. Doris explains that speed and accuracy are key in a high-volume inbound sales environment. Doris then moves on to Erica.

> *How I think this activity could be used in my organization:*

Terminology Tussle

This activity is based on the "BINGO" framework. The instructor presents techni-cal information that contains new terminology. At the end of the presentation, the instructor distributes to each trainee a "BINGO"-like board with the terms ran-domly dispersed. Every board is different. The instructor draws definitions from a hat and reads them aloud. Participants place a coin or marker on the term corre-sponding to the definition. The first player to cover five terms in a row (horizon-tally, vertically, or diagonally) wins. If there are many terms, the winner is the one who covers the whole board first.

> **Example:** Assembling boards for electronic equipment demands both precision and speed. Pham is now an instructor and realizes that for many of the new employees, the names of the different components can be extremely confusing. This is especially true for those whose first language isn't English. So he has created on his computer a number of "BINGO"-type cards each with a five-by-five matrix and pictures of each component (for example, CPU, SIMM, DIMM, BIOS, FAN) the trainees will encounter. By having the employees play the familiar game of "BINGO," in which the leader draws a component name from a hat and players cover with a token the component's picture on the printed card, he hopes to strengthen familiarity with the components and their names. In future sessions, Pham has decided he will draw out real components and ask participants to name them before covering the images on their cards.

> *How I think this activity could be used in my organization:*

They Say, We Say

The instructor organizes the class into teams of three or four members. Half the teams act as competitor sales consultants and the other half act as company consultants. The instructor randomly pairs off one competitor team with one company team. Before every round, the instructor provides a feature or function to each company team and notes that it has 15 seconds to describe its product's strength over that of the competition. Competitors then have 30 seconds to respond to all competitive challenges.

> **Example:** In one of the monthly training sessions for pharmaceutical sales representatives, Max, the marketing manager, divides his 12 reps into four teams of three. He pairs off two sets of two teams each and assigns the "competitor" role to one team and the "our product" role to the other team in each set. Selecting one set of two teams at a time, Max calls out a feature (for example, side effects). The "our product" team has to demonstrate the superiority of the company's feature convincingly within 15 seconds. The competitor team has 30 seconds to respond. Observers from the other set of teams comment, as does Max. Play now switches to the second set of teams and a new feature.

> *How I think this activity could be used in my organization:*

True Grid

Two axes of a two-dimensional grid represent two dimensions of a given subject (for example, stereo models along one axis; amplifier type, speakers, list price, and main competition along the other). Either individually, in teams, or as a group, participants place "titles" on the grid to fit the requirements of both dimensions. Participants compare their completed grids to the correct one.

> **Example:** Dynamite Sound is a high-end chain of stereo stores that believes its professional sales staff should know all the products by heart. It has created web-based learning modules about each of the models it sells and requires sales consultants to work through these individually during quiet times. One of the activities at the end of each module is a Challenge

Grid. A grid shows up onscreen with various products introduced in the e-learning module appearing along the vertical axis and specific feature categories along the horizontal axis. The sales consultant fills in all the spaces by clicking and dragging onscreen tiles to specific grid locations until the grid is filled. The computer issues a combined time and accuracy score. Top scorers are invited each month to compete online for valuable prizes.

> *How I think this activity could be used in my organization:*

Summarizing the Activities

You have just reviewed 25 activities for which you can use your imagination to adapt to almost any type of content. Already you may have identified how they can be used in your own environment. They all fit into the five-step model and can be applied in whole or in part to achieve a performance objective. Please note that all activities demand a great deal of meaningful effort on the part of the learners. Almost all of them permit meaningful interaction among learners and trainer (or training) and other learners. You can mix and match them to build an active training session—one that avoids the receptive approach. Most of the activities can be incorporated into a directive, guided discovery, or even an exploratory framework. They are yours. You now own them. Use them and adapt them as you wish.

Table 8-2 provides a final summary of the activities detailed here, suggesting where they easily fit in training. Don't feel constrained, however, by the Xs we have placed in the table. Go beyond the table. With creativity you'll find many additional learning uses for these activities.

Closing the Door on This Active Chapter

Throughout the activity portion of this chapter we have tried to engage you by asking you to imagine how you might use each activity in your organization or help one of your colleagues adopt or adapt it. Keep this in mind as you explore other existing activities produced from various sources.

Additional Resources

The web offers a wealth of free resources for creating training games and game-like activities. Here are a few examples:

* **www.thiagi.com/games.html**—more than 200 games that are easily adaptable to a variety of content.
* **www.businessballs.com/teambuilding.htm**—lots of games and other activities, especially those related to free team-building games ideas and theory for employee motivation, training, and development.
* **www.wilderdom.com/games/OtherSites.html**—listing of websites with descriptions of games to play with groups.
* **www.clubbing.com**—enchanting, free online games.
* **www.businessballs.com**—games and other activities, tools, and templates on ethical work and life learning at no charge.
* **Sivasailam Thiagarajan's and Tracy Tagliati's book,** *Jolts,* contains 50 terrific activities that are also linked to online resources. These "jolting," highly interactive activities are stimulating and thought provoking. Best of all, they can be integrated into practically any type of course or training program.[4]
* **www.traininggames.com**—both free and for purchase electronic games. You can sign up on their website and download a host of icebreaker games at no charge and ones that are easily adaptable to a variety of content.

Because websites come and go, we strongly encourage you to explore, online, the vast number of resources available in the area of games and related activities for learning. Also examine those that charge for their materials. If these fit with your objectives, they may be worthwhile purchasing for use in your organization. Make sure that you thoroughly investigate what you buy.

We conclude with a simple formula that ties all the learning activities together: teach-prompt-release. The purpose of all learning is to provide enough input to set the learner on the right path. That's the *teach* phase. Then you encourage practice with support that you fade out. That's the *prompt* phase. Finally, when the learner is sufficiently capable to try it alone, you have reached the *release* (but not abandon) phase. Some of the activities we have presented integrate into the teach phase readily (for example, Press Conference, Police Interrogation, and Listening Teams). Most help with prompting. Learners try, but receive guidance as required (for example, Confrontation, Concentration, and Terminology Tussle). A few are more adapted to release (for example, True Grid, Quiz Game, and Great Debate). Watch your learners as they gain competence and confidence. They will trigger for you the best types of activities to use. Let their transformation guide you in your training.

Table 8-2. Training Activities and Suggested Settings

Activity	Instructor-Led Large Group	Instructor-Led Small Group	Individual Learning	Peer Learning	On-the-Job Learning
Better Me					X
Concentration				X	
Confrontation		X			
Critical List	X				
Crypto Cluster		X	X		
Domino Effect		X		X	
Exam Cram	X	X		X	
Facts-in-Five	X	X		X	
Great Debate	X				
Hit-or-Myth	X		X		
Jeopardy			X		X
Jigsaw	X				
Lecture Team Quiz	X				X
Letter Game	X				
Listening Teams	X				
Mismatch	X		X		X
Ours Versus Theirs	X		X		X
Police Interrogation	X				
Press Conference	X				X
Quiz Game	X				
Slap Jack		X			
Techno Challenge				X	X
Terminology Tussle	X				
They Say, We Say	X	X	X		
True Grid			X	X	

Remember This

Ready for an activity of your own? Complete the following statements correctly by crossing out the inappropriate parenthesized word or phrase. Get them right without any prompting, and we'll release you to the next chapter.

1. Receptive training is mostly (*one-way telling / interactive*).
2. Awareness training usually (*does / does not*) result in significant behavior changes in learners.
3. Directive training is based on the belief that the learners require (*a planned learning path / room to explore and discover*).
4. Guided discovery training provides (*a totally free learning environment / cues, prompts, suggestions, and corrective feedback*).
5. Exploratory training is particularly well suited to learners with (*little prior knowledge and poorly developed metacognitive skills / considerable prior knowledge and well developed metacognitive skills*).
6. The learning activities described in this chapter (*can/cannot*) be adapted to technology-based training delivery.
7. The learning activities described in this chapter (*can/cannot*) be used easily by relatively inexperienced trainers.
8. Most of the activities described in this chapter are suited to (*practically any / very specific*) types of content.
9. The web is a (*good/poor*) resource for training professionals to discover training-learning games for working adults.
10. A simple learning formula for any type of learner, any number of learners, and any type of learning is (*say what you're going to say, say it, and say what you've said / teach-prompt-release*).

Here are our responses:

1. Receptive training is mostly one-way telling. We recommend avoiding this training architecture except for limited use to build some form of information base. It's telling and not really training.
2. Awareness training usually does not result in significant behavior changes in learners. Awareness training is not aimed at specific, verifiable behavior outcomes. It can be a precursor to changes in the learner.
3. Directive training is based on the belief that the learners require a planned learning path. It is useful for initial training to build basic competence and confidence. It also supports learners who possess poorly developed metacognitive skills or who lack confidence with respect to what they must learn.
4. Guided discovery training provides cues, prompts, suggestions, and corrective feedback. It encourages independence while offering a supportive scaffolding as required by the learner.

5. Exploratory training is particularly well suited to learners with considerable prior knowledge and well-developed metacognitive skills. It offers a rich environment for individuals to find what they require for their performance improvement.

6. The learning activities described in this chapter can be adapted to technology-based training delivery. They can be integrated into interactive, synchronous, web-based sessions; virtual classrooms; and self-study, asynchronous programs. Imagination, design skills, and some technical savvy are required.

7. The learning activities described in this chapter can be used easily by relatively inexperienced trainers. As some of the examples and table 8-2 show, peer learners can apply these for learning as can on-the-job coaches. In a workshop we ran for parents, the 20 participants created and tried out 60 learning activities to use with children. All were based on the activities in this chapter.

8. Most of the activities described in this chapter are suited to practically any content. We have adapted them to train veterinary students on bovine respiratory ailments, intellectually challenged teenagers to repair telephones, and even military personnel on passive sonar operation.

9. The web is a good resource for training professionals to discover training-learning games for working adults. Many of the resources are free. There is a huge variety to explore and from which to choose.

10. A simple learning formula for any type of learner, any number of learners, and any type of learning is teach-prompt-release. "Say what you're going to say, say it, and say what you've said" is a variation of "tell them what you're going to tell them, tell them, and tell them what you've told them." It's the receptive model of training. It's telling. It sure ain't training.

Now, on to a key question. You trained them, but did they learn? Some organizations fear to verify learning. Understandably, they do not want to create anxiety and negative feelings toward training. However, does verifying whether or not learners acquired requisite skills and/or knowledge from what you taught them demand "testing" in the form of an exam? The next chapter examines this question.

Chapter 9

Testing or Examining— What's the Difference?

Chapter highlights: ───────────────────────────────

▶ Importance and benefits of testing

▶ Differences between testing and examining

▶ Explanation of criterion-referenced testing

▶ Job aid for test method selection and creation.

───

We begin this chapter by teaching you a trick called "Lightning Squares." Although limited in mathematical range, it is an impressive stunt you can show off to wow your friends and family. What's great about it is that you don't have to be proficient at math to do it. The only prerequisite is to be reasonably competent at doing the multiplication tables you learned in primary school.

By the end of this small, fun lesson you will be able to square any two-digit number ending in "5" very swiftly. In other words, in less than 10 seconds, you will be able to give the answer to: 15^2 or 15×15; 25^2 or 25×25; 35^2 or 35×35 … right up to 95^2 or 95×95. Do you have any doubts? Let's try it out.

What is 35^2? The answer is 1225.

We got the answer in three seconds. Impressed? Try multiplying 35×35. You'll get the same answer, but it will probably take you from 15 to 45 seconds. How did we do it so fast? Watch this:

Take 35^2 and break it into 3 and 5^2. The 5^2 at the end equals 25 (5×5). We now have 3 and 25.

Multiply 3 by (3 + 1) or 4, so multiply 3 × 4. The answer is 12. The answer to 35^2 is 1225.

Here's a second example:

65^2
Break it into 6 and 5^2.
5^2 becomes 25, so you're left with 6 and 25.
Multiply 6 × (6 + 1) or 6 × 7 to get 42.
The answer is 4225. Check by multiplying 65 × 65.

Now it's your turn. The challenge is 45^2. Fill in the blanks.

45^2
Break it into _____ and _____.
_____ becomes _____, so you're left with _____ and _____.
Multiply 4 × (4 + _____) or 4 × _____ to get _____.
The answer is _____.

Turn the page upside-down to check your calculation.

Answer:
Break it into 4 and 5^2.
5^2 becomes 25, so you're left with 4 and 25.
Multiply 4 × (4 + 1) or 4 × 5 to get 20.
The answer is 2025.

The key is to take the first digit (for example, 4) and always add 1 to it (for example, 4 + 1 or 5); then multiply by the first digit (for example, 4 × 5 = 20). Then join with 25 (for example, 2025).

At this point, would you like to check to see if you've got it? Try 15^2 as fast as you can and write your answer in this box:

Your answer:

Check yourself by turning around the page.

1 × (1 + 1) or 1 × 2 = 2
Answer: 225

Would you like to test yourself before we move along with this chapter? Try the following: 25^2, 75^2, 95^2. Time yourself for solving all three. You have 30 seconds. Go!

25^2 =_____ 75^2 =_____ 95^2 =_____

Here are the answers:

> $25^2 = 625$ $75^2 = 5625$ $95^2 = 9025$

If you got all three right in less than 30 seconds, bravo! If you got all three right but it took a bit longer than 30 seconds, you're on the right track. Just practice and try again. When you do each of them in less than 10 seconds, good for you! If you made errors, review the steps and try again. You'll get it. We've never had a learner who didn't eventually succeed.

What Was That All About?

In case you haven't figured it out yet, that was our introduction to the testing chapter. First we taught you something (starting with a rationale and performance objective). Then, after a little practice in which we faded out cues (we prompted you), we gave you a "test" (we released you). Did you feel threatened by the test? Did you feel that it was natural to see if you could do it? Did you feel good about yourself and your accomplishment when you succeeded?

When we provide instruction to learner groups, either live or via some other mode, such as a book, e-learning, or video, we always build in testing. Reflect on the "Lightning Squares" lesson you just experienced. Check off the items below with which you agree:

☐ 1. I felt stressed by the three test questions.
☐ 2. I felt at ease with the three test questions.
☐ 3. The test helped me check to see if I got it right.
☐ 4. The test helped me practice and remember.
☐ 5. The test helped me find what I had missed in the lesson.
☐ 6. The test and feedback were useful.
☐ 7. Thirty seconds? I did it in a lot less time!
☐ 8. I felt great about my success. I could do it!

When we present similar exercises and then check with adult learners, here are our typical findings:

▶ About 20 percent of the learners feel stressed. With some groups, it ranges up to 30 and 40 percent. They tell us, however, that the stress isn't necessarily related to this test. It's the word "test" that affects them and often makes them freeze up.

▶ About 60 to 70 percent of the learners are totally at ease with this form of testing. Many don't even perceive it as a test. They read it as "check yourself."

▶ Almost all our learners feel that this type of testing is helpful, stressful or otherwise. It seems like more practice but is presented in a more challenging—even stimulating—manner.

▶ Almost all the adults find that this type of test-practice helps them remember longer.

▶ If learners make an error on the "test," they are happy to receive feedback and try again. In fact, in some cases the learners say they finally figured out the process through the testing and feedback.

▶ This reiterates what we just said: The testing and feedback can reinforce or add value to the lesson.

▶ We set a 30-second time limit knowing full well that most learners can do it in less time. That added sense of "I beat the test!" reinforces the learning and increases motivation. Caution: This has to be done carefully. The challenge has to be realistic and allow for satisfaction in meeting and, for those who can, beating the standard. It's a delicate balance.

▶ Achieving success leads to pleasurable feelings in most learners. They overcame what they may have perceived as a difficult challenge. The effort that results in success provides an intrinsic reward. Learners who feel competent and confident about what they learned have a higher probability of reusing it back on the job. This may not be as a result of any training per se, but of the sense of accomplishment generated by confirmation of a valued achievement.[1]

 Using the brief "Lightning Squares" lesson and debriefing, we can state the following key points about testing:

▶ Testing is a natural part of learning. It helps both learners and trainers confirm performance objective attainment or identify where something is missing and requires corrective feedback.

▶ Testing doesn't need to be threatening, but sometimes it is. (We will deal with this more in the next section on testing and examining.)

▶ Testing is an excellent way to teach. It lets the learner try out her or his learning with a bit of a challenge. The trainer or instructional component of a self-study lesson is pushed to the side. The learner, in a test situation, does all the work. Remember, the more meaningful work the learner does, the more the learner learns.

▶ Testing requires that feedback be given following the test. It either confirms objective attainment or offers corrective information specific to how the learner performed on the test, guiding her or him back on track.[2]

▶ Because testing requires active learner engagement, it should be used frequently. Meaningful engagement enhances comprehension and retention.

There is a "however" to all of this. Testing sometimes frightens adult learners, particularly those who may not have had great success with it in school. Anything that vaguely resembles a test (even a simple practice exercise with scoring or timing) can bring on anxiety and accompanying emotional push-back. This is a learned reaction to unpleasant past experiences. We'll probe this further in the next section.[3]

Testing Versus Exams

At school you may have had weekly tests and then a final exam. In a courtroom, we are familiar with the lawyers "examining" and "cross-examining" the witnesses, probing for weaknesses in their stories. In fact, the whole concept of exams has become quite terrifying. No wonder so many people experience stress if they feel they are going to participate in an exam. (Medical personnel frequently note higher blood pressure levels in patients undergoing a medical "exam.") Often those who take the exam feel as if it is not their skill and knowledge that is being examined, but they themselves. It is as if their own worth is being examined and brought into question. There's not much difference for some people between the statements "You failed the exam" and "You're a failure!" Incidentally, that perception is not restricted to low performers. Many high performers feel tremendous anxiety as well.[4]

We don't want to overdramatize the point. We also are not therapists. What we do observe is that many people confuse testing in a natural, positive, educational manner with bad exam experiences and, therefore, erect barriers to an important learning activity. We define testing as an opportunity to verify whether or not the learner has attained the pre-specified objective. If yes, the learner must receive information either naturally by succeeding with the task or from the trainer/training in the form of a message, such as, "Correct," "You've done it," or "Perfect score." If the learner has not met the performance objective, then this is an opportunity to identify where the difficulty lies and provide supportive, useful feedback with the possibility of retesting until the learner has succeeded in achieving the performance objective requirements.

One way of decreasing fear of testing is to employ terms such as "learning check" or "practice exercise." Although this may sound like a euphemism, elimination of the word "test" can lower anxiety. This discussion brings us to a fundamental perspective on training. We train adult workers so that they will be able to perform in ways both they and the organization value. Training is by no means an end. It is a way to achieve organizationally desirable work performance outcomes by building required skills and knowledge. Our training should be designed to lead the adult learners simply, naturally, and directly from where they are to where they and the organization believe they should be.

To accomplish this, we analyze our learners to determine the current levels of their skill and knowledge. We specify the desired state. Then we build our training to create a path that leads them from "here" to "there." Our performance objectives are the milestones. Our tests are checkpoints that perfectly match the objectives. This whole approach is often called *criterion-referenced instruction*—that is, instruction solidly anchored to the criteria for successful job accomplishment.[5] The testing part is called *criterion-referenced testing*. It is the natural means for ensuring that the learner has met the objective at the appropriate standard of performance.[6]

If the training were for delicatessen counter workers to be able to slice a bagel into equal halves with smooth surfaces, then the test would be for them to demonstrate this performance. If they missed something (unequal halves or rough surfaces), then they would receive feedback and be tested (or given a new practice exercise) again until they succeeded.

Imagine that the following are objectives your adult learners have to attain. How would you test them in a criterion-referenced environment? Reflect on each one. Create a test item that is a perfect match for the objective and write it in the answer block following each objective.

- Given the ABC system, display the customer file in 30 seconds and on the first try.

```



```

- Faced with a fire, select the appropriate procedure for combating it.

```



```

- Name the capitals of all the provinces of Canada, matching each capital to its province with no errors.

```



```

- From a collection of bones, identify the femur.

```



```

Table 9-1 presents our testing suggestions. Read them to learn how your ideas compare with our suggestions. Indicate your reactions to our ideas in the third column of the table.

Those four examples are intended to reinforce the idea of criterion-referenced testing. It means testing that perfectly verifies what the performance objective specifies. We will examine criterion-referenced tests in more detail soon.

Please note that the tests (or if you are getting comfortable with *learning check,* start using this term) to verify objective attainment are not necessarily exams. They could take the form of practice exercises, self-checks, team challenges, or en route checkpoints. In a formal setting they *could* become exams. What is key is that testing verifies performance objective success. In the learning environment, it should be done as naturally as possible to decrease stress that may inhibit performance. If exams are required, we recommend that you engage learners in sufficient test practice to replace their anxiety with confidence. Unless test-taking is somehow part of the job, focus on what learners are supposed to be able to do and not on the "test."

What follows is an example from our experience that illustrates the point.

Sample Scenario: I've Been Working on the Railroad

All railway personnel who operate trains must go through a certification ritual every three years. Their work requires them to take exams on nine different subjects related to every aspect of handling a train. It includes a variety of content from inspecting airbrakes to marshalling trains to reading signals to applying specific regulations for different weather and track conditions. If they don't pass all exams with a minimum of 85 percent, they don't get their cards renewed. No card, no work.

Obviously, this can be a stressful time for railway personnel as they approach their exams. For the railway, it's important to keep the locomotive engineers and conductors on the job. When we became involved at one railway, we found that the exams were mostly content centered rather than performance based and were more a set of reading tests than true verification of competency. Working with management, unions, and government examiners, we revised the exams so that they more closely matched what the engineers and conductors actually did on the job. We broke all the subjects down into major job tasks. We created lots of practice that tied closely to the tasks using clearly defined performance objectives. The practice exercises matched the objectives, and the practice tests matched the exercises. So closely was it all interwoven that training time radically decreased, and the exam success ratio shot way up. Best of all, the operational personnel found the testing easier although it was more job-application focused and contained 30 percent more test questions.

Table 9-1. Testing Suggestions Correlated to Performance Objectives

Performance Objective	Our Test Suggestion	Your Reactions
Given the ABC system, display the customer file in 30 seconds and on the first try.	Performance test: Give the learner a customer name. Have the learner interact with the ABC system to display the file. Check for accuracy, time, and number of attempts.	*(Check all that apply.)* ☐ Exactly the way I thought. ☐ Similar but not exactly the way I thought. ☐ I wish I had thought of this. ☐ I was way off base.
Faced with a fire, select the appropriate procedure for combating it.	Recall test: Show different types of fires (e.g., electrical, gas, flammable liquid). Have learner select the procedure from memory. (We have not asked her or him to combat the fire, only to select the procedure.) Verify accuracy of match.	*(Check all that apply.)* ☐ Exactly the way I thought. ☐ Similar but not exactly the way I thought. ☐ I wish I had thought of this. ☐ I was way off base.
Name the capitals of all the provinces of Canada, matching each capital to its province with no errors.	Recall test: Have learners recite the provinces and their capitals from memory. Verify accuracy.	*(Check all that apply.)* ☐ Exactly the way I thought. ☐ Similar but not exactly the way I thought. ☐ I wish I had thought of this. ☐ I was way off base.
From a collection of bones, identify the femur.	Recognition test: Display bones. Name femur. Have learner point to it.	*(Check all that apply.)* ☐ Exactly the way I thought. ☐ Similar but not exactly the way I thought. ☐ I wish I had thought of this. ☐ I was way off base.

When we used the old exam to test the engineers and conductors three months after they were recertified, many of them couldn't attain the overall 85 percent passing grade. With the new approach, more than 90 percent scored 85 percent and higher three months and even six months after recertification. As one long-time railroader put it: "Before, I hated the exams and couldn't sleep for days. With the new approach, my exam felt like all the practice tests I did on my own and in the class. No sweat!"

How Do I Go About Creating Tests?

This part of the chapter focuses on the nitty-gritty details of creating useful tests. We highly recommend you spend time on this section for three solid reasons:

- ▶ It will help you select and create valid tests.
- ▶ It has a lot of job aids that help cut down your time for test construction and guidelines for doing it well.
- ▶ We reviewed and condensed a great deal of material to prepare the few pages that follow. If you go through it, you will save all the time we had to spend.

Where to Start With Tests

Begin with your objectives. In the five-step model training session plan, you specify your overall and specific objectives. For each specific objective, you create a test item. Let's imagine that you are going to train distribution center workers on how to operate a specific forklift vehicle. There are two prerequisites: They must have a valid driver's license, and they must have written and passed the safety regulations test. Imagine that the first objective is to inspect the vehicle: "Given an XYZ-model forklift vehicle, you will be able to inspect it to determine mechanical soundness, safety status, and readiness for use, with no errors or omissions."

Going back to what you learned in chapter 4, decide if this essentially requires declarative knowledge (talk about, name, explain) or procedural knowledge (activity, do, perform). Check your choice:

- ☐ Declarative
- ☐ Procedural.

The correct answer is procedural. Learners actually have to *do* something: conduct the inspection and determine status.

Examine the information in figure 9-1. It will help you decide what type of test you should construct for the forklift training. Because this is procedural knowledge, you turn right on the chart. That takes you to the question, "Covert procedure?" In other words, is this a procedure you cannot observe, such as doing a mental calculation? If it is, you are guided to provide the learners with a written or oral test and then ask them to recount to you orally or on paper what they did. You check off each step and/or decision they made as they tell you what they have done. This is the only way to determine if the right answer was the result of the right procedure. The forklift vehicle inspection is not a covert procedure, so you can create a performance test. To verify performance, we use one of the verification tools listed in figure 9-1.

Performance Tests and Verification Instruments

A performance test is an exercise you create to verify if the learner can do what is specified in the performance objective. Suppose the objective was, "Slice a bagel so that you get two equal halves and smooth surfaces. Do not injure yourself or anyone else." Which of the following options would be an appropriate performance test?

1. Here is a bagel, a knife, and a cutting board. Slice the bagel so that you end up with two equal halves and smooth surfaces, and do not injure yourself or anyone else.
2. Explain to me the correct procedure for slicing a bagel so that you get two equal halves, smooth surfaces, and there are no injuries.
3. Here's a bagel that has been sliced. Tell me if it conforms to standards and justify your response.

The correct selection is 1, which matches the objective and calls for actual performance. If for safety, cost, resource, or other practical reasons you can't have the learner do the real thing, then you can simulate it (use a mockup or a simulator).

If that's not practical, test again but with objects that look like or represent the real thing and context. Reality is a credible way to verify (test) whether or not a person has met the performance objective. The problem: If there is any danger (that is, drive a forklift truck when you are not yet really competent or land an aircraft), then testing in a real-live manner could be disastrous. In most instances this is not a problem (that is, pull up a file from a database or slice a bagel). However, when danger exists or it is impractical to have the real thing present (for example, a locomotive airbrake in the training-testing setting), then a simulation of the real thing is the next best thing.

What is a simulation? Basically, it is a dynamic and simplified representation of a real or hypothetical system. It is based on a model of the actual system. The dynamic portion allows for manipulation of the system's elements. As an example,

Figure 9-1. Test Type Selection Job Aid

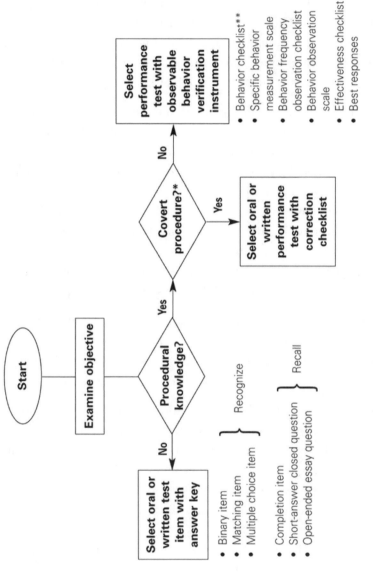

Start

Examine objective

Procedural knowledge?

No → **Select oral or written test item with answer key**

- Binary item
- Matching item   } Recognize
- Multiple choice item

- Completion item
- Short-answer closed question   } Recall
- Open-ended essay question

Yes → **Covert procedure?***

Yes → **Select oral or written performance test with correction checklist**

No → **Select performance test with observable behavior verification instrument**

- Behavior checklist**
- Specific behavior measurement scale
- Behavior frequency observation checklist
- Behavior observation scale
- Effectiveness checklist
- Best responses

* A covert procedure is one you cannot see being performed. It takes place in the learner's head. Mental arithmetic, troubleshooting, and decision making that occur inside the learner with no overt activity are examples of covert procedures.

** Most common type of performance test.

suppose you are training workers on how to troubleshoot the hydraulic system in the undercarriage of an aircraft. It would be impractical to bring in or immobilize a real airplane. So, we create a simulator that works like the real thing, but doesn't have all of the other irrelevant parts of the aircraft. The simulator (a dynamic, simplified representation of the real undercarriage) allows for manipulation. Different problems are simulated on the simulator. Trainees learn to troubleshoot and get tested. Transfer of learning to the actual hydraulic system on the real aircraft is generally pretty strong. Some additional learning activities or support may be required when confronted with reality. Obviously, more testing will be required to certify that the trainees have mastered the job tasks.

What we've described here is a "high-fidelity" simulation system. It looks and feels like the real thing. Such simulators (the equipment) allow for a wide variety of simulations (realistic events, scenarios, and actions) to be played out. High-fidelity simulators and simulations, while effective, can be costly. Therefore, we may have to back off a bit and create lower fidelity simulations. These are not quite like reality, but they are still better than just talking about objects and situations. Backing further off from this type of simulation, we turn to scenario-based learning exercises. Notice that we are getting further away from the real world. Nevertheless, scenario-based instruction is still better than dealing with only words and abstractions. Scenario-based tests are more valid than essay writing for procedural tasks.

We always want to get as close to the real job situation as possible. We back away to high-fidelity, then low-fidelity, and then to scenario-based forms of instruction and testing because of danger, cost, resource constraints, time, and other practical factors that influence what is doable in the learning-testing context.

Two other issues to bear in mind with simulation are "psychological fidelity" and transfer to the job. In nearly all cases, simulations and scenarios are far more psychologically realistic than a discourse on some topic. However, sometimes a lower-fidelity simulation may create a stronger psychological sense of reality than a physically accurate representation of the "real world." We have seen a hand-manipulated, three-dimensional cardboard pop-up visual aid displaying the organs of the body and how infection spreads affect villagers learning about reproductive health and sanitation more strongly than plastic, near-perfect representations that could be touched and handled.

With respect to transfer of learning to real life, again, simulation is more powerful than lecture or other forms of nonparticipative instruction. However, the more realistic the simulation has been, the easier it is to transfer the learning to a live situation. In all cases, guidance, practice, and support are necessary. Even with the most "authentic" physical and psychological simulations, some form of transition assistance is required. Learning checks that increasingly approximate reality and then real-world exercises and tests help cement learning and increase the probability of successful on-job performance.[7]

Creating Tests

There is no true way to measure procedural knowledge unless the learner performs for real, via simulation or through a scenario. Talking about it is not enough. Coaches can talk about successful sports plays but they cannot necessarily perform them.

The performance test is half of what you create to test the learners on the objective. The other half is the verification instrument. This helps record how well each learner has performed. It is also useful for providing feedback. Table 9-2 is a list of performance test verification instruments. Browse through them to see the variety, advantages, and drawbacks of each. Choose your instrument based on which one best fits the situation.

Let's return to the forklift example and the performance objective: "Given an XYZ-model forklift vehicle, you will be able to inspect it to determine mechanical soundness, safety status, and readiness for use, with no errors or omissions." Here is a suitable performance test: "Conduct a complete inspection of forklift vehicle 23 (model XYZ). Check it for mechanical soundness, safety status, and readiness for use. Make no errors and leave nothing out."

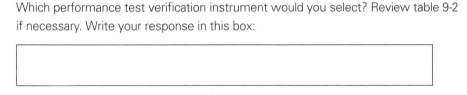

Which performance test verification instrument would you select? Review table 9-2 if necessary. Write your response in this box:

We selected the behavior checklist because we feel that the inspection largely consists of a series of actions or behaviors the learner either does or does not do (for example, verify for missing parts and check tire pressure). This selection does not eliminate additional notes made for feedback purposes.

In about 75 percent of all cases, the behavior checklist is the favored choice. It's simple and easy to use. The second most common choice is the specific behavior measurement scale. The behavior checklist elicits "yes" or "no" answers for each item, and the scale measures the observation.

Table 9-2. Variety, Advantages, and Drawbacks of Performance Test Verification Instruments

Type of Instrument	Advantages	Drawbacks
Behavior checklist: Provides an observer with a list of behaviors the learner must demonstrate during a test.	• Is easy to develop. • Is easy to train observers. • Checklist items are simple and clear. • Provides concrete feedback to the learner.	• Limits qualitative evaluation, especially for higher-level competencies. • Does not lend itself readily to situations in which there is a wide range of acceptable behaviors. • If poorly designed, results in a high degree of observer subjectivity.
Specific behavior measurement scale: Provides an observer with a set of specific behaviors and a measurement scale for each. The scale is graded by level of competence.	• Provides a means for displaying different competency levels for different learner behaviors. • Decreases observer subjectivity. • Is relatively easy to train observers to use this type of instrument. • Provides learners with feedback during the learning process.	• Takes longer to create than a checklist. • Is not useful if learner demonstrates behaviors not on the scale. • Is a bit awkward to use. • Is somewhat subjective.
Behavior frequency observation checklist: Provides an observer with a checklist that helps monitor frequency of a behavior or frequency of relevant and irrelevant behaviors.	• Produces a lot of data. • Demonstrates concretely the presence or absence of specific behaviors. • Can be used even if the learner deviates from targeted behaviors. • Can provide learners with feedback during the learning process.	• Does not measure the degree of improvement of a behavior. • Requires considerable training of observers.
Behavior observation scale: Allows an observer to judge the appropriateness of using a behavior. When a variety of behaviors have been learned, each suited to a specific situation, this permits verification of the match between situation and behavior.	• Is easy to create.	• The result depends on the ability of the observer to judge the appropriateness of a behavior.

Type of Instrument	Advantages	Drawbacks
Effectiveness checklist: Allows an observer to determine the effectiveness of a learner's behavior. Focuses on results or outcomes. What is verified is the effect of the behavior, not the behavior itself.	• Effectiveness criteria have a high degree of credibility because they focus on results. • Is easy to train observers. • Provides learners with feedback on accomplishment rather than behavior during the learning process.	• No attention to actual learner behavior. • Does not measure how the result was achieved. • Does not measure the costs of achieving the result.
Best responses: Allows for identification of several acceptable responses or solutions as best choices.	• Recognizes there are good, better, and best responses or solutions. • Recognizes that responses or solutions can be ranked in order of acceptability.	• Does not allow for different ability levels for explaining how a response or solution emerged. • An excellent response or solution can be obtained without use of a targeted behavior.

Figure 9-2 contrasts a behavior checklist for bagel slicing with a specific behavior measurement scale for that task. For bagel slicing, the behavior checklist definitely is adequate. For customer service, diagnosis, sales, conducting a sales meeting, and other less clear-cut behaviors where level of performance may be quantified along a continuum, the measurement scale may be a more appropriate model. In all cases, space for observations and comments can always be added to your instrument.

Figure 9-2. Comparison of Two Performance Test Verification Instruments

Behavior Checklist	Yes	No
Bagel sliced	☐	☐
Two equal halves	☐	☐
Surfaces smooth	☐	☐
No injuries	☐	☐

Specific Behavior Measurement Scale	Excellent	Very good	Good	Fair	Unacceptable
Bagel sliced	☐	☐	☐	☐	☐
Two equal halves	☐	☐	☐	☐	☐
Surfaces smooth	☐	☐	☐	☐	☐
No injuries	☐	☐	☐	☐	☐

Written and Oral Tests

Continuing with our forklift example, imagine that one of the performance objectives is to name each of the gauges on the vehicle dashboard and explain its use. Turn back to figure 9-1. Examine the objective. Does it require procedural knowledge?

☐ **Yes**   ☐ **No**

Naming and explaining require declarative (talk about) knowledge. The answer, therefore, is no. (On the chart, you turn left at the decision point.) To test for this performance objective we would employ some form of oral or written test with an appropriate answer key that contains the right answer. As you can see, there are several different oral and written tests. Binary or true/false items, matching tests (match the items in column A with those in column B), and multiple-choice test items are appropriate for recognizing the right answer. Here's an example:

The "C" in a European temperature reading stands for

a. Centigrade or Celsius scale.
b. Color temperature scale.
c. Central European scale.
d. Centrifugal scale.

In this case, the learner need only *recognize* the answer, which is much easier than having to *recall* it. As the chart shows, for a recall-type performance objective, you could create a completion item (for example, "The 'C' in a European temperature reading stands for _____ or _____") or a short-answer closed question (for example, "What does the 'C' in a European temperature reading stand for?"). Pushing it somewhat, you might even use an open-ended essay question ("Explain from where the 'C' in a European temperature reading is derived. What are the key benefits of this scale compared with that of the Fahrenheit scale?"). In table 9-3, we present brief descriptions of each of the types of oral and written test items and some key advantages and drawbacks.

We already have decided that for a performance objective that asks learners to name the gauges on the dashboard of a forklift vehicle and explain the uses of each one, an oral (or perhaps written) test would be appropriate. Check off the specific type of test you would select from the list below. You may check off more than one.

☐ Binary test   ☐ Completion test
☐ Matching test   ☐ Short-answer closed question test
☐ Multiple-choice test   ☐ Open-ended essay test

Table 9-3. Variety, Advantages, and Drawbacks of Oral and Written Test Items

Type of Test Item	Advantages	Drawbacks
Binary test: Offers learner two choices to select from, only one of which is correct. True/false and yes/no are the most common types.	• Is easy to correct and compile results manually, optically, or by computer. • Test instructions are easy to understand.	• Range of responses is limited to two choices. • The test creator must possess strong mastery of the learning material. • There is a 50 percent chance of getting a right answer without knowing the learning material.
Matching test: Requires learner to match an item in one column with an item in a second column. Items in the second column are generally in random order. To increase challenge, the second column usually contains more items than the first.	• Is easy to create. • Is easy to correct. • Allows for many items to be tested simultaneously. • Is especially applicable for content that lends itself to pairing items.	• Is restricted in application to objectives/content that lend themselves to pairing items. • Only tests low-level objectives. • Through process of elimination, allows for some guesswork.
Multiple-choice test: Requires learner to select the correct answer to a question from an array of three or four alternatives.	• Is easy to correct manually or mechanically. • Can include distracters that force discrimination between correct and almost-correct responses. • Permits testing of a large body of material fairly rapidly.	• Generally is limited to fact-based questions. • Does not allow for elaboration or explanation. • Takes a lot of skill and time to create excellent test items. • Requires good reading skills.
Completion test: Requires a one-word or several-words completion to a statement. Range of acceptable completion responses is limited.	• Limits the range of possible correct responses. • Is easy to correct manually using a correction guide or by computer. • Eliminates subjectivity. • Appropriate for problems with a limited number of possible correct responses.	• Not appropriate for "why" and "how" questions. • The question itself may provide clues to the correct response. • Handwritten responses are difficult to correct mechanically.

(continued on next page)

Table 9-3. Variety, Advantages, and Drawbacks of Oral and Written Test Items (continued)

Type of Test Item	Advantages	Drawbacks
Short-answer closed question test: Requires a brief, limited response from the learner.	• Is easy to create. • Is easy to check. • Is easy to insert during instruction.	• Is limited in richness of response. • Takes longer to correct (written form) than do multiple-choice, binary, or matching items. • Can result in response variability.
Open-ended essay test: Requires an extended response that can also include learner's opinion, interpretation, and vision.	• Is easy to create. • Allows for freedom of response by learner. • Appropriate for "why" and "how" types of objectives.	• Requires strong subject matter knowledge to verify and give feedback. • Correction is labor intensive. • Allows highly diverse responses.

Because the performance objective requires recall instead of recognition, we selected the short-answer closed question test. Our question would be "Name all the gauges on the XYZ forklift vehicle dashboard. Explain the uses of each one as you name it." Our answer key would contain the name of each gauge with its position on the dashboard and a list of uses for each gauge.

 As a final note on written tests of a formal nature, here are some useful guidelines to follow, regardless of the type of test items you create:

- ▶ Keep course objectives clearly in mind. The test item must match the objective perfectly.
- ▶ Start with a few easy-to-answer questions to help relieve test anxiety among trainees.
- ▶ Write the test items at the language and reading level of the learners.
- ▶ Avoid negatives and double negatives in the questions.
- ▶ Construct questions and answers that are precise and non-ambiguous. Questions should have only one correct answer.
- ▶ Do not replicate statements from the participant manual. When you do so, you test memorization of the material and not comprehension.
- ▶ Make sure that the test items do not include clues about other test items.

▶ If this is a test following a unit of instruction, make sure that the answer to one test item is not dependent on the answer to another test item.

▶ Avoid trick questions that test the learner's ability to guess, not his or her comprehension of the material.

▶ In a test covering a large body of material or a series of objectives, group same-type questions together—binary, multiple-choice, and so forth—to reduce the number of instructions and facilitate the learner's task.

▶ Provide examples for complex question types.

▶ Provide clear instructions to the instructor about the length of the test and the material required. Provide him or her with answer sheets and correction guidelines.

▶ Try out the test and revise as needed before implementation.[8]

Checking for Test Validity

You have created a test item to verify whether the learner is able to meet the objective. You may have even prepared several test items for each objective for practice, at the end of some part of the training, and to include in an overall test at the end. How do you ensure that your test items, even for practice purposes, are valid (that is, they truly test what the objective requires)? We have included a job aid to help you make this final check. Take a look at checklist 9-1.

Checklist 9-1. Test Item Verification Job Aid

Apply the checklist below to each test item, whether it is oral or written, or a performance measure. Line up each test item with its corresponding objective. For every test item, answer each question.	Yes	No
1. Does the item require the exact same performance and standards stated in the objective?	☐	☐
2. Is the learner performance in the item verifiable?	☐	☐
3. Is the type of item selected the most appropriate one for verifying objective attainment?	☐	☐
4. Is there an answer key, a correction checklist, or a verification instrument for the item?	☐	☐
5. Are all resources required to respond to the item available to the learner?	☐	☐
If you checked off even one "no," the item does not match the objective perfectly. Rework the item until you can check off every "yes" for it.		

Remember This

Given the nature of this book, we have often resorted to binary and matching end-of-chapter "tests." As you have noticed, we do this to help refresh some key chapter points, not to verify against objectives. This book is not a course; it is a sharing of our experience and research along with some exercises to illustrate and help you retain key points.[9] So, as usual, we conclude this chapter with your final exercise. Cross out the incorrect word or phrase in the parentheses below:

1. The word "test" (*often/rarely*) creates tension and stress for learners who have not had successful school experiences.
2. Generally speaking, (*low / high / both low and high*) performers suffer from test anxiety.
3. Testing (*is / is not*) a natural part of learning.
4. Testing is (*an excellent / a poor*) way to teach.
5. Key to successful testing is providing learners with (*a score/feedback*).
6. Testing should occur (*throughout / only at the end of*) training.
7. Criterion-referenced instruction is closely tied to (*the content of the course / the requirements for successful job accomplishment*).
8. The starting place for a test item is the (*performance objective / the course content*).
9. In simulation testing, the learner faces (*dynamic representations of real or hypothetical systems / abstract notions not resembling real or hypothetical systems*).
10. For procedural knowledge, use (*written or oral / performance*) tests.
11. For declarative knowledge, use (*written or oral / performance*) tests.
12. The answer to 85^2 is (*7225/4225*).

Now here's our feedback for you:

1. The word "test" often creates tension and stress for learners who have not had successful school experiences. This can also be true of high performers who are perfectionists lacking confidence. Use "test," "exam," "evaluate," and "measure" sparingly. Use "practice," "check yourself," or "game" more frequently with adult learners.
2. Generally speaking, both low and high performers suffer from test anxiety. Those who suffer from strong test anxiety usually do more poorly than those who are not as anxious. However, high-performing learners suffer almost as much as poor performers and thus lower their scores on tests.

3. Testing is a natural part of learning. A test is a trial. You learn. You want to see if you can do it and if you know it. When the test becomes a means for judging the person, however, there are dangers of inhibiting performance and diminishing motivation to learn.

4. Testing is an excellent way to teach. The key is to make it fun and challenging, not stressful. It mentally engages the learner and enhances retention.

5. Key to successful testing is providing learners with feedback. If the learner has made a response, the probability that she or he will actively attend to the feedback information is increased. Increased attention to meaningful feedback, whether corrective or confirming, helps learning.

6. Testing should occur throughout training. Frequent verification of performance objective attainment and feedback decrease the chance of learning gaps that can grow ever wider as training progresses. Testing also helps consolidate learning.

7. Criterion-referenced instruction is closely tied to the requirements for successful job accomplishment. The whole learner-centered and performance-based approach is to prepare the adult learner for the job. The ideal of criterion-referenced instruction is that 100 percent of the learners will achieve 100 percent of the performance objectives that are derived directly from the job.

8. The starting place for a test item is the performance objective. All through this chapter and right to the last job aid, the emphasis has been on perfectly matching test items to performance objectives.

9. In simulation testing, the learner faces dynamic representations of real or hypothetical systems. Simulation is a dynamic and simplified representation of a real or hypothetical system. Either a system exists such as the solar system or is made up such as Wonderland in *Alice in Wonderland*. The simulation mirrors the system, and the learner deals with its elements to try things out or solve problems.

10. For procedural knowledge, use performance tests along with performance verification instruments. For covert procedural knowledge, use correction checklists to verify what the learner did mentally.

11. For declarative knowledge, use written or oral tests. Include answer keys. These give learners the opportunity to display their talk-about knowledge.

12. The answer to 85^2 is 7225. We just wanted you to practice. Did you answer in less than 10 seconds?

You have come a long way since chapter 1. You've been inside your learners' minds; structured their training; developed strategies to strengthen learning; and developed activities to engage them and enhance their motivation, skills, and knowledge. And you've tested them to ensure that they can meet the learning objectives and perform well on the job.

We now introduce a new dimension to continue building your expertise as a training professional. The next section offers you two extensive chapters on technology and training-learning. About one third of workplace organizations in the United States employ some form of computer-driven technology to deliver online training. Technology has always been part of the training-learning world. In 1913, Thomas Edison predicted the disappearance of the classroom as a result of the introduction of the moving picture.

The next section presents a balanced approach to technology in the training world. Its purpose is to arm you with information to consider; suggestions on how best to employ the array of technological marvels available to help meet learner needs; and precautions to retain as you explore new, enticing, electronic possibilities.

Section 4

Training-Learning
With Technology and Beyond

Chapter 10

Training and Technology

Chapter highlights:

▶ Technology and learning—a partnership since prehistoric times
▶ What you can realistically expect by incorporating technology into your training
▶ Hype and promise versus reality
▶ Precautions to take and questions to ask before leaping into the technology fray.

Humanity and technology have been intertwined ever since the thumb and forefinger found one another. Early in our prehistory, humans found ways not only to create tools, but to represent their world, their issues, and their beliefs using available technological artifacts. Charcoal, animal blood, plant dyes, and mineral pigments became important means for expressing ideas, explaining events, and augmenting limited vocabularies. In addition to artistic displays on cave walls, early humans adopted music, dance, and costumes to increase the immediacy and realism of what they were sharing. They employed these means to heighten excitement and even manipulate emotions of joy, sorrow, anger, or fear.

The two chapters in this section were co-authored with Marc J. Rosenberg. We are grateful for Marc's contributions and expertise in helping readers of *Telling Ain't Training: Updated, Expanded, and Enhanced* understand the implications of technology use in training-learning. Please see his bio in the About the Authors section.

The costumes; simulations of weapons; organization of space; and inclusion of natural elements such as smoke, fire, and chemicals as mood enhancers (for example, peyote, hemp, mushrooms, and alcohol) all contributed to augment the impact of their messages.

Hence, it is not a giant leap from these early uses of media and technology to those of today—photographs, films, television, computers, 3-D, and virtual reality—to enrich communication and, of course, learning.

While the use of technology to teach has been around for a long time, it really came into its own on a massive scale during World War II, when so-called "training films" were used to teach everything from personal hygiene to weapon maintenance. Hundreds of thousands of service personnel were exposed to training films, some produced by Hollywood studios, from the 1940s through the Vietnam War. Today, the military is one of the most advanced users of learning technology.

American society also benefited from early efforts to employ mass media to teach. From the 1950s to the present, the lessons of the military's applications of learning technology were adapted for communities, public schools, and higher education. From filmstrips to film to television and, ultimately, to computers, education became the next big adopter of technology for teaching. Even preschoolers were not forgotten in the drive to apply technology for learning, as *Sesame Street* became one of the greatest success stories in the history of educational media.

From the 1970s to the 1990s, corporations also began to embrace technology for learning. Video-based training was followed quickly by computer-based training. Web-based training has become a significant part of the learning strategy of most major businesses and some smaller companies as well. Today, most of the modern approaches to the use of learning technology are combined into a broad category commonly referred to as "e-learning."

Today's students (and tomorrow's workers) have grown up around technology. They are so comfortable with it that they expect it to be part of how they learn. So the question is not "should we use technology to teach?" but "how can we use technology to teach well?"

What Is Technology and What Does It Do for Learning?

Technology has two main definitions. One focuses on artifacts and tools—from flint-chipping devices for crafting spearheads to computers and satellites for transmitting messages. The other is concerned with the application of scientific and organized knowledge: ergonomics, economics, and medicine. Both have a single aim: To solve practical problems. When we turn to learning, the practical problem is how to increase the efficiency and effectiveness of training. In other words, how we can make it cheap, fast, and really good.

Let's delve into this more deeply. You want to be an *efficient* and *effective* training professional. What does each of these words mean? Match them with their definitions:

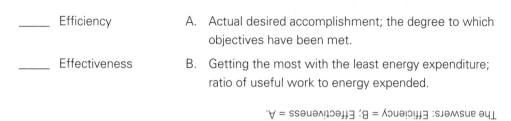

_____ Efficiency

_____ Effectiveness

A. Actual desired accomplishment; the degree to which objectives have been met.

B. Getting the most with the least energy expenditure; ratio of useful work to energy expended.

The answers: Efficiency = B; Effectiveness = A.

When it comes to training *efficiency,* the measure is fast and cheap. When it comes to training *effectiveness,* the measure is how well the learning goal is achieved—the "good" component in fast, cheap, and good.

Ideal Versus Real

Ideally, the aim is to put the two together, producing a system that is *fast,* in other words, reduces time in designing, developing, delivering, accessing, updating, and recording learning results; *cheap,* or decreases all of the costs related to training from printing, shipping, leasing classrooms, trainee travel, instructor salaries, and reduced time away from the job (productivity); and *good* by building powerful training that results in valued learning and on-the-job performance. The dream is to obtain great learning outcomes quickly and at low cost.

As in all pursuits of dreams, the reality factor is always nagging. Reality frequently fouls us up. In the workplace, time and budget pressures force us to focus on how quickly we can produce, implement, and deliver training. The critical measures of success become how fast we delivered, how little it cost, and how many bodies we put through the training pipeline. Where we seriously fall down is on measuring how well the people we trained learned to perform as desired and were able to execute successfully back on the job.[1]

An excellent meta-analysis of research on the evaluation of training by Arthur, Bennett, Edens, and Bell (2003) attests to the significant drop-off between Level 2 of Donald Kirkpatrick's evaluation levels—immediate posttraining learning—and Level 3, on-the-job application.[2] We can attribute many causes to this sad phenomenon; for example, no front-end analysis to determine whether or not training-learning was necessary or even relevant, inadequate positioning and preparation of learners by supervisors, lack of on-the-job support, hostile environmental factors such as cultural pressures and resistance to change, lack of tools and resources to apply learning, and nonexistent or counterproductive incentives to apply learning. The list could go on almost endlessly. Suffice it to say that, in the push for *efficiency* (get the training out fast and keep costs down), *effectiveness* (better performance) has been too often neglected.

What Can We Realistically Expect From the Use of Technology in Learning?

More than 60 years of research overwhelmingly answers what we can realistically expect from using technology in learning.[3] Media and technology can substantially improve the efficiency of training and learning, which is extremely important. However, they have little to no impact on the effectiveness of learning. There are, however, exceptions. Technology can become effective in training when the skills and knowledge to be acquired are of a technological nature and are taught using the technology for which the skills and knowledge are required. Use of spearhead chippers to teach how to make better spearheads makes eminent sense. So does the use of electronic hardware and software to train learners on the navigation of complex databases.

Other than in instances in which the "medium" itself is what is to be learned, the medium is not the message. On the contrary, it is how training is *designed* that makes the learning effectiveness difference, not the technology for transmitting and delivering the learning message. Long ago, computer programmers coined the term "GIGO" with respect to how well programs a programmer wrote produced results. GIGO simply means, "Garbage in, garbage out." The same applies to training with technology.

Should We Ignore Technology?

The history of humanity has often been dramatically altered by technology. Drawing animals and hunting scenes or using props and costumes to represent weapons and prey in prehistoric times helped deliver important survival messages or communicated significant events and critical lessons learned. Probably the most powerful technology to affect learning and the history of humanity from the 15th century onward was the printing press. Coupled with a first century technological development, paper (originally invented in China and slowly passed on to Europe by the 11th century), these two technological innovations vastly expanded access to knowledge with such explosive force that even fierce church opposition could not withstand the powerful transformation in learning this dynamic technology duo engendered (somewhat analogous to the Internet today).

Printing reduced time to reproduce books and other knowledge-laden documents. Paper tremendously lowered the cost of written and illustrated materials. Together they made knowledge long withheld from commoners accessible. These technological vehicles helped democratize information and laid the foundation for the overthrow of elites who up until then were the only ones who could afford to possess written words. As Francis Bacon, in his 1597 "Religious Meditations," expressed, "knowledge is power." The printing press and paper, much as the Internet does today, spread power to the people.

What Can You Reasonably Expect From Technology?

Technology can enable efficiency. Like the printing press and paper, "learning technologies" offer unprecedented opportunities for connecting learners with skill and knowledge content. However, they are only the means of access and interaction. They are *not* the content and methodology for triggering learning. Technologies are also subject to the rule of GIGO.

Table 10-1 lists benefits of technology with explanations of what you can reasonably expect to obtain from technology applied to training-learning.

Caveat Emptor (Let the Buyer Beware)

All of the benefits listed in table 10-1 are *potential*. The possibilities are available. Yet, vendors present a great deal of misleading hype to organizations and purchasing decision makers. So, *let the buyer beware!* Here are 10 promises that vendors and technology evangelists often trumpet. These promises are frequently based on potential and a few dramatic examples. Watch for the price tags and time consumption associated with the development of miraculous benefits. Remember this old saw: If it sounds too good to be true....

Promise 1: Technology-Based Training Offers Enormous Cost Savings

Be cautious about promises of giant savings from lower facility, instructor, and travel costs. These are definite possibilities, but only under certain conditions. First, technology-based learning requires an appropriate technological infrastructure of equipment, software, communications, storage, delivery, security, technical expertise, and instructional design capability. The cost of obtaining and installing these when they are not already present is generally steep, offsetting promised delivery savings, at least in the beginning.

Table 10-1. Technology Benefits for Training-Learning

Benefit	Explanation
Accessibility	More than by any other means, learning content via computers and the web, information repositories, and portable storage devices is infinitely easier to access than in the past. Attending a class or visiting a library is no longer required. Learning management systems (LMSs) make locating courses or even brief, just-in-time learning modules a touch-of-the-fingers exercise. Registering for online courses via an LMS is also usually simple. Modern computers and high-speed Internet access deliver learning material to learners not only instantaneously, but also with a high probability that it will flow smoothly, thus increasing the likelihood of a positive learning experience.
Instantaneous response and feedback	With new technologies, learning can be delivered quickly, sometimes within moments of a request, adapting, based on the design of the learning program, to learner progress. If learners require help, termi-nology definitions, or examples, these can be included in the learning and immediately delivered. Similarly, feedback on learner responses requires no discernable delay. Feedback that either simply confirms or rejects a response or elaborates on the learner's response and provides guidance to assist toward attaining success can be built into a training program.
Instantaneous testing and feedback	The technology for developing e-learning and associated tests is continually improving. Today, not only can we capture and record test responses and results, but we can have these interpreted and pro-grammed to adapt presentation of content based on how a learner responded to test items. Feedback to the learner is not only timely, it is seamless, presenting appropriate messages and either new material or, via links, previously encountered content for review. New software is making the testing and feedback features of electronically delivered learning increasingly more "intelligent" in helping learners.
Consistency of message	Delivering the same message, without live instructor variation, can be a desirable benefit when consistency is essential. Once developed, the learning material can be quickly disseminated to all parts of an organiza-tion and across the globe simultaneously. This is a savings in both time and effort to control message content delivery.
Rapidity of delivery	The cost of getting training to everyone who requires it in a timely man-ner has often been a major issue. The cost of recruiting and training sufficient numbers of instructors and then scheduling classes can cre-ate serious lag times in training delivery. Imagine sending 10 instructors to deliver two-day classes on regulatory changes to 6,000 employees with 20 employees per class. This would require each instructor to teach 30 classes. Without breaks, this would end up taking three months (at 20 working days per month). More realistically, it probably

Benefit	Explanation
Rapidity of delivery (continued)	would take six months, given people's schedules and the unlikelihood of filling every class. While excellent technology-delivered training could require a longer development time, delivery to all 6,000 employees would be almost immediate, thus offering considerable time savings.
Simultaneity of training delivery	Continuing the above scenario, all 6,000 employees would be able to receive simultaneous access to the required training. Despite the diversity of people's schedules and operational constraints, all employees could still receive training within a short timeframe. What is more, there are no border crossings to deal with when it comes to delivering the instruction. The electronic highways have few barriers to delay transmission of materials and instructional expertise across national boundary lines.
Ease of update	Updating instructor and student materials for a course is a demanding and often frustrating experience. Paper substitutions can be haphazard and incomplete, regardless of how well a system has been designed. Learning programs delivered via technology require much less effort and time to update, modify, and transmit the new release. Everyone on the distribution list receives the changes simultaneously. It is even possible to have a new release trigger deletion of a previous iteration of the same training program.
Reusability	Aside from being able to retake an e-learning or other technology-delivered course, parts of these can be reused and reworked into handy sets of on-the-job application tools. The same content, illustrations, and guidelines can be reformatted for uses other than learning. Parts of courses can be lifted and adapted or repurposed for different learning groups. There is a great deal written on reusable learning objects (RLOs) and standards for creating such items and then reusing them in multiple ways. One can build up libraries of learning parts (content loaded or instructional strategy loaded, such as a game whose content can be replaced), seriously saving development time.
Flexibility of use	Two terms frequently applied to online or e-learning (but can be applied with other technologies) are "synchronous" and "asynchronous." These refer to whether or not the learners participate in a training-learning session while it is actually being taught (synchronous) or at any time of their choosing (asynchronous). The advantage of synchronous training-learning is that with a knowledgeable instructor and some useful, but not expensive materials (for example, colorful visuals, real objects, and sample cases), a webinar (seminar via the web) can be scheduled to allow many learners in disparate locations to log on and participate in the activity simultaneously. Asynchronous learning requires considerably more time and cost to develop. Its key advantage, however, is flexibility of use. Anyone, at any time, in any place, can sign up and take the training on his or her own schedule—a distinct advantage, especially in a global setting. Synchronous sessions can

(continued on next page)

Table 10-1. Technology Benefits for Training-Learning (continued)

Benefit	Explanation
Flexibility of use (continued)	be recorded for independent, individual use, but even with interactive elements included to increase individualized use, the result is not as effective. Most organizations use combinations of synchronous and asynchronous technology-delivered training for greater flexibility in meeting both learner needs and organizational constraints. They also frequently combine the technology-based instruction with live learning sessions, tutorials, mentoring, or even on-the-job practical assignments, thus creating a versatile and comprehensive approach to training.
Interactivity	Technology-delivered training-learning, especially various forms of e-learning and simulations, requires active responding on the part of learners. This leads to increased attention and retention. The kicker here is in the nature of the instructional design. Meaningful interactivity strongly affects learning. Questioning, problem solving, especially if introduced in gradually more challenging exercises, and thought-provoking activities are all feasible by computer. However, you can also create senseless, dull, meaningless button-pushing and clicking lessons that do not stimulate mental engagement and generate learning. Technology offers great possibilities for intriguing and stimulating learners to think, infer, store, and retrieve knowledge and skills. It provides a platform for applying what is learned. The key is in the design of what is programmed into the technological medium.
Adaptability	Once you have developed a basic course, you can easily adapt it to different learning populations, locations, and needs. If more advanced or different examples are necessary, replacements or additions require minimal effort to insert or replace. Similarly, if certain parts of a program are not relevant for geography, deletions are easy to execute, seamlessly reconnecting what is needed. Introductions and guidelines are also simple to reword.

This is why investment in e-learning is best done organization-wide, to get the economies of scale needed to justify the expense. The ratio of instructional design time to training delivery time is high for any true quality instruction. Estimates for development of excellent e-learning, for example, run anywhere from four to 10 times longer than typical times for classroom training. Some vendors quote low design and development ratios per hour of output. Examine their final products. Many are nothing more than online page turners, primitive in presentation and poor in instructional quality. Developing quality, asynchronous instruction can take weeks or months. This is a time lag cost that must be considered.

Most examples of low-cost delivery per learner are based on large numbers of learners. If an online training program costs $200,000 to develop (and generally this *excludes* amortization and maintenance of infrastructure costs) and there are 5,000 employees to train, the cost per employee is only $40—a remarkably low cost. However, if there are only 250 employees who will participate in the program, the cost escalates to $800 per employee. At this point, live delivery of the program with 20 participants per delivery might be considerably cheaper. (In both cases, we are not including employee time in training or lost opportunity costs, which become a critical calculation in deciding whether or not to go the technology route.)

Where technology-delivered training does offer cost savings is in its efficiency. Carefully designed e-learning and other forms of self-paced learning generally eliminate unnecessary chatter and time wasters associated with a live class. The technology-based version can be tightly engineered, sticking to the essential. The result is that a five-day instructor-led class may be reduced to three days thus returning the learner to the workplace two days early. This adds to worker productivity and is one of the major benefits of more efficient e-learning. Travel and hotel costs are also eliminated—a desirable bonus.

There is a need for some caution here, however. Often live training serves multiple purposes such as team-building, social interaction to facilitate later communication, and a sharing of passion and commitment usually absent in the more sterile atmosphere of the electronic environment.

Promise 2: Delivered to the Desktop

The benefit of desktop delivery offered by purveyors of technology-delivered instruction is intuitively attractive. There is no travel, ready accessibility, just-in-time delivery, and minimal cost. However, you must make sure that the desktop equipment is able to handle the technical requirements of the learning program (that is, bandwidth, sound card, streaming software, and memory). You also must have in place a suitable information technology infrastructure to facilitate access, delivery, and support. Any lapses in the system will quickly discourage use. This is even more critical as more organizations allow employees to participate in e-learning from home; on the road; and, even unfortunately, on vacation. This gives rise to a special kind of e-learning known as "m-learning" (mobile learning).

Now, for the most important aspect of desktop delivery—the workplace environment and culture. In most enterprises, employees spend a large part of their time juggling priorities to meet demanding, shifting, and competing deadlines. Under pressure conditions, despite high quality and useful, relevant, desktop-delivered training, a major question is, "Will workers actually set aside the time to take the training and will their bosses let them?" Learning requires some form of isolation and considerable concentration, especially if the instruction is challenging and engaging. The workplace is rife with task interferences from people dropping by to phone calls and emails to continual requests for attention, help, support, and demands for answers to questions or simply to "find things."

The workplace is not an ideal setting for engaging in any type of formalized training, especially when done while teeming life continues all around the learner, so strong efforts must be made to create a space that is conducive to learning, away from distractions such as phone calls and email and with the strong support of local managers. An advantage to live classroom instruction is that it isolates learners and focuses their attention without the distractions of the normal workplace. This, then, is an extremely important factor to consider when presented with the seduction and allure of on-the-job desktop training delivery. Learning in the workplace is possible, and sometimes preferable, but the organizational culture—the "learning culture"—must be right.

Promise 3: Greater Active Engagement

While the promise of greater active engagement is absolutely true *potentially*, the reality is that most technology-based learning is expository with much of it in the form of page turning. The learner reads from a screen and occasionally responds to questions. Even when accompanied by audio, average e-learning, for example, is often nothing more than overloaded visual displays with droning or text explanations (also known as "death by slides"). All the technology in the world cannot compensate for lack of true engagement built into the training design. Engagement requires creative instructional designers and trainers working with truly knowledgeable subject-matter experts—ones who also know the job of the learners—to develop an engaging training program. So, bear in mind that "greater active engagement" is not a natural outcome of employing technology for learning, but rather the result of your investment in designing to make it happen. Telling ain't training, and, as with any medium, you have to work to ensure that the training is not a technologically delivered *telling* session.

Promise 4: More Tailored and Targeted Instruction

Developing technology-delivered training so that it responds to every learner in an individualized manner can become prohibitively expensive. For this reason, as with any other form of delivery, learner analyses are required to determine the characteristics of those who are to be trained along with significant learner population variations. You can then construct modules of interaction which, based on learner diagnoses, self-evaluations, or pretests, allow the system to assign appropriate modules. These can range from basic skills and knowledge in a particular content area to advanced training. Specific modules can deal with specialized aspects that are accessed by those requiring the specific content they contain. Tailoring and targeting are definite possibilities. However, they come at a price. Some flexible modularity based on simple diagnostic/assessment mechanisms is the more likely option.

Promise 5: More Up-to-Date Instruction

While most technology-delivered instruction *can* be updated rapidly, in reality, redoing visuals, exercises, and tests with feedback can be time consuming. Someone, or a team, must be assigned the task of updating a course or program. Our experience is that while technology-based training can be readily brought up to date, maintaining currency in training is far too frequently neglected. Up-to-date instruction requires, just as for all training, a firm commitment and assigned resources to make it happen.

Promise 6: Just-in-Time Learning

You may have a huge catalog of instructional modules a worker can access on an as-and-when-needed basis. The problem may be, however, lack of guidance to help make the appropriate selection at the right time. If your organization has not taken suitable care to ensure that the repertoire of training perfectly matches job-specific needs, then someone attempting to take the training just in time for the job requirement will be disappointed with what is presented. Just-in-time training in the proper dosage at the moment of need is a wonderful delivery *capability* of most computer-based learning systems. However, it is mostly a buzzword, unfortunately, if not designed and built to serve the just-in-time need.

Promise 7: Any Time, Any Place Learning

This promise is similar to that of desktop delivery. The infrastructure must permit access to the organization's intranet from any location. Bandwidth is an issue if the learning materials contain sophisticated graphics, animation, video, and sound. The equipment or terminals on the receiving end must contain sufficient memory and capability to handle the available training. Security may be an additional consideration. Just how much "any place" can an organization really tolerate without compromising protection of confidential information? Finally, as with desktop delivery, is "any place" delivery appropriate for fostering learning?

Promise 8: Built-In Testing

Most modern e-learning systems come equipped with testing engines that facilitate the creation, delivery, and correction of tests and mechanisms for recording of test results. While this is a great feature, its usefulness to support learning and retention is only as good as the tests themselves. Test development is a professional skill. Poorly developed test items lacking validity, or tests that are statistically unreliable, can only distract and discourage learners. They also may provide inaccurate information about learner progress. This can lead to misinterpretation of results generated by unskilled test developers. Testing capability in technology-based learning systems offers an excellent opportunity to allow learners to demonstrate that they have indeed learned. The capability must not be confused with the real work of quality test design and construction.

Promise 9: Accurate, Up-to-Date Training Records

Accurate, up-to-date training records are an excellent feature of most LMSs. They can capture an array of learner information, including the number of key strokes per exercise and number of seconds these took. The danger is TMI—too much information. When training organizations become awash in TMI they may end up drowning in detail and unable to discern what is essential. What constitute meaningful data and significant trends? As with each of the hyperbolic promises about what a technology-based learning system can deliver, judgment and ability are required to harness the potential, apply it with skill, and delete or ignore the superfluous.

Promise 10: Reusability of Training

Being able to store and retrieve instructional components for reuse can produce significant savings in costly and time-consuming instructional design. There are two ways to approach reusability. The more formal one, which most vendors favor, requires adoption of standards for developing and encoding learning "objects" and then entering these into repositories according to well-defined rules.[4] Labeling of each object must be clear and based on explicit conventions. This, in itself, requires that training content developers master the standards and conventions. Review and maintenance of the reusable learning objects (RLOs) residing in the database are essential. You must purge old content regularly to avoid the risk of learners accessing outdated instruction. The proper management of an RLO treasure trove requires the assignment of knowledgeable personnel to maintain reusability protocols, content currency, and appropriate accessibility.

With respect to the formal approach, we have some fundamental concerns and questions about this "RLO system" of instructional design. A potential danger exists that in creating a learning object capable of being reused with a variety of audiences, each with its own learning needs, the object itself may lose an essential quality, that of being specifically tailored to the characteristics of a distinct learner group. A "one size fits all" piece of instruction may end up not being appropriate for anyone. Like an article of clothing made for all sizes, ages, and genders, it may, in fact, be fit for no one. An essential requirement of sound instructional design is that the instruction be an excellent match with the intended learners.

Granularity, or the size of an object, is also an issue. If too small in size, the resulting training package may resemble a patchwork quilt. Tiny bits of instruction do not necessarily combine seamlessly to create a coherent whole. If the size of the objects is too large, then decreased flexibility may limit their range of use.

Another consideration is that of language. The nature, style, vocabulary, and type of examples required for a sales audience may strongly differ from those needed by a technician, or a customer service agent, or a customer. What type of language should one employ in developing an object destined to be used with a variety of audiences? Again the question arises, "If it is destined to fit everyone, will it fit anyone?"

The second, or more informal approach to reusability, offers some immediate, cost- and time-savings benefits. Graphics, game frameworks, various types of challenge activities, test templates, and even task analyses developed for one training program can be readily reused in others, generally with some tweaking. Procedural instructions, job aids, product descriptions, examples, and cases may fit into other training materials and modules, even ones destined for different audiences. With technology to assist, all of these can be lifted easily out of one program and inserted, sometimes with adaptation, into another. This form of reusability is available to you, as a trainer, without requiring any form of specialized training or formalized protocols.

To conclude, reusability is a long-sought goal that promises all sorts of efficiency benefits. You must decide, however, how it can work best within your learning context. The formal approach is a long-term investment with many issues to resolve. The informal path is one you can set out upon today. However, it will not provide a consistent method for systematic exploitation of the training capital you possess.

Promises, Promises, Promises

To summarize major promises and claims made by technology vendors and the precautions you should bear in mind about them, we offer exercise 10-1, Promise Versus Precaution. Read each vendor/enthusiast promise and then match it with the most suitable precaution and questions you must ask.

Exercise 10-1. Promise Versus Precaution

Our system offers you	Great, but...
1. enormous savings through lower instructional and travel costs	A. some of our current training is information dumping with slides— pretty much one-way telling. Will the technology make what we do more engaging and interactive? Will it alter long entrenched training habits?
2. desktop delivery	B. we will have to conduct systematic learner and task analysis to develop instruction tailored to job needs and our learners' characteristics and backgrounds.
3. greater active engagement	C. there are the same problems as for desktop delivery in terms of technical infrastructure to deliver training. Also, do we really want our learners to be taking training in just any place? What about security and confidential information? Does any place mean the best place to learn?
4. more tailored and targeted instruction	D. can our desktop terminals handle the training delivery technical requirements? Is the work site the best learning environment? Can or will workers take time to stop what they are doing at work and engage in training?
5. more up-to-date instruction	E. what data do we really want to record and report about training? We will have to sort through the mass of data the system generates to tailor reports that are helpful and meaningful for decision making. Who will do this? What skills are needed for this task?
6. just-in-time learning	F. are we technically capable of replacing classes with technology-delivered learning (for example, asynchronous e-learning)? What about instructional design costs compared to delivery costs? And the time to design and develop effective online learning? What about swiftly changing content? Do we have enough learners per course to achieve sufficient cost/benefit ratios?
7. any time, any place learning	G. what standards will we adopt for developing and labeling reusable learning objects? What exactly will a reusable piece of instruction look like? Who will create and maintain the database? What special training will be required to train on designing for reusability? If we reuse existing pieces of instruction informally, are we missing the benefit of a comprehensive approach to efficiently repurpose our training capital?
8. built-in testing	H. does our system have a well-designed test engine? What are its exact capabilities? Do we have in-house expertise to verify the validity of automatically generated tests?

Our system offers you		Great, but...
9. accurate, up-to-date training records	I.	does our current catalog of training match immediate job needs? Are our courses designed for just-in-time? How much modification will they require? What investment is needed to create "doses" of training tied to a job-task need? Will our workers, on their own, pull up the training just in time? How do we get them to do this naturally?
10. reusability of training	J.	how well do we currently update and maintain our training? Will we be more likely to do this in a training technology environment? What skills will people require to do this? Will we assign personnel to update and purge?

Answers: 1-F; 2-D; 3-A; 4-B; 5-J; 6-I; 7-C; 8-H; 9-E; 10-G.

You probably found this to be a tough exercise. Promises and precautions overlap considerably. Nevertheless, if you come away from this exercise with a strong set of questions to pose when technology-driven solutions for training are touted, then the effort was worthwhile. Technology, as we have stated in several ways, offers great learning advantages for empowering the efficiencies of learning. It is up to you to ensure that effectiveness is not forgotten. It is also up to you to realistically assess what it will take to gain the most from the technology. Otherwise, you will end up with technologically enhanced telling and not training.

Remember This

This chapter contained a lot of information about technology and its promises. Did you retain the chapter's lessons? Cross out the inappropriate alternative in these statements. Then check your responses against ours.

1. Humans have a (*short/long*) history of using technology for communicating and learning.

2. The aim of technology is to (*solve practical problems / discover new tools*).

3. Today, the U.S. military is (*an advanced / a reluctant*) user of technology for learning.

4. Efficiency refers to the (*degree to which objectives have been met / ratio of useful work accomplished to energy expended*).

5. Effectiveness refers to the (*degree to which objectives have been met / ratio of useful work accomplished to energy expended*).

6. Often neglected in measuring training success is (*how fast and cheaply we trained large numbers of trainees / how well trainees performed as a result of their training*).

7. Kirkpatrick's Level 3 evaluation focuses on (*on-the-job application posttraining / satisfaction with the training*).
8. We (*should / should not*) ignore technology for training-learning.
9. Technology applied to training increases (*accessibility, flexibility, and immediacy of feedback / the probability that learners will learn better*).
10. Asynchronous training allows (*all participants to take the training as it is being delivered / individual participants to take the training at a time of their own choosing*).
11. Technology (*decreases/increases*) the amount of time wasters associated with live classroom training.
12. Technology-delivered training can decrease costs if there are (*large numbers of trainees / any number of trainees*).
13. RLO stands for (*retrofit learning organization / reusable learning object*).

Here is how we would respond to these statements:

1. Humans have a long history of using technology for communicating and learning. Early cave paintings and artifacts dating back to prehistoric times show that humans used the technology of the times to communicate and celebrate events in their lives.
2. The aim of technology is to solve practical problems. Science aims at making discoveries about the workings of the universe. Technology puts those discoveries to work solving the practical problems we encounter.
3. Today, the U.S. military is an advanced user of technology for learning. Not only today, but going back into its early history, the military has systematically embraced technology as a powerful means for helping train millions of its personnel. It is not only an avid user and advocate of technology in training, it is an innovator in this arena and a model for many corporate and nonprofit organizations in using learning technologies.
4. Efficiency refers to the ratio of useful work accomplished to energy expended. Efficiency focuses on reducing time, costs, effort, and resources used to achieve desired ends. The lower the expenditures of all of these, the greater the efficiency.
5. Effectiveness refers to the degree to which objectives have been met. How well a goal is met is the measure of the effectiveness of the means for achieving success. The greater the goal success, the greater the effectiveness.
6. Often neglected in measuring training success is how well trainees performed as a result of their training. Sadly, organizations, in their rush to check off that training was done, ignore following up to verify if the training did the job. That is why technology is so attractive to training decision makers. "Faster and cheaper" is easily calculated and sounds good.

7. Kirkpatrick's Level 3 evaluation focuses on on-the-job application posttraining. Level 1 is participant reaction evaluation. Level 2 refers to immediate learning at the end of a training session. Level 4 focuses on results—did anything change organizationally as a result of the training?

8. We should not ignore technology for training-learning. Anything that increases efficiency of learning is important. The printing press and paper increased access to knowledge by disseminating it more rapidly and at much lower cost than before. The result in history has been enormous.

9. Technology applied to training increases accessibility, flexibility, and immediacy of feedback. Yes to all of these. Effectiveness of training depends on its design.

10. Asynchronous training allows individual participants to take the training at a time of their own choosing. This is self-explanatory. Asynchronous means not at the same time.

11. Technology decreases the amount of time wasters associated with live classroom training. No roll-call is required, or lunch breaks, or discussions of extraneous subject matter. Technology-based instruction sticks to the essential (if well designed).

12. Technology-delivered training can decrease costs if there are large numbers of trainees. Because of high infrastructure, design, and maintenance costs, amortization of these requires large numbers of trainees to take the training. If all groups are small, other delivery means, including live classroom delivery, may be less costly.

13. RLO stands for reusable learning object. In the formal approach to reusability, instructional designers create "objects" or pieces of instruction that follow specific standards and conventions for easy storage in repositories. These can be retrieved, repurposed, and reused for a variety of training-learning audiences and requirements.

With this foundational chapter as a base for integrating technology into your training, you are now ready to discover, from a practical perspective, what is out there for you to choose from. This is what the next chapter offers.

Chapter 11

Learning With Technology: Making It Work

Chapter highlights:

▶ Mythconceptions about technology and learning

▶ Quality in online learning

▶ Launching into online learning—thinking it through

▶ Blended learning—a continually evolving concept

▶ Web 2.0 and the future of training.

One of the gravest mistakes training organizations make when they decide to embrace new learning technologies[1] as means for strategically "upgrading" their services is to focus too heavily on the "technologies" and too little on the "learning." True, you can't turn to learning technology, as the term is currently used, without the computers, networks, software, and infrastructure to make it work. However, if *learning* is weak and doesn't result in skills and knowledge applied on the job, you simply end up spending a lot of money to deliver time-consuming, ineffective training.

Hit or Myth?

Let's start off, then, with a brief quiz. For each of these statements, indicate whether you feel the statement is a "hit" (H) or a "myth" (M).

1. _____ The hardest part of technology-based learning is deploying it to all the learners who need it.

2. _____ A great instructor-led course can be readily transferred to technology-based delivery. After all, a great learning experience works no matter how it's delivered.

3. _____ The most resistance to technology-based learning comes from the learners themselves; many just don't want it.

4. _____ The greater the percentage of all your courses that you move online, the better your overall e-learning program will be.

5. _____ Over the next 10 to 15 years, technology-based learning will eliminate almost all classroom training in the workplace.

As you probably guessed, all of these statements are myths. Here are some explanations:

1. While getting learning technology to work is no simple task, good standards and practices exist to help you do it right.[2] And by forming a close partnership with your information technology organization, you obtain the expertise necessary to make it work. More challenging is designing the right type of online training, making sure it is relevant and interesting for your learners, measuring the results in a meaningful way, and creating an atmosphere in the organization in which people want to learn via technology.

2. It is true that a great instructor-led course makes it easier to transition to online training, but a simple shifting of the same content and exercises to the new medium often doesn't work. Instructional design for online training definitely includes the principles of sound training-learning, but it also requires mastery of new interactive learning techniques, textual and visual design, multimedia presentations, and more to transform what was designed for the classroom into excellent, technologically delivered instruction.[3]

3. The argument that learners don't want to learn via technology only holds true when the technology-based course is poorly designed, is difficult to navigate or control, or offers little perceived value. Build a great and meaningful online experience that is readily accessible, and learners will flock to it. For them, it is faster and offers more flexibility in their learning schedule than having to wait for a live course to be announced. In addition, future employees, born and raised with technology, will increasingly demand this approach to training. Even executives are becoming much more supportive of learning technology because of its efficiency. Surprisingly, in too many organizations, the greatest resistance to learning technology comes from

training organizations themselves.[4] So, before you start down the training-with-technology path, investigate to determine the extent to which your own team is on board. If it is not yet fully convinced and ready to engage in this exciting new venture, getting your team members to become enthusiastically supportive should be your first priority.

4. Many organizations believe that having lots of courses available online is a great accomplishment. However, quantity is no substitute for quality, relevant instruction. If courses are not used or of marginal value to the people in an organization, they are a waste. The best e-learning programs offer online courses that are precisely geared to individual and business needs. If this means fewer, but more impactful courses, then this is the wiser path to choose rather than overstuffing training program repositories.

5. A number of e-learning prognosticators suggest that classroom training is an anachronism, outdated and ready for the junkyard. However, every organization that has tried to eliminate classroom instruction has had to retrench. There is still a great deal of value in bringing people together to learn, solve problems, and try new things as a team. Classroom training is not going to rapidly disappear; however, it likely will take on a different appearance. Your role will be to decide when, where, and in what form live, group-based instruction will be most beneficial.

What Makes for Quality Online Learning?

A constant theme that permeates most discussions of online learning is that of *quality*. With any form of training, one aspect of quality is that the training supports specific learning and organizational objectives. After all, any course that doesn't deliver this shouldn't be offered. For technology-based learning, an important aspect of quality is its instructional soundness and versatility. How do you maintain high-quality learning effectiveness in a medium where no instructor is present to answer questions or adjust the content based on expressed learner interests? The short answer is through well-designed instruction based on analyses that draw out, in advance, learner and organizational needs.

Poorly designed online learning hurts quality. Even when the technology works well, the screens are beautiful and exciting, and a large amount of multimedia is available, if no meaningful learning results from all of this, everyone's efforts—yours, the learners, and their managers—have been wasted. The careful, systematic crafting of online instruction, complete with tryout and revision cycles using real learners, is an essential characteristic of quality online learning design.

E-learning, or, for that matter, any technology-based instruction, can be disappointing in many ways. Think of the last time you interacted with an online course. In this list, check off any item that matches one of your experiences:

1. _____ The content was incomplete, incomprehensible, boring, or just plain wrong.

2. _____ There was no alignment between what was taught and what was really needed on the job and no alignment between the course and the organization's goals.

3. _____ The online course was primarily a lecture on the computer, or a seemingly endless run of slides, with little for the learner to do except read pages of text, watch long-winded "talking heads," and press "next" to continue.

4. _____ There was more form than substance. Lots of "clicky-clicky bling-bling" (a term coined by Cammy Bean at the e-learning design firm, Kino), referring to too many animations, extraneous sounds, and superfluous graphics that overwhelm the instructional message.[5]

5. _____ Interactive exercises within the course were not challenging and the feedback following the exercises was not comprehensive enough to let learners know where they required more study or practice. Overall, learners received little guidance on how they were doing.

6. _____ The course focused more on entertaining learners than on educating them. While the course may have been fun, little applicable learning was produced.

7. _____ The course was of low value after it was completed. Information in the course proved too hard to retrieve back on the job, so there was no way to "refresh" without enrolling in the online course all over again—something most learners are loath to do.

8. _____ The learners perceived the online tests as being afterthoughts that failed to measure the most important skills and knowledge acquired from the course.

9. _____ The course was complicated from a navigational perspective. Learners got lost and could not locate required content. If they stopped before they completed a lesson, they had to start over. There was no mechanism within the course to track and record where a learner had left off.

10. _____ Little to no reinforcement or support followed the online instruction. While this is important for all types of training, it is particularly critical with online learning. Because learning online is frequently an individual experience, often learners need to talk with others about what transpired to confirm that they had learned correctly and had focused on what was essential.

The preponderance of online courses is not designed perfectly, hence many will show some of these weaknesses. Fairly good ones, with the guidance of competent and experienced training professionals, can be much improved. However, too many online learning experiences are riddled with so many weaknesses that learning is significantly hindered and improvement is simply not practical. In these cases, the wisest choice is to start over—a sadly expensive course of action to undertake.

To avoid the necessity of having to begin again, do it correctly the first time. Here are 10 ways to increase the probability of developing your online learning so that it produces desired results right from the start:

- ▶ **Right content.** First and foremost, make sure you are training on the right content. This means that the information you include should be accurate, relevant, complete, and interesting for the target audience. You achieve this by conducting a proper front-end analysis or needs assessment[6] and gaining access to one or more truly qualified subject-matter experts. Testing the content with actual learners can go a long way toward eliminating problems before they become embedded in the course and, thus, much more expensive to fix.

- ▶ **Strong alignment.** Assuring strong alignment between the course and business goals is essential if the learner is to gain the value that was intended from the course. Vetting the course with key stakeholders will help here.

- ▶ **True interactivity.** Making the course truly interactive is a hallmark of excellent online learning. From simple, well-thought-out knowledge quizzes to complex simulations, taking the time to create a highly interactive experience that requires the learner to exercise the brain in addition to the mouse button-finger provides large payoffs in learning gain. Remember, in a simulated, e-learning environment, the learner can try out techniques and ideas that might not be practical in the real world. This "safe failure" capability can be a powerful interactive approach, helping people learn from their mistakes without risk to others. Our best advice here is to provide as much opportunity for practice as you can. Then, find ways to provide even more. Just remember: Telling ain't training.

- ▶ **Valued experience.** Making a course fun is not necessarily bad. However, focusing on "edutainment"[7] at the expense of learning is a growing problem. Learners appreciate value—online courses that give them what they need, in the shortest period of time. If they get that, whether or not they had fun will not be an issue.

- ▶ **Few distractions.** Moderation and purpose are key when considering which "special features" of your authoring tool to use and how often to use them. Bear in mind that just because you can use exciting animations, doesn't mean you should. The test question is always, "Will it contribute to the learning process?"

- ▶ **Useful on the job.** Design the course so that the learner can easily refer back to specific, application-oriented parts of it once back on the job. If the course has job aids and other tools embedded in it, create simple and easy ways to access those tools once the instruction has ended.

- ▶ **Powerful feedback.** Always keep in mind that the online learner usually has no one at hand to assist in case of a problem or a lack of understanding. That is why your feedback and model answers for every activity should be as comprehensive as possible. If the learner can understand where a problem lies and remediate it quickly, learning and retention skyrocket. The probability of transferring back to the job what was learned also increases significantly.

- ▶ **Valid assessments**. At the end of an online experience, most learners want to know how they've done. If an end-of-course assessment is going to be used, make sure it's designed well and measures what's truly important. Tie test items closely to the objectives of the course.[8]

- ▶ **Good human factors.** Create a great user experience. If learners become frustrated with the interface or navigation within the course, they may leave and never come back.

- ▶ **Integrated follow-up.** When learners have had a good learning experience and feel both competent and confident that they can apply what they acquired, support at their worksites is essential to ensure they try out what they have gained. Therefore, when you launch your online learning programs, make certain support resources in the form of immediate supervisors or knowledgeable colleagues, who are familiar with the content and who are able to serve as posttraining coaches, are available to help learners integrate new skills and knowledge into the job.

Online Learning Is *Not* the First Decision You Make

In making a decision to implement any form of technology-based training-learning, especially the online variety, people often forget that several decisions come before this—decisions that ultimately affect whether or not the online approach is appropriate. There are actually seven key design questions for which you require answers. The question of whether or not to go "online" is at the end of the list, not the beginning.

► **Who is this course for and why?** This is your key needs assessment question. How many people will require this training? (Of course, you have determined that training is required to close the gap between desired and current performance.) Where are they located? Do they have the time and ready access to the learning system? Is the course for technical people, business-oriented customers, or managers? Is it for novices or more experienced performers? Is it focused on a key, high-risk performance, or on background knowledge? The answers to these questions strongly influence how the learning program is designed and whether or not online learning might be appropriate.

► **What are the content and the context?** Here you want to focus on the subject matter itself and the necessary conditions for learning. What should be taught? Under what conditions will the learners have to perform? How must the content be organized? Is the learning context dependent (for example, how to operate a drill press) or independent (for example, verify a balance sheet)? How stable is the content? What are the learning and performance objectives? Clearly, knowing the precise nature of *what* should be taught and with what contextual requirements or constraints helps define *how* it should be taught.

► **How deeply should it go?** Related to content and context is the question of level of learning. Perhaps some aspects of the content need only be dealt with in basic overview form, while other parts require drilling down. For the same content, some people may only require a briefing while others must absorb a great deal of detail to be able to perform. For example, for technical, high-risk content, engineers may have to acquire great depth to carry out their jobs while their managers may need a less detailed overview of the same material.

► **What type of learning is needed?** A useful question to ask concerns the nature of the required learning. The answer will direct you in developing instruction that is both appropriate and effective. "Must the learners commit to memory what they have to learn?" In other words, will they have to perform from memory on the job without referring to any outside reference material or job aid? If the answer is yes (for example, when landing an aircraft that suddenly loses power and altitude, there is no time to look things up or follow a step-by step procedural job aid), then your learning design will focus on drilling into the learners' minds the appropriate steps to take. The learning program will include numerous, varied situations that permit them to practice until they reach the point of "automaticity" (perform automatically without thinking.) If the answer is no (for example, when assembling a bicycle) and learners can refer to manuals, job aids, or online resources, then instruction will center on resource selection and use of whatever tools contain the appropriate guidance. The answer to this question provides direction about the type of learning required and hence the nature of how the training will be designed. It will also help determine the level of learning and performance learners will have to demonstrate to certify that they will be able to apply their learning in the real world.

▶ **How much time do you have?** Often overlooked is the question of the amount of time the organization can tolerate for development *and* delivery of the course to all who need it. This can be a critical factor to consider in your decision making, especially if a new product launch date has been set. Online learning takes much longer to develop, but much less time to deliver, so coming up with a business rationale (business case) for an online approach is important. You want to be sure to have the training ready and deployed to all affected employees or customers when it will do the most good. You don't want to have a negative impact on the business by being late.

▶ **How will the training be delivered?** Now you are ready to decide if online learning is the right way to go. The previous five questions should help inform this decision and ensure that you deliver the best training in the most efficient way possible. Part of the decision making, at this point, concerns whether or not the delivery will be synchronous or asynchronous. We discussed these two terms in chapter 10. Do you wish to have all the learners log in at the same time (synchronous) and participate in a webinar (popular with many organizations because it requires few resources and is generally not costly)? There are great advantages. Everyone, no matter where she or he is located, can be present at the same event. When well designed, the synchronous webinar is similar to a live learning session. With great materials and an excellent instructor or facilitator or group of dynamic experts, the webinar session can be highly impactful. Software to produce and deliver webinars is relatively inexpensive. The webinar can be received virtually anywhere online access is available and requires no specialized environment for delivering the content. Our own experience with webinars has been extremely positive. Not only can the instructor or facilitator directly interact with individual learners, but the learners themselves can communicate with each other and the leader during a session using text chat modes. The software allows for considerable interactivity, including using whiteboards, teamwork, surveys, testing, and question-and-answer sessions. The key drawback is that each webinar is a one-time event. Watching a recording of a webinar at a later time loses the immediacy and excitement of the live happening. Webcasts, usually in the form of conference-style presentations and often used to communicate important announcements, are also synchronous events. Some interaction can be built in.[9]

Asynchronous e-learning and other forms of self-paced, technology-delivered training have the advantage of availability according to individual learners' schedules and needs. In general, asynchronous training is more expensive to design and produce. It usually requires far more time to develop a learning package that must compensate for the lack of an instructor's presence before being ready for dissemination. Much more instructional design investment is necessary to develop quality asynchronous training that maximizes the power of technology while adhering to adult learning principles than for synchronous learning. However, the result of this front-end effort is paid back with highly flexible and reusable instruction. Presentation of material can be adapted based on learner progress. Testing and individual learning results can be recorded and reported.[10]

▶ **What are the metrics?** Finally, you have to determine how you will evaluate the success of the course—whether it is online or not. Is learning gain enough? What about business value? And performance? Be sure you have a comprehensive approach to evaluation and that your client or customer is involved in this planning.

These seven questions certainly don't completely cover all aspects of online training design, but they do convey two important things. First, deciding that a course should be online, before issues of need, content, context, depth, approach, and time are determined, is likely to result in less-than-optimal results. Second, a simple checklist that incorporates these questions can help you avoid mistakes in your planning and provide common discussion points for your team as you contemplate what training works best online for you, your learners, and your organization.

All of the preceding content may leave you with the impression that you are being asked to decide between classroom and online or other forms of technology-based learning. This is absolutely not the case. The use of technology in learning and the notion of online learning itself is changing into something much broader and more sophisticated than most people realize.

Blended Learning

With the idea that online training will eliminate classroom training rejected as a myth, but with online training here to stay as a significant component of our instructional strategy repertoire, it stands to reason that a combination of the two might be useful in many instances. This combination has come to be known as blended learning.

Traditional blended learning supports the idea that classroom training can be augmented with online training in ways that shorten classroom time (efficiency) by moving basic content online. Freed from the introductory material, the classroom instructor can concentrate on more advanced content and spend more time in class enabling learners to practice, experiment, and work in teams. This changes the classroom dynamic from a passive lecture mode to one of high engagement and activity. The instructor transitions from the "sage on the stage," to the "guide on the side."[11]

Today, e-learning, for example, is often used as the pre-course and post-course components of classroom training. In curriculum planning, online courses are positioned in a learning path alongside classroom training. Decisions are made on how best to optimize both approaches so that the end result is more cost-effective and efficient training, offering more scheduling flexibility for the learner, while retaining the same or even higher levels of quality.

How Would You Blend?

Table 11-1 presents four sample scenarios. For each of these, come up with a way that blended learning might be used.

Table 11-2 presents some suggestions for how you might apply a blended solution to each scenario.

Beyond Traditional Blended Learning

While it's appropriate to think about blended learning as the combination of online and classroom training, there is much more to consider.

Ask yourself how many hours (or days) per year a typical employee or customer spends in training (either classroom or online). If you said anything more than 40 hours or five days, congratulations! You work in a progressive place. Most organizations provide, on average, less than one week of *formal* training per year.[12]

Table 11-1. Four Sample Scenarios

Scenario	Explanation
Computer Manufacturer In three months, the company is releasing a new billing system that 1,000+ engineers worldwide must implement. It is radically different from the existing one.	
International Real Estate and Relocation Company New customer service center launch for national and international relocation. One thousand new customer service agents will be immediately required in a variety of positions. Must be productive within six weeks. Projected volume of 100 additional new agents per month. Agents have to relocate employees and their families from a variety of companies to new job locations.	
High-Tech Solutions Company Ensure that company and third-party partner engineers on four continents apply "best practices" for customer benefit and service consistency.	
Wireless Telephone Company Reduce time and cost to produce a steady stream of productive, consistently performing new-hire customer service agents across geographically dispersed call centers.	

Table 11-2. Some Suggestions for Blended Learning Scenarios

Scenario	Blending Suggestion
Computer Manufacturer In three months, the company is releasing a new billing system that 1,000+ engineers worldwide must implement. It is radically different from the existing one.	*Pre-course e-learning module that reviews the upcoming changes and helps the engineers understand what needs to be done. This allows more practice time during the actual face-to-face training, which can be more "lab" oriented.*
International Real Estate and Relocation Company New customer service center launch for national and international relocation. One thousand new customer service agents will be immediately required in a variety of positions. Must be productive within six weeks. Projected volume of 100 additional new agents per month. Agents have to relocate employees and their families from a variety of companies to new job locations.	*Move as much content as possible to online learning so that most of the 1,000 employees can be trained, at least on the basic content, as fast as possible. Then bring them into a real call center (or a lab) for field-based training and practice, with possible additional coaching by seasoned performers.*
High-Tech Solutions Company Ensure that company and third-party partner engineers on four continents apply "best practices" for customer benefit and service consistency.	*E-learning modules on each best practice can be developed and placed into an online course library that engineers can access as needed. These courses can be in multiple languages. In addition, these can be positioned outside the company firewall so that third-party engineers can have access without gaining entry to more sensitive content within the company. Local live instruction to practice on a variety of cases can be provided that uses locally relevant examples. The instructor and colleagues can give immediate feedback to learners. Follow-up support by the instructors helps fine-tune best-practice application on the job.*
Wireless Telephone Company Reduce time and cost to produce a steady stream of productive, consistently performing new-hire customer service agents across geographically dispersed call centers.	*E-learning course that simulates some of the screens and interactions that the employees will have with the new system. In addition, a follow-up course can be provided for those who need additional practice. This can improve time to competence, allowing slower learners more time to practice skills by using the optional e-learning tools provided. On-the-job tutorials by supervisors and/or lead agents provide individualized assistance as required.*

The word *formal* is important. Formal training is scheduled training that generally includes a start and stop time. Formal training has a specific design plan that has all learners go through the learning experience in much the same way. Now consider this, if approximately somewhat less than a week per year is devoted to formal training, what do employees or customers do during the remaining 51+ weeks in the year when they require new skills or knowledge? Certainly they continue to learn, but how?

We know that people learn in many different ways. We also know that most learning takes place on the job. In addition to receiving instruction, we certainly learn from reading and listening, doing and observing, trial and error, adjusting and adapting, and from guided and unguided practice. We grow our competencies via many different sources, as well. Beyond instructors, we learn from our colleagues and our bosses, from experts, from websites and documents of all kinds, and from our own experiences.

Between 70 and 80 percent of all our learning in the workplace is *not* delivered to us through formal courses.[13] We acquire most of what we learn *informally*. Informal learning is highly personal. It is unscheduled and totally guided by individual interests and needs. There are no course schedules or start and stop times, and, because people's interests and capabilities differ, what one individual learns is likely to be different from what anyone else acquires and retains.

So while the design of formal training is centered on structured, highly organized learning programs, informal learning is more like a free-form library, where learners explore resources and select those that are most useful and efficient for them at any particular moment.

Think about your college learning experience. In any one semester, you scheduled about 15 formal hours a week in class, but you spent (or should have spent) as much or probably more informal learning time in the library, in study groups, working on projects, and conducting research. In the workplace, for those 51+ weeks during which you are not in a formal class of any kind, you are still learning, albeit informally.

So the new view of blended learning is not simply the combination of classroom and online training, although that is part of it. Rather, it is the combination of formal and informal learning, in the broadest sense of these terms.

New Informal Learning Approaches

The world of training is exploding with new approaches to informal learning. Instruction is augmented by information and collaboration. All three are critical.

Think of the combination as a three-legged stool (see figure 11-1). Remove one leg and the entire stool becomes unstable and collapses.

Instruction, the first leg of the stool, is the deliberate act of guiding learners to acquire skills and knowledge they lack, but require to perform well. It is what we have been dealing with to date in this volume.

Information, the second leg, has become a massive challenge for all organizations. While the rate of information growth is accelerating, the half-life of that information is shortening. In other words, we have more knowledge out there, but the rate at which knowledge becomes obsolete and replaced by new knowledge has never been faster.[14] The challenge of every organization is to manage its knowledge in information repositories that house and distribute content in the form of documents, presentations, financial and customer data, video and audio files (for example, podcasts), and much more. Tools from the simple to the sophisticated are now available to manage organizational knowledge in ways that let people access and update it more reliably, while at the same time maintaining the appropriate levels of intellectual property protection.

Collaboration is the third leg of the three-legged stool. The importance of collaboration in learning success, between colleagues, with experts, and even among learners, cannot be understated. The ability of workers to seek out answers, test ideas, find others who have the same interests and needs, and work in teams or

Figure 11-1. New Blended Learning

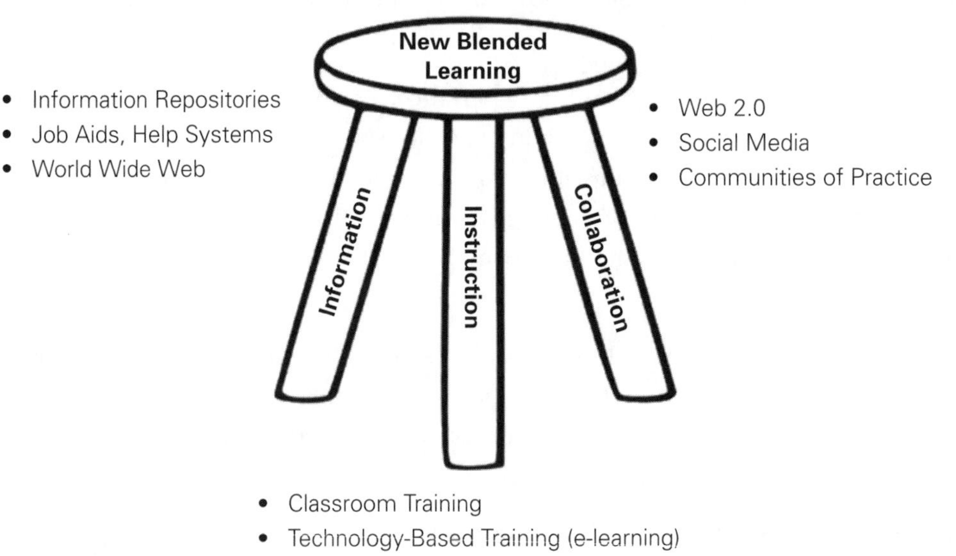

- Information Repositories
- Job Aids, Help Systems
- World Wide Web

New Blended Learning

- Web 2.0
- Social Media
- Communities of Practice

Information Instruction Collaboration

- Classroom Training
- Technology-Based Training (e-learning)

communities of practice, is not only a natural way to learn, it can be much more efficient. When an individual poses a question and can obtain an answer quickly, that person can get right back to work instead of stopping to take a course that may not be available at the moment of need.

A true learning organization is not the organization with the largest collection of training programs or the most courses online. Rather, it is the organization where knowledge is most freely shared through increasingly effective information exchange and collaboration approaches and tools. The sharing of knowledge is a highly social act. It was learning guru John Seely Brown, formerly of Xerox's Palo Alto Research Center (PARC), who first championed the notion that *all learning is social*. Social learning is the new frontier of online learning.[15]

The Rise of Web 2.0

Today, the Internet is more than interactive; it is social. Everyone is a content creator and a content consumer. The tools for creating and distributing content are easier than ever to master. The new World Wide Web, Web 2.0, is defined by this idea of information connectedness.

Learn More...

With the explosion of web applications such as YouTube, Twitter, Facebook, Wikipedia, Flickr, and many others, as the expression goes, "you'd have to be sitting under a rock" not to be aware of the changes taking place on the Internet and the rise of Web 2.0. Tools that let people collaborate, collect and share information, and build communities are everywhere.

Instead of reviewing tools such as blogs, wikis, RSS feeds, social networking, podcasting, and webcasting, why not use these tools to learn on your own?

You can use search engines like Google and Bing and content sites such as YouTube and Wikipedia, among other resources, to find out more about social media and Web 2.0 tools and how they can be used in learning and in other situations. Besides, accessing continually updated media to get the latest information is likely a better way to keep abreast of changes in the Web 2.0 world than just relying on what can be fit into this short chapter.

How's that for an example of informal learning? Try it.

You can also explore some of the resources listed in the endnotes.

From YouTube to Wikipedia, from podcasts to webcasts, and from hundreds of thousands of blogs and wikis, and half a billion members on social networks, a new dynamic and personal web has embraced us. For training, Web 2.0 (also referred to as social media, the real-time web, and the collaborative web) creates great opportunities for informal learning.

Using Web 2.0 and social media tools for informal learning is not without its challenges. Here are some that have been raised recently. Check off those with which you agree.

☐ 1. Social media leads to less thoughtful reading and writing, which can't be good for learning.
☐ 2. Relying on social media leads us to communicate with people who mostly have only cursory knowledge about a subject.
☐ 3. Social media hurts the ability to have conversations, which is bad for collaboration.
☐ 4. Social media is training us to think in "sound bites."
☐ 5. When everyone can create content, more bad content proliferates.
☐ 6. Users of social media tend to have poor research and information quality evaluation skills.

Most people believe all of these statements contain some truth. After all, poor implementation or too much of a good thing can damage the benefits of any innovation. In addition, some always resist new technology. Fear of abuse and a lack of security always temper organizational technology initiatives. It took years for companies to fully embrace email and e-learning. But it did happen, and there is no turning back. For Web 2.0 and social media, the best way of thinking about barriers is that, eventually, "these too, shall pass."[16]

Despite criticisms, many point to social media and Web 2.0 as a great opportunity. With how many of these points do you agree?

☐ 1. Social media represents another change in how we communicate; we survived television, email, and the Internet, and we'll master this too.
☐ 2. Social media is encouraging more writing in blogs and other online publications. The medium may be different, but good writing is never out of style.
☐ 3. Social networking is resulting in the formation of better teams—ones that would never have formed without these new tools.
☐ 4. Social media may be troublesome to today's workers, but will be second nature to tomorrow's workers.
☐ 5. Social media may be the only way to keep up with the explosion of information on a global scale.
☐ 6. Social media enables more access to more people, which is great in terms of relationships and understanding. How can this be bad?

The debate about social media will continue for a considerable time, probably until some new technological phenomenon bursts on the scene. Our recommendation for now is to neither run from Web 2.0 and social media nor blindly embrace it without inhibitions. We must understand and manage it better, including balancing the hype and the promise with the realities of new media. We cannot be smart users of technology if we are not also smart consumers of technology-delivered content. By maintaining a proper balance and using new media wisely, it is possible to exploit Web 2.0 and add great value to the overall learning technology equation.

Integrating Web 2.0 Into Training

What are some interesting ways of integrating Web 2.0 into an overall learning technology strategy? Adding information access and collaboration opportunities, especially back on the job following formal training, is one good approach. Another is by considering information and collaboration tools as opportunities to move content out of training so that precious training resources can be devoted to higher-order learning opportunities (from lecturing on facts to facilitating simulations and experimentation). Re-examining the four scenarios presented in tables 11-1 and 11-2, what ideas come to mind for using informal Web 2.0 tools to enhance learning and performance? Write down your ideas in table 11-3.

Table 11-4 presents some suggestions on how you might incorporate Web 2.0 approaches and tools into your overall learning strategy.

There are certainly more, and perhaps better, ideas for each. What did you come up with?

Resources and Examples: Ideas for Using New Media in Learning

The web is a vast library of information, more than any one individual can sift through. Looking for information on new ways to use technology for learning? Table 11-5 presents some interesting resources in a variety of new media formats. Review them and then come up with ideas on how you might use these tools to meet the learning needs of your students.

What ideas did you come up with? Check table 11-6 for more.

The New Blended Learning and the Future of Training

As learning technology moves toward the future, its very nature is being redefined. Going beyond simply blending online courseware with instructor-led training, the

Table 11-3. Your Ideas for Incorporating Web 2.0 Into Blended Learning Scenarios

Scenario	Blending Suggestion	
	Formal Online Training	**Informal Web 2.0 Ideas**
Computer Manufacturer In three months, the company is releasing a new billing system that 1,000+ engineers worldwide must implement. It is radically different from the existing one.	Pre-course e-learning module that reviews the upcoming changes and helps the engineers understand what needs to be done. This allows more practice time during the actual face-to-face training, which can be more "lab" oriented.	
International Real Estate and Relocation Company New customer service center launch for national and international relocation. One thousand new customer service agents will be immediately required in a variety of positions. Must be productive within six weeks. Projected volume of 100 additional new agents per month. Agents have to relocate employees and their families from a variety of companies to new job locations.	Move as much content as possible to online learning so that most of the 1,000 employees can be trained, at least on the basic content, as fast as possible. Then bring them into a real call center (or a lab) for field-based training and practice, with possible additional coaching by seasoned performers.	
High-Tech Solutions Company Ensure that company and third-party partner engineers on four continents apply "best practices" for customer benefit and service consistency.	E-learning modules on each best practice can be developed and placed into an online course library that engineers can access as needed. These courses can be in multiple languages. In addition, these can be positioned outside the company firewall so that third-party engineers can have access without gaining entry to more sensitive content within the company.	

Scenario	Blending Suggestion	
	Formal Online Training	**Informal Web 2.0 Ideas**
High-Tech Solutions Company (continued)	Local live instruction to practice on a variety of cases can be provided that uses locally relevant examples. The instructor and colleagues can give immediate feedback to learners. Follow-up support by the instructors helps fine-tune best-practice application on the job.	
Wireless Telephone Company Reduce time and cost to produce a steady stream of productive, consistently performing new-hire customer service agents across geographically dispersed call centers.	E-learning course that simulates some of the screens and interactions that the employees will have with the new system. In addition, a follow-up course can be provided for those who need additional practice. This can improve time to competence, allowing slower learners more time to practice skills by using the optional e-learning tools provided. On-the-job tutorials by supervisors and/or lead agents provide individualized assistance as required.	

new blended learning transcends instruction itself to bring information access and collaboration to the forefront of learning.

The new blended learning represents a significant expansion of the trainer's toolkit and a significant opportunity to reach out beyond instructional settings to improve learning and performance directly within the workplace. To do so successfully requires strong partnerships with IT, HR, line organizations, senior leaders, and employees and customers. In the end, the new blended learning opens an important doorway through which training professionals can have true impact on the day-to-day performance of individual people and whole organizations.

The web is like a widely cast net that allows you to collect from the ether ocean neat techniques and methods for conveying information, for communicating, for gathering content, or simply for spicing up an already existing training-learning

Table 11-4. Suggestions for Incorporating Web 2.0 Ideas Into Blended Learning Scenarios

Scenario	Blending Suggestion	
	Formal Online Training	Informal Web 2.0 Ideas
Computer Manufacturer In three months, the company is releasing a new billing system that 1,000+ engineers worldwide must implement. It is radically different from the existing one.	Pre-course e-learning module that reviews the upcoming changes and helps the engineers understand what needs to be done. This allows more practice time during the actual face-to-face training, which can be more "lab" oriented.	• *Distribute a podcast of the chief information officer talking about the new system and its importance to the company.* • *Create an information repository of resources that support the use of the new system and make it accessible to all. Teach how to use it in the training.*
International Real Estate and Relocation Company New customer service center launch for national and international relocation. One thousand new customer service agents will be immediately required in a variety of positions. Must be productive within six weeks. Projected volume of 100 additional new agents per month. Agents have to relocate employees and their families from a variety of companies to new job locations.	Move as much content as possible to online learning so that most of the 1,000 employees can be trained, at least on the basic content, as fast as possible. Then bring them into a real call center (or a lab) for field-based training and practice, with possible additional coaching by seasoned performers.	• *Build a comprehensive help function into the new system that serves as an information repository with content that goes beyond the training.* • *Create a social network of coaches and mentors that new employees can quickly tap into whenever they have a question or problem.* • *When speed matters, communication is key. Use a blog to keep customer service managers up to date on how the training program is moving along.*
High-Tech Solutions Company Ensure that company and third-party partner engineers on four continents apply "best practices" for customer benefit and service consistency.	E-learning modules on each best practice can be developed and placed into an online course library that engineers can access as needed. These courses can be in multiple languages. In addition, these can be positioned outside the company firewall so that third-party engineers can have	• *Build a best-practice repository that contains demonstrations and practical stories of how people have used the new practice to improve their performance. Create the capability for people to contribute their stories, thus growing the knowledge base over time.*

Scenario	Blending Suggestion	
	Formal Online Training	**Informal Web 2.0 Ideas**
High-Tech Solutions Company (continued)	access without gaining entry to more sensitive content within the company. Local live instruction to practice on a variety of cases can be provided that uses locally relevant examples. The instructor and colleagues can give immediate feedback to learners. Follow-up support by the instructors helps fine-tune best-practice application on the job.	• *Establish a network of experts in each best practice who are available for online consultation.*
Wireless Telephone Company Reduce time and cost to produce a steady stream of productive, consistently performing new-hire customer service agents across geographically dispersed call centers.	E-learning course that simulates some of the screens and interactions that the employees will have with the new system. In addition, a follow-up course can be provided for those who need additional practice. This can improve time to competence, allowing slower learners more time to practice skills by using the optional e-learning tools provided. On-the-job tutorials by supervisors and/or lead agents provide individualized assistance as required.	• *Create a knowledge base of "best calls" and "worst calls," based on real experiences (although simulated to protect privacy) so that employees can hear and discuss strategies for responding to these calls. Use this knowledge base inside the training program but also make it available "on the floor" with expert commentary on how to respond.* • *Improve call center computer screens (usability, navigation, etc.) to allow more seamless integration of learning and support tools with the application.*

program. Like our prehistoric ancestors who called upon the technologies of their time to enhance their messages and lessons, we, too, should gather what is available to us to help improve our learners' skills, knowledge, and ability so that they, in turn, can produce valuable contributions to their own lives and to those of others.

Table 11-5. How Would You Use These New Media in Training?

New Media Format	How Would You Use This Medium in Training?
Video: YouTube From the silly to the profound, YouTube contains millions of videos on almost every subject. Here's how to view a great set of videos that simply and eloquently explains new Web 2.0 tools: Go to YouTube and in the search bar type in "_____ in Plain English." For example, "Social Media in Plain English," "Twitter in Plain English," or almost any other Web 2.0 term. In wonderful short videos, Lee Leefever explains it all. (You can also go directly to his company's website, www.commoncraft.com.)	
Information Repository One of the best information resources on new learning technology can be found at The Center for Learning and Performance Technologies in the United Kingdom. In this incredibly current and rich resource, Jane Hart provides a treasure trove of resources and ideas that are practical and easy to use and share. Some examples include • **The State of Learning in the Workplace;** http://c4lpt.co.uk/handbook/state.html • **Introduction to Social Media;** http://c4lpt.co.uk/academy/ism/index.html • **Top Social Media Resources;** http://janeknight.typepad.com/pick/2010/12/2010-in-review-pt-1-top-10-c4lpt-resources.html • **Learning Tools Directory;** http://www.c4lpt.co.uk/Directory/index.html • **100+ Free Websites to Find Out About Anything and Everything;** http://c4lpt.co.uk/Showcase/100anything.html	
Blogs Blogs provide a wonderful way to keep everyone informed about what is going on in your work, your project, your organization, or your life. Here are some interesting blogs in the e-learning space: • **Learning Circuits;** http://learningcircuits.blogspot.com/ • **eLearning Technology;** http://elearningtech.blogspot.com/	

New Media Format	How Would You Use This Medium in Training?
Blogs (continued) • **Life in Perpetual Beta;** http://www.jarche.com/ • **Jane's Pick of the Day;** http://janeknight.typepad.com/pick/ • **Learning Trends;** http://trends.masie.com/ • **eLearning Post;** http://www.elearningpost.com/ • **Internet Time;** www.internettime.com	
Wikis A wiki is a quick and easy way to collect and organize information for others to view and share. You can have as many or as few contributors as you like. In addition to Wikipedia, here are some wikis in the e-learning arena: • **eLearn Space;** http://www.elearnspace.org/ • **Teaching with Technology;** http://twt.wikispaces.com/eLearning • **Wiki Educator;** http://wikieducator.org/Main_Page	

Remember This

This chapter contained a great deal of content and ideas to consider. What did you retain? Here are statements for you to straighten out. As usual, just cross out the portion of each statement that is, in your opinion, not correct. Then, examine what we selected along with some additional feedback.

1. The most resistance to technology-based learning comes from the (*learners themselves / members of training organizations*); many just don't want it.
2. The preponderance of online courses (*is / is not*) designed perfectly.
3. In a simulation e-learning environment, the learner can try out techniques and ideas that (*are always / might not be*) practical in the real world.
4. Online learning as your delivery mode is (*the first / one of the last*) decisions you make.
5. Combining online and classroom training is (*extremely useful / not worthwhile*).
6. The world of training is witnessing (*an increase / a decrease*) in informal learning.
7. Collaboration (*decreases/increases*) efficiency in learning.

Table 11-5. How Would You Use These New Media in Training?

New Media Format	How Would You Use This Medium in Training?
Video: YouTube From the silly to the profound, YouTube contains millions of videos on almost every subject. Here's how to view a great set of videos that simply and eloquently explains new Web 2.0 tools: Go to YouTube and in the search bar type in "_____ in Plain English." For example, "Social Media in Plain English," or "Twitter in Plain English," or almost any other Web 2.0 term. In wonderful short videos, Lee Leefever explains it all. (You can also go directly to his company's website, www.commoncraft.com.)	• Create a YouTube "channel" of guest speakers and other experts that learners and workers can explore anytime and anywhere. • Create videos of your presentations (or those of your students) that can be accessed by class participants. • Record webinars and webcasts for future viewing.
Information Repository One of the best information resources on new learning technology can be found at The Center for Learning and Performance Technologies in the United Kingdom. In this incredibly current and rich resource, Jane Hart provides a treasure trove of resources and ideas that are practical and easy to use and share. Some examples include • **The State of Learning in the Workplace;** http://c4lpt.co.uk/handbook/state.html • **Introduction to Social Media;** http://c4lpt.co.uk/academy/ism/index.html • **Top Social Media Resources;** http://janeknight.typepad.com/pick/2010/12/2010-in-review-pt-1-top-10-c4lpt-resources.html • **Learning Tools Directory;** http://www.c4lpt.co.uk/Directory/index.html • **100+ Free Websites to Find Out About Anything and Everything;** http://c4lpt.co.uk/Showcase/100anything.html	• Create online resources for students to access in class and after they are back on the job. Keep adding to the knowledge base and let everyone know when new information is posted. • Work with other parts of your organization to provide "primary" sources of information to your learners. • Create one-stop locations for all information related to a particular topic. Work with corporate librarians to ensure ease of access and use. • Create your own resource of online information to augment in-class materials.
Blogs Blogs provide a wonderful way to keep everyone informed about what is going on in your work, your project, your organization, or your life. Here are some interesting blogs in the e-learning space: • **Learning Circuits;** http://learningcircuits.blogspot.com/ • **eLearning Technology;** http://elearningtech.blogspot.com/	• Create a blog to let your students (current and former) know what is going on with your courses and your curricula. • Post interesting, even controversial items on your blog and allow students to react to them. • When forming learning teams, allow each team to share their progress through blogs.

New Media Format	How Would You Use This Medium in Training?
Blogs (continued) • **Life in Perpetual Beta;** http://www.jarche.com/ • **Jane's Pick of the Day;** http://janeknight.typepad.com/pick/ • **Learning Trends;** http://trends.masie.com/ • **eLearning Post;** http://www.elearningpost.com/ • **Internet Time;** www.internettime.com	• For multiple course curricula, use blogs to communicate with students between sessions.
Wikis A wiki is a quick and easy way to collect and organize information for others to view and share. You can have as many or as few contributors as you like. In addition to Wikipedia, here are some wikis in the e-learning arena: • **eLearn Space;** http://www.elearnspace.org/ • **Teaching with Technology;** http://twt.wikispaces.com/eLearning • **Wiki Educator;** http://wikieducator.org/Main_Page	• Have students use wikis to compile results from research or projects. • Use a wiki to enable the entire class to contribute content on one or more subjects. Consider allowing students to contribute to the wiki over time so that it becomes a robust resource that people can use in class and back on the job.

8. A true learning organization is one with (*large amounts of / highly targeted*) training programs available online.

9. With more than a half billion members on social networks, this has created a (*personal/impersonal*) web.

10. Information and collaboration tools provide opportunities to move more content (*out of / into*) training so that precious resources can be devoted to higher order learning opportunities.

11. A blog is a (*quick and easy way to collect and organize information for others to view and share / wonderful way to keep everyone informed of what is going on in your work, projects, organization, or life*).

This is what we selected and why:

1. The most resistance to technology-based learning comes from the members of training organizations; many just don't want it. As we stated at the beginning of this chapter, the argument that learners don't want to learn via technology only holds true when the technology-based course is poorly designed, is difficult to navigate or control, or offers little perceived value. Build a

great, meaningful, online experience that is readily accessible, and learners will flock to it. However, technology-based learning can be threatening to training professionals who are faced with changes for which they are not prepared. The result is resistance until they begin to see benefits for themselves and for their learners.

2. The preponderance of online courses is not designed perfectly. In the rush to get the training out, organizations often cut instructional design corners. They also succumb to vendor promises that for little cost, they can turn classroom training into e-learning. Truly effective online training requires careful crafting and knowledgeable decision making. Alas, we find these two to be in short supply when we review what so many organizations have put online for their learners.

3. In a simulation e-learning environment, the learner can try out techniques and ideas that might not be practical in the real world. A simulation environment encourages learners to try things out, make errors and then grow from these. It offers opportunities for "safe failure." In such a low risk setting, learners attempt things that might not work in the real world, discover why this is so, and receive immediate feedback that improves their actions and decision making.

4. Online learning as your delivery mode is one of the last decisions you make. Does the problem you wish to solve require improved skills and knowledge, or is it one that can only be handled by other means (for example, better tools, greater incentives, or clearer expectations)? Is there an adequate IT infrastructure in place? Are the learners independent enough to be able to get the most from an online approach? Do you have adequate resources? Many questions must be answered and many decisions must be made before you finally can say that online learning will be the most cost-effective and efficient way to go.

5. Combining online and classroom training is extremely useful. Yes, each can be exploited to the best advantage based on strategy, costs, accessibility, and impact. Examine the possibilities for effective combinations.

6. The world of training is witnessing an increase in informal learning. With so many free resources at our disposal, from online information and learning tools to communities of practice and other forms of networking with knowledgeable experts, you can plug yourself into the Internet and find almost limitless ways to bake a cherry pie, repair a vintage car engine, or deepen your knowledge of poetry. Obviously, you have to take precautions about the quality and credibility of what you discover. Informal learning also allows you to encounter wrong or misleading information.

7. Collaboration increases efficiency in learning. We learn a great deal through collaboration—by participating in a demonstration, asking questions of experts, or trying out something and receiving feedback from an experienced practitioner. We don't have to wait for an instructor to run a class or go to a library to find an answer. The web offers numerous resources and search engines such as google.com or yahoo.com that continue making it easier to find the right person or group to help us learn rapidly.

8. A true learning organization is one with highly targeted training programs available online. Quantity does not equal quality. Available programs must be tightly linked to on-the-job requirements. Otherwise, the learning experiences are frustrating and turn-offs to learners. Adults want to solve problems and move ahead in their work. Lots of available and irrelevant training will not do it for them. Focus on the necessary and make it highly accessible and easy to navigate. This contributes to building a learning organization in the truest sense of the term.

9. With more than a half billion members on social networks, this has created a personal web. There are so many members and so much information about each one that you can select your personal network of people and content. With excellent tools to help you access whom and what you desire, social networks allow you to create a world of your own choosing.

10. Information and collaboration tools provide opportunities to move more content out of training so that precious resources can be devoted to higher-order learning opportunities. The web is a vast storehouse of learning content. You can go into it as a learning professional and uncover what will allow learners to acquire relevant knowledge and skills on their own. You can encourage learners to explore for themselves. This saves you time and permits you to invest your precious resources on pulling things together, sharing in what has been learned, focusing attention on essentials, and fostering higher-order thinking and decision making.

11. A blog is a wonderful way to keep everyone informed of what is going on in your work, projects, organization, or life. Blogs are being used with increasing frequency to communicate and share information about work, new initiatives, problems encountered, events, or simply about day-to-day life.

Closing Out on Learning With Technology: Making It Work

This chapter has been a lengthy one, filled with a great amount of content on technology, online learning, e-learning, blended learning, the Internet, Web 2.0, social networks, and other exciting innovations. Almost every day, we hear about new options to consider that have potential for improving the way we can help people learn. We have to pace ourselves in absorbing all of the glittering possibilities. Just keep remembering that technology offers us means not ends. Don't forget GIGO. Otherwise, you will end up with technology-driven telling and little effective training.

On that note, we are ready to enter the final section of *Telling Ain't Training: Updated, Expanded, and Enhanced*. In it, we focus once again on the fundamentals— what science and best practice have demonstrated to be reliable truths about training-learning. In this last section, we also, sadly, say farewell to you. Please stay with us to the end for some last thoughts and reflections on our voyage through this book.

Section 5

Wrapping It Up

Chapter 12

Hit or Myth:
What's the Truth?

Chapter highlights:

▶ Hit-or-myth game that separates fact from fiction about learning

▶ Research-based debriefing

▶ Practical advice on remaining vigilant in the face of tradition.

So much of what passes for accepted practice or stable truths in training is often counterproductive to the learning process and to workplace performance. Yet these apparent truisms get passed along from generation to generation of trainers. We have read whole treatises on how examining the shape of learners' skulls and feeling their cranial bumps can help you better instruct them (that is, the 19th- and early 20th-century phrenology movement). Teachers and trainers took that seriously along with maintaining the balance of the body's humors (still alive in some new-age writings). In studying the history of training, we have seen firmly held beliefs concerning racial differences in learning and about what content and methods are more appropriate for each gender (for example, don't teach too much mathematics and science to women because they haven't the reasoning capacity for those subjects).

At the start of the 20th century, teaching and training leaned heavily on memorization as an excellent means for strengthening the brain, which was viewed as a muscle that required exercise. That and other myths for building "character" and "reasoning abilities" have been debunked scientifically as no more than intuitive myths formulated on the basis of flawed logic and pseudoscience. Surely training has progressed far beyond these primitive beliefs? Perhaps.

This chapter provides some additional pieces of the learning puzzle. Some of them don't fit neatly with the preceding chapters, but they are valuable and we want to share them with you. We have created a series of statements that we've tied together into a "Hit-or-Myth" game, one of the activities we described in chapter 8. Here's how it works.

In worksheet 12-1 are a dozen statements that relate to training and workplace performance. Read each one and decide whether you believe it is true—a hit—or false—a myth. Check off your choices on the worksheet. When you've finished, we will debrief the exercise with you and share what we have discovered about each statement.

Have you checked off your choices? Please force yourself to choose in each case. It will make what follows more meaningful and fun for you.

1. Experts who perform well generally know what they are doing and are the best people to explain their successes.

That statement feels intuitively sensible, but it contradicts what the field of knowledge engineering has discovered. Early in this book we discussed how differently experts and novices process information. Many experts cannot articulate the knowledge they use when demonstrating expertise. They can relate what they do in specific cases, but can't recommend general principles that apply in all cases. An experiment done with New York taxi drivers illustrates this point. The drivers could say why they were taking a particular route from one part of Manhattan to another, but could not give general principles for navigating the city. They just "know" what to do each time based on traffic, time of day, the latest information, and weather conditions. Most of all, they *sensed* what was the best route to take as a result of their experience. The first statement is a myth.[1]

2. Attention to learning styles is necessary for effective teaching. Some learners are more visual and others are more auditory. Still others are highly kinesthetic. Matching instruction to these styles results in improved learning results.

We alluded to this earlier. Research has shown there to be differences in which senses individuals favor for attending to and processing learning information. In recent years, much press has been given to the importance of learning styles. What exactly is this? Is it preference, habit, or inborn trait?

Worksheet 12-1. Hit-or-Myth Game

Statement	Hit	Myth
1. Experts who perform well generally know what they are doing and are the best people to explain their successes.	☐	☐
2. Attention to learning styles is necessary for effective teaching. Some learners are more visual and others are more auditory. Still others are highly kinesthetic. Matching instruction to these styles results in improved learning results.	☐	☐
3. The more enjoyable the instructional methods, the greater the learning achievement.	☐	☐
4. All other things being equal, media and technology make a major difference in learning effectiveness.	☐	☐
5. Working out problems on your own results in better problem-solving performance than studying those that have already been worked out.	☐	☐
6. The more content you give to learners, the more they take away.	☐	☐
7. A well-designed training program will overcome a poor implementation plan.	☐	☐
8. Technology is the key to future workplace learning success.	☐	☐
9. Lack of workplace performance results mostly from a lack of required skills or knowledge.	☐	☐
10. Successful performance during training usually results in improved performance on the job.	☐	☐
11. Attending to right brain–left brain scientific findings helps us to aid learners who have either right or left hemispheric dominance. Instruction focused toward the right hemisphere can enhance creativity; to the left hemisphere it can foster logical thinking.	☐	☐
12. Good, old-fashioned common sense is a natural best friend of science. It is a sure guide for making sound training decisions.	☐	☐

General consensus is that a learning style is a mode of learning that is most effective for a person. It helps the individual obtain superior learning results. Here's the bad news: More than 25 years of research on this and related themes has not provided any form of conclusive evidence that matching the form of instruction to a learning style improves learning or even attention.[2]

More powerful than those differences is the overall effect of stimulus variation. In simpler terms, research suggests that varying the training message to affect more than one sensory input channel has a greater learning impact than focusing on a single sense for each learner type. By targeting sight, hearing, touch, smell, and even taste, we increase attention because the learner simultaneously engages several senses in a complementary (nonconflicting) manner. This results in heightened comprehension and retention. (For example, see an apple, bite into it to touch and taste it, smell the apple, and hear the crunch.)

So, although it's true that some learners are more visual and others are more auditory, the difference is not important for effective learning. Learners process what they learn at deeper levels (involving meaning) than merely at the sensory levels. It's another myth. Stimulus variation offers a greater payoff.

Oh, just one more interesting point. Although the marketplace is replete with learning-style tests dealing with 13 categories of identified learning styles, an indepth review of them by researchers *not* related to the developers' tests found that only three of the 13 learning style models came even close to demonstrating internal consistency, test-retest reliability, and predictive value.[3]

3. The more enjoyable the instructional methods, the greater the learning achievement.

We would like this to be true, but the results of research on learner enjoyment or satisfaction and learner success vary from a negative correlation of .80 to a positive .75. There is no stability in the findings. Some studies conducted with high- and low-ability students and structure found the following to be true: High-ability students prefer structure but do better in exploratory modes; low-ability students prefer less structure but do better in the structured, more directive mode.

Overall, enjoyment and satisfaction do not seem to be the critical variables for learning. Persistence or time on task appears to be far more powerful. If enjoyment makes learners persist longer, then that works. But studying unhappily for hours and sweating it out works just as well, and if the learner is meaningfully mentally engaged, perhaps it works even better.

To add one more layer, enjoyment and satisfaction as a *cause* of improved attention and learning requires that the learning activities, themselves, be deemed "enjoyable" by the learners. However, in some studies, enjoyment or satisfaction was expressed as a result of the learning event. In other words, it was not necessarily the enjoyment factor in the instruction or learning activity itself, but the positive consequence of what took place: high test score, valued accomplishment, or a sense of having overcome a difficult learning endeavor.[4] Score another myth.

4.   All other things being equal, media and technology make a major difference in learning effectiveness.

This has been one of the most persistent myths we have seen over the past 50-plus years. In 1913, Thomas Edison predicted the demise of traditional teaching with the invention of the "moving picture." At various times, particularly after World War II in the late 1940s and 1950s with the audiovisual boom, in the 1960s with television, and from the 1980s to the present with computers, enthusiastic educators have lauded the power and potential of the "new media." Studies on the impact of individual media, media combinations, even on various media attributes—comparing one to another or to "conventional" training—have all more or less ended up in the same place. When all the dust has settled, the media have not shown superiority among themselves or against other training modes over time.

Media and technology-based delivery systems, especially computer-driven ones, have improved accessibility to training, permitted cost savings for large learner populations, and provided greater consistency of training messages. Their potential to improve efficiencies in learning is still being studied, again with varying results. All other things being equal, the use of media and technology-based learning systems to improve learning effectiveness to any large degree has not been demonstrated.

It is worthwhile mentioning a large and rigorous study conducted in 2009 and revised in 2010 on the use of online learning, including Web 2.0 applications and systems. The study systematically examined the research literature involving computer usage in various configurations—alone and including a variety of media and blended use (both computer and live classroom)—from 1996 through July 2008.

The report authors identified more than 1,000 empirical studies of online learning. They thoroughly analyzed the studies that contrasted an online to a face-to-face condition, measured student learning outcomes, applied a rigorous research design, and provided adequate information to calculate an effect size (how big the difference was between different treatment groups). They then conducted a meta-analysis on the retained studies. This allowed them to discover, on average, students in online learning conditions performed *modestly* better than those who had received face-to-face instruction. The highest performance results came from those learners who had been taught with a blend of online and face-to-face instruction. The blended instruction often included additional learning time and instructional elements not received by students in the face-to-face condition. The analyst-authors conclude that the positive effects associated with blended learning should not be attributed to the media or technology. They noted that *the studies in this meta-analysis do not demonstrate that online learning is superior as a* medium. *In many of the studies showing an advantage for online learning,* the online and classroom conditions differed in terms of time spent, curriculum, and pedagogy. *It was the combination of elements in the treatment conditions (which were likely to have included additional learning time and materials and additional opportunities for collaboration) that produced the observed learning advantages.* The studies included in the meta-analysis were drawn from a broad spectrum of contexts including school, higher education, and workplace settings.[5] Yes. Another myth.

5. Working out problems on your own results in better problem-solving performance than studying those that have already been worked out.

Particularly in instances where learners may encounter a variety of unique problems in their work, recent research suggests something that appears initially surprising. Don't have learners work out each problem. Rather, provide them with worked out (or partially worked out) problems and have them study the model solutions before attacking similar new problems or troubleshooting occurrences. This appears to lighten the learners' cognitive load and increase problem-solving success. Once again, we may have been tempted to believe that solving everything on one's own builds superior problem-solving capabilities. Further reflection based on research gives us pause. Yet another myth![6]

6. The more content you give to learners, the more they take away.

Based on our observations of many training programs delivered live, via manuals, or online, we are amazed by how much content trainers and training developers attempt to cram into a session. Time and again, we have heard trainers express the fear that "we didn't give the learners everything they might need."

Learners, as we pointed out earlier, are born with cognitive load limits. Through the use of information chunking and leveraging of cognitive strategies, we can increase the amount of skills and knowledge learners can acquire and retain. But human ability to process information is fixed and has been for thousands of years. By prioritizing and culling extraneous information, we can help our learners retain what is essential. Less is more. Hosing down learners with high-pressure information flows will not make them absorb more knowledge. It will only drown them. Myth![7]

7. A well-designed training program will overcome a poor implementation plan.

So many excellent training programs are sitting on shelves collecting dust. The reason: poor implementation planning. This particular myth is not a scientifically researched issue. This has been examined more in the management of training literature. No matter how well the training has been conceived, it will have low impact if

- ► no time is budgeted for workers to take the training
- ► insufficient instructors, equipment, or learning time is available
- ► no pretraining preparation or posttraining support is available for the learners
- ► resources to exploit the training are inadequate
- ► there are no incentives to apply the training on the job
- ► no changes in policies and procedures have been created to integrate newly acquired skills and knowledge.

Implementation is key to the success of any training. Even partial or not perfectly designed training has a higher probability of on-the-job success if the factors listed above are accounted for than does a wonderfully created training program with a poor implementation strategy. If you pit great training against an unprepared environment, expect the environment to win. Myth number 7.

8. Technology is the key to future workplace learning success.

The bottom line in deciding whether this statement is a hit or a myth is a lack of supporting evidence. Although technology suppliers and enthusiastic technophiles have touted the future-world of learning as being upon us, facts have not supported that assertion. Despite the launching of an armada of e-learning and related technology-based training systems, few convincing research findings have demonstrated the effectiveness of these ventures in terms of superior learning gains or better performance from workers.[8]

Recently, even such taken-for-granted assertions as technology-based learning solutions save time and money (not having to travel to a course, no instructors, and no hotel and per-diem costs) are being called into question. High initial costs of hardware and software plus high costs associated with technology-based training development are not being sufficiently amortized through large-scale, repeated use. Rapid obsolescence of equipment, learning software, and courseware have reduced savings.[9]

A recent trend has been the development of automated systems for training and the breaking down of learning content into reusable chunks or objects that are housed in information repositories. Although a great deal of experimentation and effort is being made in these areas, much uncertainty still exists as to how viable the new approaches will be.[10] Remember that technology only amplifies and accelerates. If what we provide is more telling material, technology will tell louder and faster. But it won't result in valued transformation.

The most recent information we have obtained shows that although the mid to late 1990s and early years of the 21st century experienced a decrease in live training and an increase in technology-based training in North American work organizations, that trend has slowed and even reversed in some cases. Count number 8 as a myth!

> 9. Lack of workplace performance results mostly from a lack of required skills or knowledge.

Another way to state this is that the most effective way to improve workplace performance is through training. Building skills and knowledge is worthwhile, but many other factors have been found to supersede skill or knowledge deficiencies. In studying workplace performance, researchers have identified the following to be key causes of performance problems: lack of clarity in expectations; limited access to required information, resources, incentives, or consequences; inadequate feedback systems; and poor selection of people to perform the tasks. In many cases, people already know how to do their jobs. Training and development are important for increasing their performance. Without attending to all of the other factors, however, much of training's potential contributions are lost. Score another myth.[11]

> 10. Successful performance during training usually results in improved performance on the job.

The sensible, logical conclusion that one is tempted to draw is that, if people perform well during training, they will continue to do so on the job. If not, why train? Sadly we report that the research evidence does not support that assertion. Training is necessary in many instances. Rarely, however, is it sufficient to achieve sustained, improved posttraining performance. A quote from Baldwin and Ford, who in 1988 published an extensive review of training research, seems appropriate here: "American industries annually spend more than $100 billion on training … not more than 10 percent of these expenditures actually result in transfer to the job." Ten years later, Ford and Weissbein (1997) updated Baldwin and Ford's review and arrived at the same conclusion.

As in statement 9, training cannot succeed without support from other factors such as information, resources, incentives and consequences, selection, communication, process design, and adequate control of task interferences. Once again, it's another myth.[12]

11. Attending to right brain–left brain scientific findings helps us to aid learners who have either right or left hemispheric dominance. Instruction focused toward the right hemisphere can enhance creativity; to the left hemisphere it can foster logical thinking.

There has been so much hype about lateral hemispheric dominance in the media and in publications that it seems one should pay close attention, especially since Roger W. Sperry won a Nobel prize for his work in this area. However, from a learning perspective, a scientific finding does not necessarily translate into practical, research-supported applications. Sperry did his work mostly on people who had undergone surgery that severed connections in the corpus collosum between the two hemispheres.

In the 1960s and 1970s, the discoveries Sperry and others made, including those by his postgraduate student and colleague Michael Gazzaniga, provided great insights into the working of the brain. Educators and entrepreneurs became excited, extrapolating from this work in the learning arena. Since then, hemisphere dominance tests have populated the educational and training worlds along with curricula to address each of the parts of the brain. Here are some notes of caution.

Most functions require both hemispheres to operate optimally. While brain imaging shows structural differences between the hemispheres, little evidence suggests that these correlate with functional differences. What recent neuroscientific studies are showing is that brain functions tend to be housed in specific areas of the brain and in both hemispheres. An intensive review of 67 recent brain imaging studies on creativity concluded that there was lack of empirical evidence to substantiate the belief in any form of hemispheric dichotomy with respect to creativity.[13]

12. Good, old-fashioned common sense is a natural best friend of science. It is a sure guide for making sound training decisions.

If only this were true. The answer for this final statement is a resounding "myth." Pick up any research textbook and in the early chapters you'll discover the warning that what we euphemistically call "common sense" is one of the greatest enemies of science.

Based on common sense, authority insisted that the sun circled the earth, even after scientific and systematically gathered empirical evidence showed otherwise. Some people today still believe in a flat earth. In the name of common sense, great injustices have been visited on whole groups of people who were "obviously inferior" (that is, by observing how they live and what they believe, it makes good, common sense for us to dominate and exploit them). Doesn't the larger physical size and strength of men suggest that they should command women?

Common sense is in the eye of the beholder who selects data to draw conclusions. Common sense is generally derived from local lore, reinforced by small samples of selected data, and subjectively filtered to arrive at convenient conclusions. This has been true of the training world where we have enshrined such common sense notions as these:

- ▶ *Spare the rod, spoil the child.* This has led to the justification for beating learning into schoolchildren.
- ▶ *Girls lack the reasoning capability necessary for mathematics and science.* This spilled over into other forms of gender discrimination and injustice in learning.
- ▶ *Tell them what you're going to tell them. Tell them. Tell them what you've told them.* This has resulted in the one-way, overloaded information-dumping that is still prevalent in training today.

More modern common sense notions in training relate to some of our previously cited myths about overemphasizing learning styles or overdependence on technology to improve learning. Despite a lack of supporting scientific evidence, many people still strongly argue for large-scale, technology-driven learning systems without considering the uses to which they will be put and that will miraculously empower the worker just in time and with just what is required.

Common sense is whatever we make of it. It's not a best friend of science. It's not a sure guide for making sound training decisions. If we could offer the training community a motto, it would be "Let data talk, and beware of common sense."

Let us close on this myth with two quotes from famous scientists:

"Common sense is nothing more than a deposit of prejudices laid down in the mind before you reach eighteen."

—Albert Einstein[14]

"Good sense is of all things in the world the most equally distributed, for everybody thinks himself so abundantly provided with it, that even those most difficult to please in all other matters do not commonly desire more of it than they already possess."

René Descartes[15]

The Bottom Line on Learning

How did you score on worksheet 12-1? We deliberately set up the Hit-or-Myth game to state only commonly held myths. Our purpose was not to put one over on you, but to arm you in your mission to transform your learners. Part of the job is to combat and counter tradition ("but we've always done it this way"), enthusiastic hype ("it's the latest and the greatest"), and false reasoning ("just follow your—meaning *my*—common sense") when it comes to helping people learn.[16]

Based on what we have derived from our combined 80 years of research and practice, our counsel to you is to demand hard evidence that objectively supports what others try to sell you in training. Keep your eye on the key criteria for success and on the bottom line:

- ▶ Is it learner centered?
- ▶ Is it performance based?
- ▶ Can we demonstrate results?

Your mission and ours is *not* enthusiastic telling. It is effective transformation that leads to both learner and organizational success.

Hit-or-Myth—A Final Match-Up

To close this chapter, we've created a brief match-up game in worksheet 12-2. In column A of the worksheet, we have randomly listed our dozen myth-conceptions. Any or all of them may be thrown at you someday. Column B contains a list of counterarguments. Your job is to match the appropriate counterargument to each myth statement. Have fun!

If you matched most of the myth statements to their appropriate counterarguments, you have a good sense of what will work in training … and what won't.

Now we turn to our final chapter to tie some loose ends together on telling ain't training, share some reflections, and bid you farewell but not good-bye.

Worksheet 12-2. Countering the Myths

Your Match		Column A		Column B
_____	1.	Attention to learning styles is necessary for effective teaching. Some learners are more visual and others are more auditory. Still others are highly kinesthetic. Matching instruction to these styles results in improved learning results.	A.	Many experts cannot articulate the knowledge they use when demonstrating expertise. They possess procedural, but not declarative, knowledge to explain.
_____	2.	A well-designed training program will overcome a poor implementation plan.	B.	Common sense is based on local lore, reinforced by small samples of selected data and subjectively filtered to arrive at convenient conclusions. It tells us that the earth is flat.
_____	3.	Working out problems on your own results in better problem-solving performance than studying those that have already been worked out.	C.	The research on learner enjoyment or satisfaction varies from a negative correlation of −.80 to +.75. There is no stability in the research findings. Persistence has been demonstrated to be more powerful.
_____	4.	The more enjoyable the instructional methods, the greater the learning achievement.	D.	American industries annually spend more than $100 billion on training... not more than 10% of these expenditures actually result in transfer to the job. Regardless of the success of the training effort itself, without proper transfer conditions—an all-too-common state—the training investment is soon lost. Anticipated performance change does not occur.
_____	5.	Lack of workplace performance is due mostly to lack of required skills or knowledge.	E.	Although there are many individual differences in the senses learners lean more toward, and although learners may have some discernible learning preferences, habits, or "styles," these are not that important for learning. Research suggests that learners process information at a "meaning" level and engage all appropriate senses for acquiring and retaining information. Stimulus combinations and variations have more effect on acquisition and retention than a continual favoring of a single form of instruction,

___ 6.	Good, old-fashioned common sense is a natural best friend of science. It is a sure guide for making sound training decisions.	F. Yes, there is well documented research showing the asymmetry of the two hemispheres. However differences in structure don't necessarily result in differences in function. Recent neuroimaging research suggests that both hemispheres are required for most meaningful mental activities. The right brain–left brain "dichotomania" is too simplistic a notion to direct instruction.
___ 7.	Experts who perform well generally know what they are doing and are the best ones to explain their successes.	G. Many other factors have been found to supersede skill or knowledge deficiencies such as lack of clear expectations, feedback, resources, incentives, consequences, and access to needed information.
___ 8.	The more content you give to the learners, the more they take away.	H. Studies on the impact of media on learning over the past 50 years generally end up with the same conclusions. All other things beings equal, media is not the key variable in effectiveness of learning.
___ 9.	Technology is the key to future workplace learning success.	I. Many excellent training programs sit on shelves collecting dust. No matter how well the training has been conceived, it will have low impact if it cannot be implemented adequately. Time, budget, resources, culture, incentives, policies, and procedures are key to performance in the workplace.
___ 10.	All other things being equal, media and technology make a major difference in learning effectiveness.	J. Recent research suggests that showing learners model solutions partially or fully worked out is more effective than having them work out all the problems by themselves. This is especially true for nonrecurring problems.
___ 11.	Attending to right brain–left brain scientific findings helps us to aid learners who have either right or left hemispheric dominance. Instruction focused toward the right hemisphere can enhance creativity; to the left hemisphere it can foster logical thinking.	K. Despite technophile enthusiasm and industry hype, few studies demonstrate the superiority of technology-based training on learning. Recent data on technology-based training does not show a dramatic increase in use.
___ 12.	Successful performance during training usually results in improved performance on the job.	L. Learners have cognitive load limits. Unlike computers, their information-processing capacity has not increased. Information overload has a negative effect on learning and retention.

Chapter 13

Concluding Reflections on Telling Ain't Training

Chapter highlights:

▶ Summary of the book's contents
▶ Review of key messages
▶ Model of instruction drawn from the work of Carl Jung.

This final chapter has three purposes. The first is to pull together the contents of this book into a coherent summary and to leave you with a rationale and memory of the journey you have undertaken with us. The second is to revisit and reemphasize the key messages we have shared with you. We wanted this book to be a conversation. As in all engaging dialogues, we sometimes ramble on and digress from the main points. We won't feel right until we make sure those points have been realigned and restated. The third purpose is to share some final reflections on training and telling. Through this, we wish to leave you with some food for thought as you go forth and figure out what to do with what you've learned.

A Rapid Review of Telling Ain't Training

Chapter 1 was a teaser chapter designed to whet your appetite for more. If you've made it to this point, we succeeded. We are so delighted! More important, the teaser was created to trigger reflection about how *you* have learned. Our guess is that it wasn't mostly from telling.

In chapter 2, you encountered four key terms: training, for reproducing behaviors; instruction, for generalizing learned behaviors to novel instances; education, for building general mental models and values that guide us in how we deal with life's events; and learning, the change in mental structures and behavior repertoires that allows us to face the world and survive. You also became acquainted with the now familiar mantra: learner centered, performance based. No matter whom you train, what the subject is, and how you deliver it (live or otherwise), this mantra should remain with you as a constant guide.

With the rationale for focusing on learner-centered and performance-based training established and with the goal of transforming our learners so that they can perform in ways they and their organizations value, we turned to the learners themselves. To transform, you have to know how learners perceive, process, store, and retrieve information. You have to identify facilitating and inhibiting characteristics of the learners. Finally, you have to be able to use your knowledge of the learner's learning capacities and limits to trigger successful transformation. That's what we shared with you in chapter 3.

If I know so much, why can't I make people learn? That's a question frequently asked by SME trainers frustrated because they can't seem to "make them learn." Here's where you encountered declarative (talk-about) and procedural (do) knowledge. In chapter 4, you also came face-to-face with the paradox of taking SMEs with highly developed procedural knowledge and having them explain things declaratively so that learners can perform procedurally. What a mess!

Chapter 5 introduced you to four key adult learning principles: readiness, experience, autonomy, and action. It demonstrated how consideration of adult learning characteristics greatly assists you in building an effective instructional message. In chapter 6 you discovered the five-step model for structuring training, based on six universals from learning research. That simple model pulls together all the pieces you encountered earlier. It takes into account the mantra, the learner's characteristics, and the adult learning principles to provide a solid structure for building high-probability-of-success training sessions. Chapter 7 added more detail on how you can structure successful learning sessions and help the learner learn more easily by taking into account metacognitive skills and exploiting or enhancing cognitive strategies. In that way you shore up specific weaknesses while strengthening the overall ability of your learners to learn more efficiently.

Chapter 8 introduced four major approaches to training that are used in the workplace and described their features, benefits, and limitations. It also presented you with a large array of ready-to-use activities that can be broadly applied in terms of learners and content, are easily adaptable, and totally respect the principles of *Telling Ain't Training*.

Testing was the theme of chapter 9. You now possess a set of tools you can apply to develop appropriate tests. As we explained in that chapter, testing is a great way to enhance learning if it's done right. Chapter 9 provided you with guidance and support to do it correctly.

Chapter 10 was an important chapter that connected training with technology and attempted to present a balanced view of what to expect when you turn to technology to support or deliver training. It also offered cautions about the overpromise and underdelivery frequently associated with technology hype. Key to exploiting technology appropriately is determination of precisely what your goal is; critical review of not just the technological options, but the hard evidence of successful application; prudent decision making based on fact, not hope; and, finally, well supported implementation with evaluation of results. Technology is just as capable of delivering *telling* as any poor trainer.

Chapter 11 examined the numerous ways you can make technology work for you to produce effective and efficient learning. Starting out with commonly held "myth-conceptions" about learning and technology, it swiftly drew you into dealing with such issues as what drives quality online learning and what decisions you and your organization first have to make before investing in technology-based learning. This chapter also introduced blended learning in its various guises, emphasizing how true blending requires intimate integration of information and collaboration with instruction. Closing out the chapter, you encountered an array of Web 2.0 resources you can begin exploring today and exploiting tomorrow.

Finally, chapter 12 presented a number of training myths—ones to beware of. It also provided you with ammunition to do battle against those who would impose these myths on your organization, your learners, and you.

So here we are. We've traveled far together in a short time. We've shared with you much of what it's taken us many years to learn on our own. Accept it with our best wishes and support. Hold on to the key messages:

- ► Your success is the result of your learners' success.
- ► Learning effectiveness is not in the packaging, but in the design and structuring.
- ► Information is inert. It gains value only when learners seek it out and mold it to their characteristics and needs.
- ► Telling ain't training.

One more key message to retain: live or virtual, synchronous or asynchronous, on-the-job or in the classroom, one-on-one or one-on-many or many-on-one, face-to-face or technology delivered—it's all the same in terms of learning. Begin with the learner. Determine the desired outcome. Design training to help learners progress from where they are to where they ought to be. Adapt the delivery system to the characteristics of the learners and the content. Avoid pseudoscientific ways of determining and labeling learner characteristics. Those are the essentials.

Something to Think About—Reflections From Carl Jung[1]

We are not Jungians. We are learning and workplace researchers and practitioners. A number of years ago, however, we found a model of teaching-learning inspired by the work of Carl Jung that intrigued and touched us (see figure 13-1).

The teacher consciously (T_C) formulates a message to which the learner consciously (L_C) attends. They engage in conscious dialogue (1). However, the teacher doesn't consciously plan every word she or he will say. Unconsciously, the teacher (T_U) draws from inside the right words, analogies, and responses. She or he sets up a dialogue between the conscious self and the unconscious self (2). Similarly, as the teacher's message reaches the learner, he or she also sets up an internal dialogue between conscious and unconscious (3). While this is occurring, the teacher begins to respond not only to the learner's conscious remarks, but also to nondeliberate but nevertheless important cues emanating unconsciously from the learner (L^U) who, in turn, unconsciously responds to the teacher's remarks (4). Similarly, the learner consciously reacts to unconscious teacher cues (5) and vice versa.

Figure 13-1. Teaching-Learning Model Inspired by Carl Jung

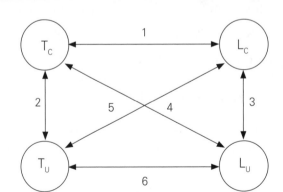

Ultimately, a more profound dialogue emerges. In this deeper communication, one type of dialogue takes place consciously and on the surface (1); the other, which is much more meaningful, occurs unconsciously (6). It is at this unconscious level that, irrespective of the words, the true messages are conveyed.

One of our favorite classics is the late 19th-century novel by Edward Eggleston titled *The Hoosier School-Master.*[2] At one point, the young schoolmaster walks a servant girl home after a spelling bee, which she has won much to everyone's surprise. Although not in a teaching-learning context, what follows well illustrates this deeper dialogue that Jung has described.

> You … wish me to repeat all their love talk. I am afraid you'd find it dull…. Ralph talked love when he spoke of the weather, of the crops, and spelling school—these were what his words would say if reported. But below these commonplaces there vibrated something else. One can make love a great deal better when one doesn't speak of love. Words are so poor! … The solemnest engagements made have been without the intervention of speech….

> Hannah lay awake until the memory of that walk through the darkness came into her soul like a benediction…. She recalled piece by piece the whole conversation—all the commonplace remarks about the weather; all the insignificant remarks about the crops; all the unimportant words about the spelling school. Not for the sake of the remarks. Not for the sake of the weather. Not for the sake of the spelling school. But for the sake of the undertone.

Notice how the real message each has sent to the other is not explicitly articulated. It occurs at that deeper, Jungian, unconscious level.

We leave you with this final reflection. In training, especially as the pressure of accelerating new knowledge requirements tempts us to head for the content and exploit increasingly sophisticated technological means for conveying it, there is a danger of losing our most important message to our learners. If we focus only on words and the superficial, do we lose the essential transformation we seek? As you reflect on those who influenced and taught you most and best, was it via their words? Or was it something else?

Our aim is not to leave you with some mystical meditation. We simply raise a caution about maintaining a focus—what it is that the learners, the organization, and you value most. We have tried to follow our own principles within this book format. We have taught you through the words and activities we offered you. We have prompted you to try out some of the strategies, job aids, tactics, and activities and have offered cues and suggestions for their use. Now we release you to go forth and train well. We hope that beneath the words we have conveyed to you our deep passion and commitment to helping adult learners and you achieve success. Reflect on what you want to make of your training role. As the Jung model and the contents of this book suggest, training is one heck of a lot more than simply telling.

Endnotes

The contents of this book derive from many scientific and professional sources. To make *Telling Ain't Training* easy to read, we refrained from citing too many references for fear of interrupting the flow of each chapter. Instead, we opted to create a substantial endnotes section keyed to specific topics and/or assertions found within the chapters. What follows is a list of references and interesting readings for those who wish to delve more deeply into a subject of personal interest. Please note that we frequently comment on the references, which are organized by chapter and then by topic. Topics are presented sequentially as they appear in the text. There are no endnotes for chapter 1. We also retained most of the original references from the first edition because, in many cases, they still remain valid and offer excellent information even though some may be dated.

Chapter 2: An Introduction to Some "Familiar Terms"

Training, instruction, education, learning

[1]All of the following provide much more depth about what we do as trainers/instructors/educators and the impact of each on learning:

Driscoll, M.P. (2004). *Psychology of Learning for Instruction,* 3d edition. Needham Heights, MA: Allyn & Bacon. This textbook covers a wide range of teaching-learning theories and their applications from primary school to corporate learning and development.

Gagné, R., and K.L. Medsker. (1996). *The Conditions of Learning: Training Applications.* Orlando, FL: Harcourt Brace and Co. Still a foundational document for anyone connected with training.

Sawyer, R.K., ed. (2006). *The Cambridge Handbook of the Learning Sciences.* New York: Cambridge University Press. This volume provides a modern view of learning, what methods are most effective, and what is wasteful or counterproductive. The chapters provide excellent guidance and examples of how training, instruction, and education combine to produce learning.

Performance-based instruction

[2]Brethower, D.M., and K.A. Smalley. (1999). *Performance-Based Instruction*. San Francisco: Jossey-Bass Publishers. See also Pucel, D.J. (2005). *Developing and Evaluating Performance-Based Instruction,* 3d edition. New Brighton, MN: Performance Training Systems.

Media and learning

[3]Clark, R.E. (2001). *Learning From Media: Arguments, Analysis, and Evidence.* Greenwich, CT: Information Age Publishers.

Clark, R.E. (1999). Media Will Never Influence Learning. *Educational Technology Research and Development* 47(2): 21-29.

Both publications by Clark provide powerful arguments and evidence that media, per se, have little to no impact on learning effectiveness.

[4]A more recent and nuanced summary of the research on media and learning is Fadel, C., and C. Lemke. (2008). *Multimodal Learning Through Media: What the Research Says.* San Jose, CA: Cisco Systems. One interesting citation is "A recent meta-analysis in which over 650 empirical studies compared media-enabled distance learning to conventional learning found pedagogy (the method of instruction) to be more strongly correlated to achievement than media" (Clark, R.E., and D.F. Feldon. {2005}. Five Common but Questionable Principles of Multimedia Learning. In R.E. Mayer, ed., *Cambridge Handbook of Multimedia Learning.* Cambridge: Cambridge University Press, 97-116).

Interactive learning

[5]The following provide considerable information on effective means for creating interactive teaching-learning situations:

Engle, R.A. (2006). Training Interactions to Foster Generative Learning: A Situative Explanation of Transfer in a Community of Learners Classroom. *The Journal of the Learning Sciences* 15(4): 451-498. Concerning interactivity in learning and its effectiveness, periodicals such as *The Journal of Interactive Online Learning* or *The Journal of Interactive Learning Research* provide current articles on research in this arena.

Rieber, L.P. (1996). Seriously Considering Play: Designing Interactive Learning Environments Based on the Blending of Microworlds, Simulations, and Games. *Educational Technology Research and Development* 44(2): 43-58.

Stolovitch, H.D. (1984). Frame Games and Gamechains: A Technology for Interactive Teaching-Learning. In R.K. Bass and C.R. Dills, eds., *Instructional Development: The State of the Art, II.* Dubuque, IA: Kendall/Hunt Publishing Company.

Meaningfulness in learning interactions

[6]Meaningfulness in learning has been a topic of interest globally for many years. Here are a few references to clarify what is meant by meaningfulness and what its effect on learning can be:

Boettcher, J. (2000). Designing for Learning: What Is Meaningful Learning? *Syllabus* 14(1): 54-56.

Satheim-Smith, A. (1998). *Focusing on Active, Meaningful Learning: IDEA Paper No. 34.* Manhattan, KS: Kansas State University.

Wilson, A., and L. Burket. (1989). What Makes Learning Meaningful? *Proceedings of the Annual Meeting of the American Association for Adult and Continuing Education,* Atlantic City, NJ, October 1989. (ERIC Document ED 313 586)

Yasin, M., M.N. Daud, H. Musa, and S.S. Imam. (2007). Effect of Meaningfulness of Learning Materials on Speed of Learning. *e-IPRC Proceedings,* Srinakharinwirot University, Bangkok, Thailand.

Chapter 3: The Human Learner

Physiology and evolution of human learning

[1]The following references on the physiology and evolution of human learning provide an excellent base for understanding how learners came to be who and what they are today:

D'Aracangelo, M. (2000). How Does the Brain Develop? A Conversation With Steven Peterson. *Educational Leadership* 58(3): 68-71.

Jenkins, M. (1999). *Evolution.* Lincolnwood, IL: NTC Publishing Group.

Kingdon, J. (1993). *Self-Made Man.* New York: John Wiley & Sons.

Ornstein, R. (1991). *The Evolution of Consciousness: The Origins of the Way We Think.* New York: Simon & Schuster.

Palumbi, S.R. (2001). *The Evolution Explosion.* New York: W.W. Norton & Company.

Sousa, D.A. (2001). *How the Brain Learns: A Classroom Teacher's Guide,* 2d ed. Thousand Oaks, CA: Corwin Press.

Sprenger, M. (1999). *Learning and Memory: The Brain in Action.* Alexandria, VA: Association for Supervision and Curriculum Development.

The senses

[2]For a great book about the latest research on the senses, read Rosenblum, L.D. (2010). *See What I'm Saying: The Extraordinary Powers of Our Five Senses.* New York: WW Norton and Company. Neuroscientific and cognitive research have uncovered the amazing capabilities of all our senses—some unimaginable even a few years ago. This is also an inspiring book on overcoming sensory deficiencies.

[3]Thalheimer, W. (2004). *Bells, Whistles, Neon, and Purple Prose: When Interesting Words, Sounds, and Visuals Hurt Learning and Performance—A Review of the Seductive-Augmentation Research.* This is a meta-analytic research report examining the impact of "seductive elements" such as music, animation, sound, and other exciting effects in instructional programs. Thalheimer examines 29 studies and concludes that unless absolutely necessary for the instructional objective, these elements, overall, have a decremental effect on learning and retention. Available at http://www.worklearning.com/seductive_augmentations.htm.

[4]Mayer, R.E. (2001). *Multimedia Learning.* New York: Cambridge University Press. For more extended information and a review of the research in this area, see also Clark, R.E., and D.F. Feldon. (2005). Five Common but Questionable Principles of Multimedia Learning. In R.E. Mayer, ed., *The Cambridge Handbook of Multimedia Learning.* New York: Cambridge University Press.

Autonomic nervous system

[5]For a succinct description of the autonomic nervous system, how it functions, and how influential a role it plays in directing our daily activities, read Dr. David H.P. Streeten's online article, The Autonomic Nervous System, published by the National Disautonomia Research Foundation. Available at http://www.ndrf.org/ans.html#General%20Organization%20of%20the%20Autonomic%20Nervous%20System).

Three somewhat dated but still useful references are

Backs, R.W. (1995). Going Beyond Heart Rate: Autonomic Space and Cardiovascular Assessment of Mental Workload. *International Journal of Aviation Psychology* 5(1): 25-48.
Microsoft Encarta Online Encyclopedia 2001. (2001). Alternative Medicine. Available at http://encarta.msn.com.
Miyake, S. (1997). Factors Influencing Mental Workload Indexes. *Journal of Occupational and Environmental Health* 19(4): 313-325.

For a general overview of "arousal," go to http://en.wikipedia.org/wiki/arousal. At the Rockefeller Institute, a team of researchers, led by Donald W. Pfaff, have uncovered even more specific factors affecting arousal. Consult the Internet for various papers Dr. Pfaff and his team have published in the Proceedings of the National Academy of Sciences. Additional references of interest are:

Microsoft Encarta Online Encyclopedia 2001. (2001). Alternative Medicine. http://encarta.msn.com.
Walsh, V. (1998). Skill Learning: Bringing Cognition to Its Senses. *Current Biology* 8(16): 572-574.

Short-term memory

[6]Cowan, N. (2001). The Magical Number 4 in Short-Term memory: A Reconsideration of Mental Storage Capacity. *Behavioral and Brain Sciences* 24: 97-185. Cowan has extended his examination of both short-term and working memory in Cowan, N. (2005). *Working Memory (Essays in Cognitive Psychology)*. New York: Psychology Press. This volume encompasses a wide range of research on both short-term and working memory, with clear distinctions between the two (storage versus working attention).

Oberauer, K. (2002). Access to Information on Working Memory: Exploring the Focus of Attention. *Learning, Memory, and Cognition* 28(3): 411-421.

Some additional references are

Banikowski, A.K., and T.A. Mehring. (1999). Strategies to Enhance Memory Based on Brain Research. *Focus on Exceptional Children* 32(2): 1-6.
Gathercole, S.E. (1996). *Models of Short-Term Memory*. East Sussex, UK: Psychology Press.
Microsoft Encarta Online Encyclopedia 2001. (2001). Memory (psychology). Available at http://encarta.msn.com.
Schooler, J. (1998). A Multiplicity of Memory. *Exploring* 22(1): 4-6.
Sprenger, M. (1999). *Learning and Memory: The Brain in Action* (chapter 4). Alexandria, VA: Association for Supervision and Curriculum Development.

Chapter 4: Getting Learners to Learn

[1]Chi, M.T.H. (2006). Laboratory Methods for Assessing Experts' and Novices' Knowledge. In K.A. Ericsson, N. Charness, P.J. Feltovich, and R.R. Hoffman, eds., *The Cambridge Handbook of Expertise and Expert Performance*. New York: Cambridge University Press, 167-184.

Two other readings that help clarify how experts process information differently from others:

Comptelli, G., and F. Gobet. (2005). The Mind's Eye in Blindfold Chess. *European Journal of Psychology* 17: 23-45
Hoffman, R.R., G. Trafton, and P. Roebber. (2006). *Minding the Weather: How Expert Forecasters Think*. Cambridge, MA: MIT Press.

The greater the expertise, the greater the difference in thinking from novices

[2]Chase, W.G., and H.A. Simon. (1973). Perception in Chess. *Cognitive Psychology* 4(1): 55-81.

The following readings are also enlightening for training professionals:

Brandsford, J., A.L. Brown, and R.R. Cocking. (2000). *How People Learn: Brain, Mind, Experience, and School,* expanded ed. Washington, DC: National Academy Press.

Clark, R.C. (2008). *Building Expertise: Cognitive Methods for Training and Performance Improvement,* 3d edition. San Francisco: Wiley-Pfeiffer.

Daley, B. (1999). Novice to Expert: An Exploration of How Professionals Learn. *Adult Education Quarterly* 49(4): 133-147.

Stepich, D. (1991). From Novice to Expert: Implications for Instructional Design. *Performance and Instruction* 30(6): 13-17.

Declarative and procedural knowledge

[3]The following two references clarify the differences between declarative and procedural knowledge. In the process, they add extra nuances and layers to the terse distinctions generally made between the two:

Jiamu, C. (2001). The Great Importance of the Distinction Between Declarative and Procedural Knowledge, *Analise Psicológica* 4(19): 559-566.

ten Berge, T., and R. van Hezewijk. (1999). Procedural and Declarative Knowledge; An Evolutionary Perspective. *Theory Psychology* 9(5): 605-624.

Also, see

Gagné, R., and K.L. Medsker. (1996). *The Conditions of Learning: Training Applications.* Orlando, FL: Harcourt Brace and Company. This volume is a classic. Most professionals in the training-learning profession have read it. It is a must-have on your bookshelf.

Smilkstein, R. (1993). Acquiring Knowledge and Using It. *Gamut.* Seattle: Seattle Community College District. (ERIC Document ED 382 238)

[4]If you want to know more about the indicative and subjunctive moods, here are two brief, but clear references online: For the indicative mood, see http://www.lousywriter.com/verbs_indicative_mood.php; for the subjunctive mood refer to http://englishplus.com/grammar/00000031.htm.

[5]Although somewhat technical, the following reference brings home this point in a programming context: Rosenbloom, P.S. (2010). Combining Procedural and Declarative Knowledge in a Graphical Architecture. In D.D. Salvucci and G. Gunzelmann, eds., *Proceedings of the 10th International Conference on Cognitive Modeling,* Philadelphia, PA: Drexel University, 205-210.

Ability, prior knowledge, motivation

[6]A recent study by two Turkish university researchers underscores the roles ability, prior knowledge, and motivation play in learning. Although the study used eighth grade science students as the subjects, their findings are in line with past discoveries

of the relationships among these three variables and learning outcomes. Araz, G., and S. Sungur. (2007). The Interplay Between Cognitive and Motivational Variables in a Problem-Based Learning Environment. *Learning and Individual Differences* 17(4): 291-297.

[7]Probably the most cited proponent of multiple intelligences is Howard Gardner of Harvard University. A good reference for learning more about this:

Armstrong, T. (2009). *Multiple Intelligences in the Classroom,* 3rd ed. Alexandria, VA: Association for Supervision and Curriculum Development.

[8]Not everyone is convinced of this belief concerning the innate abilities model. Read Colvin, G. (2008). *Talent Is Overrated: What Really Separates World-Class Performers From Everybody Else.* New York: Penguin Group. He presents the results of a great deal of investigation and some convincing research-based arguments against the "born with talent" postulate for outstanding achievement. So, for that matter, does Malcolm Gladwell in a well-argued piece in *The New Yorker* titled "Talent Myth: Are Smart People Overrated?" (July 22, 2002).

[9]Much has been written on the topic of prior knowledge and its influence on learning. A neat, clean study demonstrates the relationship succinctly. Its reference section is also brief, but to the point:

Halikari, T., N. Kanjavuouri, and S. Lindblom-Ylanne. (2008). The Relevance of Prior Knowledge in Learning and Instructional Design. *American Journal of Pharmaceutical Education* 72(5): 1-8.

[10]The three variables of value, confidence, and mood form the basis for what is known as the CANE model of motivation, developed by R.E. Clark of the University of Southern California. This model can easily be accessed online. A recent study applying the CANE model illustrates how value, confidence, and mood play vital roles in affecting motivation:

Condly, S.J., and R. Di Pietro. (2004). *Motivation in the Hospitality Industry.* New York: Site Foundation. (A summary of the report is available at http://www.incentivecentral .org/employees/whitepapers/motivation_in_the_hospitality_industry.1903.html.)

[11]What affects learning has many facets. The following readings have been around for a number of years, but are still frequently cited. Browse through these to gain more insights into the roles ability, prior knowledge, and motivation play in transforming learners:

Bandura, A., C. Barbaranelli, G.V. Capara, and C. Pastorelli. (1996). Multifaceted Impact of Self-Efficacy Beliefs on Academic Functioning. *Child Development* 67(3): 1206-1222.

Clark, R.E. (1999). The CANE (Commitment and Necessary Effort) Model of Work Motivation: A Two Stage Process of Goal Commitment and Mental Effort. In J. Lowyck, ed., *Trends in Corporate Training.* Leuven, Belgium: University of Leuven Press.

Dochy, F.J.R.C. (1988). *The "Prior Knowledge State" of Students and Its Facilitating Effect on Learning: Theories and Research.* Heerlen, The Netherlands: Open University, Secretartiaat. (ERIC Document ED 387 486)

Dochy, F.J.R.C., et al. (1996). The Importance of Prior Knowledge and Assessment for Increasing Efficiency of the Learning Processes, Especially in "Problem-Based" Learning Environments. *European Journal of Agricultural Education and Extension* 3(3): 141-166.

Kaplan, A., and C. Midgley. (1997). The Effect of Achievement Goals: Does Level of Perceived Academic Competence Make a Difference? *Contemporary Educational Psychology* 22(9): 415-435.

Mager, R.F. (1997). *Making Instruction Work.* Atlanta: Center for Effective Performance.

Stipek, D. (1998). *Motivation to Learn—From Theory to Practice.* Los Angeles: Allyn & Bacon.

The instructor as a compensation for what the learner lacks

[12]These two readings allude to the notion of the instructor as a flexible support for compensating for what learners lack:

Watson, D.L., and N.A. Stockert. (1987). Ensuring Teaching and Learning Effectiveness. *Thought and Action* 3(2): 91-104.

Yelon, S.L. (1996). *Powerful Principles of Instruction.* Reading, MA: Addison-Wesley.

Chapter 5: Adult Learning Principles

[1]The field of adult learning or "andragogy" became a popular center of interest and study from the late 1960s into the 1990s. It has continued to have a powerful influence on the training world. The following are some useful readings that summarize key principles and currents within the adult learning domain:

Birkenholz, R.J. (1999). *Effective Adult Learning.* Danville, IL: Interstate Publishers.

Brookfield, S.D. (1991). *Understanding and Facilitating Adult Learning: A Comprehensive Analysis of Principles and Effective Practices.* San Francisco: Jossey-Bass Publishers.

Cohen, S.L., D.W. Dove, and E.L. Bachelder. (2001). Time to Treat Learners as Consumers. *Training & Development* 55(1): 54-57.

Davenport, J., III, and J.A. Davenport. (1985). Knowles or Lindeman: Would the Real Father of American Andragogy Please Stand Up. *Lifelong Learning* 9(3): 4-5.

Van Houten, C. (2000). *Awakening Will: Principles and Processes in Adult Learning.* Herndon, VA: Anthroposophic Press.

———. (2000). *Practicing Destiny: Principles and Processes of Adult Learning.* Herndon, VA: Anthroposophic Press.

Principles of adult learning in action

[2]There is vast literature on adult learning theory and research and best practices in diverse areas such as adult literacy, adult learning methodologies, English as a second language, and workplace training. Here is an enlightening paper on adult learning:

Thompson, M.A., and M. Deis. (2004). Andragogy for Adult Learners in Higher Education. In *Proceedings of the Academy of Accounting and Financial Studies* 9(1): 107-111.

[3]The National Center for the Study of Adult Learning and Literacy (NCSALL) in the Graduate School of Education, Harvard University, maintains an up-to-date database of research in this area and provides links to other organizations that conduct adult learning research.

[4]For information about Malcolm Knowles, his writings, and his life, go to http://en.wikipedia.org/wiki/Malcolm_Knowles.

[5]An excellent resource for helping to create readiness to learning:

Merriam, S.B., R.S. Caffarella, and L.M. Baumgartner. (2007). *Learning in Adulthood: A Comprehensive Guide,* 3rd ed. San Francisco: Jossey-Bass.

[6]Tashiro, A., M. Hiroshi, and F.N. Gage. (2007). Experience-Specific Functional Modification of the Dentate Gyrus Through Adult Neurogenesis: A Critical Period During an Immature Stage. *The Journal of Neuroscience* 27(12): 3252-3259.

[7]It is always exciting to discover studies that actually examine the effects of a phenomenon such as "self-directedness in learning" with adults. Loibl, C., and T.K. Hira. (2005). Self-Directed Financial Learning and Financial Satisfaction. *Financial Counseling and Planning* 16(1): 11-21 offers such an example. The results demonstrate the effectiveness of self-directed financial learning and the role good financial management practices play in the relationship of financial learning with financial satisfaction and workers' satisfaction and with their career progression.

The following references from the first edition of *Telling Ain't Training* still offer interesting and useful information for training professionals:

Beitler, M.A. (2000). *Self-Directed Learning Readiness at General Motors Japan.* (ERIC Document ED 447 266)

Brockett, R.G., and R. Hiemstra. (1991). *Self-Direction in Adult Learning: Perspectives on Theory, Research, and Practice. Routledge Series on Theory and Practice of Adult Education in North America.* New York: Routledge, Chapman and Hall.

Piskurish, G.M. (1994). Self-Directedness, Quality, and the Learning Organization. *Performance and Instruction* 33(7): 32-35.

Tobias, S. (1993). Interest and Prior Knowledge. *Proceedings of the Annual Meeting of the American Education Research Association*, Atlanta, April 12-16. (ERIC Document ED 362 480)

Dieting, weight loss programs, and regaining of lost weight

[8]Curioni, C.C., and P.M. Lourenço. (2005). Long-Term Weight Loss After Diet and Exercise: A Systematic Review. *International Journal of Obesity* 29: 1168–1174.

Chapter 6: A Five-Step Model for Creating Terrific Training Sessions

[1]Most of the ways we learn to adapt to our environment are bound up in what is genetically programmed within us. Our cultural and physical circumstances may affect *how* we engage in learning, but the mechanisms that trigger learning appear to be universal. Researcher Patricia Greenfield has written extensively on research in this area.

Greenfield, P.M., H. Keller, A. Fuligni, and A. Maynard. (2003). Cultural Pathways Through Universal Development. *Annual Review of Psychology* 54: 461-90.

[2]We will likely return to the issue of individual differences and learning styles. However, while some insist on the importance of learning styles, ways of measuring these, their classifications (now up to more than 70), and diverse viewpoints on what to do about them, considerable confusion still exists about this shaky construct. What should one do when teaching shapes (triangle, square, polygon) to a child who is classified as "aural"? Is it better to speak and describe, or should one employ pictures? Frequently, the content itself dictates how it should be presented during instruction. A wonderful, highly readable essay on this topic with numerous recent citations is "Do Learning Styles Exist?" by Hugh Lafferty and Keith Burley (2009), easily accessed online at http://www.learningstyles.webs.com/.

[3]An early experimental study demonstrated that personally perceived value of a topic enhanced desire to learn, even more than curiosity, which was also studied:

Rossing, B.E., and H.B. Long. (1981). Contributions of Curiosity and Relevance to Adult Learning Motivation. *Adult Education Quarterly* 32(1): 25-36.

[4]To add to the comment, "regardless of the type of learner," two experimental studies on two different types of learners generated the same consistent results (also found elsewhere) concerning the personally meaningful "why":

Choi, J., J. Fiszdon, and A. Medalia. (2010). Expectancy-Value Theory in Persistence of Learning Effects in Schizophrenics: Role of Task Value and Perceived Competency. *Schizophrenia Bulletin* 36(5): 957-965.

Hye-Yeon, L. (2007). Effects of Attributions and Task Values on Foreign Language Use Anxiety. *Journal of Education and Human Development* 1(2): 1-20.

In the latter case, the more students perceived the value to them of acquiring the foreign language, the lower their anxiety.

[5]Although written more than 35 years ago, the findings of the following article have been sustained to today:

Lawson, T. (1974). Effects of Instructional Objectives on Learning and Retention. *Instructional Science* 3(1): 1-22. Providing a true sense of where the instruction is heading, what is important, and what to focus on do have a strong impact on learning.

See especially the work of David Ausubel going back to the 1960s. The foundational reading for this is

Ausubel, D.P. (1960). The Use of Advance Organizers in the Learning and Retention of Meaningful Verbal Material. *Journal of Educational Psychology* 51: 267-272.

Concerning the orienting of learners on what is to be acquired, here are some useful resources. While taking a more general approach to advance organizers, they nevertheless provide excellent guidance on directing learners concerning expectations and on what they should focus.

Mayer, R. (2002). *The Promise of Educational Psychology.* New Jersey: Pearson Education, Inc.

Mayer, R. (2003). *Learning and Instruction.* New Jersey: Pearson Education, Inc.

Woolfolk, A. (2001). *Educational Psychology,* 8th ed. Boston: Allyn and Bacon.

[6]Bromley, K., L. Irwin-DeVitis, and M. Modlo. (1995). *Graphic Organizers.* New York: Scholastic Professional Books. This book deals with the importance of structure in learning and retention.

A good example of how structure of any sort (visual, text, or both) affects learning and retention is presented in

Colaso, V., A. Kaml, P. Saraiya, C. North, S. McCrikard, and C.A. Shaffer. (2002). Learning and Retention in Data Structures: A Comparison of Visualization, Text, and Combined Methods. In P. Barker and S. Rebelsky, eds., *Proceedings of the 14th 2002 World Conference on Educational Multimedia, Hypermedia & Telecommunications.* Denver, CO, June 24-29. In a series of studies, they demonstrated that all forms of structure positively affected learning and retention, but that the combination of structures worked best.

[7]Excellent examples of this can be found in two more recent studies. Both find a decided edge for the covert response in terms of learning and retention, although learners enjoy the use of overt response mechanisms such as clickers.

Haggas, A.M., and D.A. Hantula. (2002). Think or Click? Student Preference for Overt Versus Covert Responding in Web-Based Instruction. *Computers in Human Behavior* 18(2): 165-172.

Martyn, M. (2007). Clickers in the Classroom: An Active Learning Approach. *Educause Quarterly* 30(2) (online publication).

[8]Although somewhat dated, this is our favorite review of the feedback literature going back to the 19th century. It covers practically everything one could ask for about feedback research and findings and offers well-supported keys to practice.

Kluger, A.N., and A. De Nisi. (1996). The Effect of Feedback Interventions on Performance: A Historical Perspective, a Meta-Analysis, and a Preliminary Feedback Intervention Theory. *Psychological Bulletin* 119(2): 254-284.

Here are two recent studies on this topic. Both present more up-to-date information and variations on what we know about feedback, and both make excellent reading:

Austermann Hula, S.N., D.A. Robin, and E. Maas. (2008). Effect of Feedback Frequency and Timing on Acquisition, Retention, and Transfer of Speech Skills in Acquired Apraxia of Speech. *Journal of Speech, Language, and Learning Research* 51: 1088-1113.

Smith, T.A., and D.R. Kimball. (2010). Learning From Feedback: Spacing and the Delay-Retention Effect. *Journal of Experimental Psychology: Learning, Memory, and Cognition* 36(1): 80-95.

[9]A large number of studies on the use of rewards and incentives for learning have shown a link between the two, although it is not as linear and straightforward as some might suggest. Recent examination of this connection has been conducted by neuroscientists using sophisticated electronic means for tracking brain activity when rewards are presented or anticipated. One interesting study found that when tested 24 hours post scan, subjects were significantly more likely to remember scenes that followed cues for high-value rather than low-value reward. The researchers were able to localize areas of the brain that deal with rewards and influence learning and retention. This form of research is not only exciting in and of itself, it also represents a trend toward how newer types of research studies on learning and retention will be conducted over the next decade.

Adcock, R.A., A. Thangaval, S. Whitfield-Gabrielli, B. Knutson, and J.D.E. Gabrielli. (2006). Reward-Motivated Learning: Mesolimbic Activation Precedes Memory Formation. *Neuron* 50: 507-517.

[10]All of the advice provided derives from Kluger and DeNisi's (1996) review of feedback research cited in endnote 8.

[11]To close out the five-step model and the six universals of research on which it is founded, here are additional readings:

On the importance of knowing why (reason for learning) and what

Choi, I., and D.H. Jonasson. (2000). Learning Objectives From the Perspective of the Experienced Cognition Framework. *Educational Technology* 40(6): 36-40.

Keller, J.M. (1987). Strategies for Stimulating the Motivation to Learn. *Performance and Instruction* 26(8): 1-7.

Klein, J.D., J.C. Cavalier, and C. Jamie. (1999). Using Cooperative Learning and Objectives With Computer-Based Instruction. *Proceedings of Selected Research and Development Papers Presented at the 21st National Convention of the Association for Educational Communications and Technology (AECT)*, Houston, February 10-14. (ERIC Document ED 436 134)

Morse, J.A., and P.K. Morse. (1978). Effects of Instructional Objectives on Relevant and Incidental Learning for Experienced and Inexperienced Possessors. *Proceedings of the Annual Meeting of the 62nd American Educational Research Association*, Toronto, Ontario, Canada, March 27-31. (ERIC Document ED 173 357)

On structure and learning

Bills, C.G. (1997). Effects of Structure and Interactivity on the Achievement of Students Receiving Internet-Based Instruction. *Proceedings of the Interservice/Industry Training, Simulation, and Education Conference*, Orlando, FL, December 1-4. (ERIC Document ED 416 317)

Dowaliby, F.J., R. Curwin, and L. Quinsland. (1981). Classroom Structure and Student Participation: An Aptitude by Treatment Interaction Approach to Instructional Research for the Hearing-Impaired. *Paper Series #47*. Washington, DC: Rochester Institute of Technology, NY National Technical Institute for the Deaf. (ERIC Document ED 224 257)

Gregg, L.W., and S. Farnham-Diggory. (1989). *Content and Structure in Learning*. Rockville, MD: National Institute of Mental Health.

Inteligen. (2001). *Human Memory, Encoding, Storage, Retention, and Retrieval*. Available at http://www.brain.web-us.com/memory_encoding.htm.

On overt and covert responding

Dwyer, C., M. Moore, and F. Dwyer. (1992). Covert and Overt Rehearsal Strategies Used to Complement Visualization. *Proceedings of the 24th Annual Conference of the International Visual Literacy Association*, Pittsburgh, September 30-October 2. (ERIC Document ED 363 290)

Elred, J.P. (1996). Incorporating Experiential Learning in the Teaching of the Nonverbal Communication Course. *Proceedings of the 82nd Annual Meeting of the Speech Communication Association*, San Diego, CA, November 23-26. (ERIC Document ED 408 627)

Shettel, H.H., and R.H. Lindley. (1961). *An Experimental Comparison of Two Types of Self-Instructional Programs for a SAGE System Paired-Associate Task.* Pittsburgh: American Institute for Research in Behavioral Sciences. (ERIC Document ED 130 605)

Wilder, L., and D.J. Harvey. (1971). Overt and Covert Verbalization in Problem Solving. *Report From the Project on Variables and Processes in Cognitive Learning.* Madison, WI: Wisconsin University—Research and Development Center. (ERIC Document ED 062 001)

On meaningful engagement and learning

Ausabel, D.P. (2000). *The Acquisition and Retention of Knowledge: A Cognitive View.* New York: Kluwer Academic Publishers.

Cavallo, A.L. (1992). Students' Meaningful Learning Orientation and Their Meaningful Understandings of Meiosis and Genetics. *Proceedings of the Annual Conference of the National Association for Research in Science Teaching,* Boston, March. (ERIC Document ED 356 140)

Nystrand, M., and A. Gamoran. (1990). *Student Engagement: When Recitation Becomes Conversation.* Washington, DC: Office of Educational Research and Improvement. (ERIC Document ED 323 581)

On importance of feedback in learning

Kulik, J.A., and C.C. Kulik. (1988). Timing of Feedback and Verbal Learning. *Review of Educational Research* 58(1): 79-97.

Ovando, M.N. (1992). Constructive Feedback: A Key to Successful Teaching and Learning. (ERIC Document ED 404 291)

On corrective and confirming feedback

Hodes, C.L. (1984). *Relative Effectiveness of Corrective and Non-Corrective Computer Feedback on Cognitive Learning of Science.* Master's thesis. Pennsylvania State University. (ERIC Document ED 311 883)

Latham, A.S. (1997). Learning Through Feedback. *Educational Leadership* 54(8): 86-87.

Silverman, S., L. Tyson, and J. Krampitz. (1992). Teacher Feedback and Achievement in Physical Education: Interaction With Student Practice. *Teaching and Teacher Education* 8(4): 333-344.

On feedback on performance versus feedback toward self

Geddes, D., and F. Linnehan. (1996). Exploring the Dimensionality of Positive and Negative Performance Feedback. *Communication Quarterly* 44(3): 326-344.

Tosti, D., and S. Jackson. (1999). Feedback Systems. In H.D. Stolovitch and E.J. Keeps, eds., *Handbook of Human Performance Technology: Improving Individual and Organizational Performance Worldwide.* San Francisco: Jossey-Bass/Pfeiffer.

On immediate and delayed feedback, effect on learning

Cope, P., and S. Simmons. (1994). Some Effects of Limited Feedback on Performance and Problem-Solving Strategy in a Logo Microworld. *Journal of Educational Psychology* 86(3): 368-379.

Nishikawa, S. (1988). A Comparison of the Effects of Locus of Control With Feedback Strategies on Factual Information Recall and Retention During Computer-Assisted Instruction. *Proceedings of the Annual Meeting of the Association for Educational Communication and Technology*, New Orleans, January 14-19. (ERIC Document ED 295 655)

Sturgess, P.T. (1978). Immediate vs. Delayed Feedback in a Computer-Managed Test: Effects on Long-Term Retention. *Technical Report #NPRDC-TR-78-15, March-August 1976*. Chico, CA: California State University. (ERIC Document ED 160 635)

On frequent, specific feedback, effect on learning

intime (integrating new technologies into methods of education). (2001). Frequent Feedback. Available at http://www.intime.uni.edu/model/learning/freq.html.

Poertner, S., and K. Massetti Miller. (1996). *The Art of Giving and Receiving Feedback. AMI: How to Series*. Urbandale, IA: Provant Media.

On too-detailed feedback, effect on learning

Sasaki, Y. (1997). Individual Variation in a Japanese Sentence Comprehension Task—Form, Function, and Strategies. *Applied Linguistics* 18(4): 508-537.

On reinforcement and learning

Lee, K., and J. David. (1998). The Perceived Impacts of Supervisor Reinforcement and Learning Objectives: Importance on Transfer of Training. *Performance Improvement Quarterly* 11(4): 51-61.

On intrinsic and extrinsic rewards in learning

Bishop, J., S. Kang, and C. Wilson. (1985). *Incentives, Learning, and Employability*. Washington, DC: National Institute of Education. (ERIC Document ED 268 378)

Ryan, R.M., and E.L. Deci. (1985). Intrinsic and Extrinsic Motivations: Classic Definitions and New Directions. *Contemporary Educational Psychology* 25(1): 54-67.

Stolovitch, H.D., R.E. Clark, and S.J. Condly. (2001). *Incentives, Motivation, and Workplace Performance: Research and Best Practice*. New York: Society of Incentives and Travel Executives Research Foundation.

On objectives and learning, positive effects

Choi, J., and D.H. Jonassen. (2000). Learning Objectives From the Perspective of the Experienced Cognition Framework. *Educational Technology* 40(6): 36-40.

Lee, K., and J. David. (1998). The Perceived Impacts of Supervisor Reinforcement and Learning Objectives: Importance on Transfer of Training. *Performance Improvement Quarterly* 11(4): 51-61.

Main, R. (1979). Effect of Intended and Incidental Learning From the Use of Learning Objectives With an Audiovisual Presentation. *Proceedings of the Annual Convention of the Association for Educational and Communications Technology,* New Orleans, March. (ERIC Document ED 172 794)

Chapter 7: Getting Learners to Remember

[1]The terms *metacognition* and *metacognitive skills* have taken on various meanings over time. Writings about them, however, have two things in common. They tend to agree that knowing about knowing or being aware of your thinking and learning skills helps you strategize more effectively to learn something new. Although the terms may discuss different skills required to learn effectively, they also agree that metacognitive skills are a key differentiator between excellent and poor learners.

[2]The concept of the mind's operating system is drawn from Clark, R.C. (2008). *Building Expertise.* San Francisco, CA: Pfeiffer-Wiley. We suggest the recommendations presented on pages 313-336.

[3]Even beyond the findings that superior metacognitive skills are highly correlated with learning success of various types, despite equal intellectual capabilities, some researchers have found only a slight correlation between intelligence and metacognitive skills. See for example

Desoete, A., H. Roeyers, and A. Huylebroeck. (2006). Metacognitive Skills in Belgian Third Grade Children (Age 8 to 9) With and Without Mathematical Learning Disabilities. *Metacognition and Learning* 1(2): 119-135.

Veenman, M.V.J., and M.A. Spaans. (2005). Relation Between Intellectual and Metacognitive Skills: Age and Task Differences. *Learning and Individual Differences* 15(2): 159-176.

[4]Jean Piaget, the famous psychologist who studied developmental stages of children, indirectly referred to what we now commonly call metacognitive skills. Here is a useful article dealing with metacognitive skills at the third-grade level:

Goldberg, P.D., and W.S. Bush. (2003). Using Metacognitive Skills to Improve 3rd Graders' Math Problem Solving. *Focus on Learning Problems in Mathematics,* September 2003, available at http://www.accessmylibrary.com/article-1G1-117322859/using-metacognitive-skills-improve.html.

[5]This article provides empirical evidence of the successful impact of cueing to help learners develop metacognitive capabilities:

Veenman, M.V.J., R. Kok, and A.W. Blote. (2005). The Relationship Between Intellectual and Metacognitive Skills in Early Adolescence. *Instructional Science* 33(3): 193-211.

[6]Introduced in the 1980s by researcher Patricia Palincsar, the basic concept and procedure of reciprocal teaching is to "be used to not only help poor comprehenders improve their rate of comprehension, but to enable them to maintain that progress over time and to transfer those critical thinking skills to different learning tasks (p. 169)":

Palincsar, A.L., and A.L. Brown. (1984). Reciprocal Teaching of Comprehension-Fostering and Comprehension-Monitoring Activities. *Cognition and Instruction* 1(2): 117-175.

A more recent description of reciprocal teaching is found in Philicia Randolph's and Jeanice Lewis's essay, "Reciprocal Teaching," online at http://red6747.pbworks.com/Reciprocal%20Teaching.

[7]There are many definitions given to the term *cognitive strategies*. We have selected to use the one that fits with designing and delivering effective training:

West, C.K., J.A. Farmer, and P.M. Wolff. (1991). *Instructional Design Implications From Cognitive Science*. Englewood Cliffs, NJ: Prentice-Hall.

[8]We have already referred to David Ausubel and his work on advance organizers. Here is a recent study on the use of advance organizers in the accounting arena:

Togo, D.F. (2002). Topical Sequencing of Questions and Advance Organizers Impacting on Students' Examination Performance. *Accounting Education: An International Journal* 11(3): 203-216.

[9]The psychological literature is replete with research studies on the use of analogies, metaphors, and the like. Here is an interesting take on their use in science education that offers analogous implications for other disciplines:

Aubusson, P.J., A.G. Harrison, and S.M. Ritchie. (2006). Metaphor and Analogy in Science Education: Serious Thought in Science Education. *Science & Technology Education Library* 30: 1-9.

[10]The 1970s and 1980s were years in which the use of memory aids, especially mnemonic devices and strategies, were studied as means to facilitate retention and recall for a variety of populations from young children and older students to learning-disabled persons, the elderly, and even Alzheimer patients. Overall, memory aids and mnemonic devices and strategies were found to be effective for retention and recall. To read more about these, we suggest three friendly readings you can access online:

Ehren, B.J. (2002). *Mnemonic Designs*, reading 5. Lawrence, KS: University of Kansas, Center for Research on Learning.

http://elearndesign.org/teachspecialed/modules/ocada304_norm1/15/18_5.html. This online article provides a number of mnemonic illustrations that are highly effective. We informally tested these on random adult subjects and found that retention was significantly higher than for equivalent word mnemonics.

Mnemonic Strategies and Techniques—Components of Mnemonic Techniques, Varieties and Uses of Mnemonic Techniques, Educational Applications of Mnemonic Techniques. Available at http://education.stateuniversity.com/pages/2241/MnemonicStrategies-Techniques.html.

[11]These three books are worthwhile examining, if you are interested in mnemonics:

Evans, R.L. (2007). *Every Good Boy Deserves Fudge*. New York: Perigee Book-Penguin. The volume inundates you with a deluge of mnemonics drawn from an almost endless array of topics. It is a great reference book for finding mnemonics on just about anything.

Holliman, C. (2009). *The Mnemonics Book: 30 Ways in 30 Days to Maximize Your Memory*. Chapel Hill, NC: Professional Press. We particularly like this book because it teaches the reader how to strengthen memory through the strategic use of mnemonics. The author is a professor at Old Dominion University and tutors students on how to prepare for their SAT exams. The author proposes a Velcro Theory of Memory—the more hooks we put into our associations, the better we will recall them. This publication is almost a training manual and draws heavily from cognitive psychological principles.

Stevens, C. (2008). *Thirty Days Has September: Cool Ways to Remember Stuff*. New York: Scholastics Inc. This book covers a large number of topics, provides mnemonics for each, and then explains how each mnemonic works.

[12]The following references were included in the first edition of *Telling Ain't Training* and still have relevance today:

On metacognition

Hacker, D.J., J. Dunlosky, and A.C. Graesser. (1998). *Metacognition in Education: Theory and Practice*. Mahwah, NJ: Lawrence Earlbaum Associates.

Metcalfe, J.S., and A.P. Shimamura. (1996). *Metacognition*. Cambridge, MA: MIT Press.

Rampp, L.C., and J.S. Guffey. (1999). *Metacognition: A New Implementation Model for Learning*. (ERIC Document ED 440 088)

On metacognitive skills

Clark, R.E., and S. Blake. (1997). Analyzing Cognitive Structures and Processes to Derive Instructional Methods for the Transfer of Problem Solving Expertise. In S. Dijkstra and N.M. Seel, eds., *Instructional Design Perspectives. Volume II, Solving Instructional Design Problems*. Oxford, UK: Pergamon.

Hall, Y.C., and M. Esposito. (1984). What Does Research on Metacognition Have to Offer Educators? *Proceedings of the Annual Meeting of the Northeastern Educational Research Association,* Ellenville, NY, October 24-26. (ERIC Document ED 254 552)

Mayer, R.E. (1998). Cognitive, Metacognitive, and Motivational Aspects of Problem Solving. *Instructional Science* 26(1-2): 49-63.

On well-developed metacognitive skills and learning success

Carr, M., and H. Thompson. (1995). *Metacognitive Intervention and Interest as Predictors of Memory for Text.* Reading research report No. 35. Athens, GA: National Reading Research Center. (ERIC Document ED 387 791)

El-Hindi, A.E. (1996). Enhancing Metacognitive Awareness of College Learners. *Reading Horizons* 36(3): 214-230.

On metacognitive skill variation, achievement, and intelligence

Davis, E.A. (1996). Metacognitive Scaffolding to Foster Scientific Explanations. *Proceedings of the Annual Meeting of the American Educational Research Association,* New York, April 8-14. (ERIC Document ED 394 853)

Gilbert, L.C. (1986). Inducement of Metacognitive Learning Strategies: Task Knowledge, Instruction, and Training. *Proceedings of the 70th Annual Meeting of the American Educational Research Association,* San Francisco, April 16-20. (ERIC Document ED 271 486)

Romainville, M. (1994). Awareness of Cognitive Strategies: The Relationship Between University Students' Metacognition and Their Performance. *Studies in Higher Education* 19(3): 359-366.

Veenan, M.V., J.J. Elshout, and A. Meijer. (1997). The Generality Versus Domain Specificity of Metacognitive Skills in Novice Learning Across Domains. *Learning and Instruction* 7(2): 187-209.

On reciprocal teaching

Kincannon, J., C. Gleber, and J. Kim. (1999). The Effects of Metacognitive Training on Performance and Use of Metacognitive Skills in Self-Directed Learning Situations. *Proceedings of the 21st National Convention of the Association for Educational Communications and Technology,* Houston, February 10-14. (ERIC Document ED 436 146)

Rosenshine, B., and C. Muster. (1991). Reciprocal Teaching: A Review of Nineteen Experimental Studies. *Proceedings of the 72nd Meeting of the American Educational Research Association,* Chicago, April 3-7. (ERIC Document ED 394 683)

West, C.K., J.A. Farmer, and P.M. Wolff. (1991). *Instructional Design: Implications From Cognitive Science.* Englewood Cliffs, NJ: Prentice Hall.

On cognitive strategies

Clark, R.C. (1994). The Causes and Cures of Learner Overload. *Training* 31(7): 40-43.

Rabinowitz, M. (1988). On Teaching Cognitive Strategies: The Influence of Accessibility of Conceptual Knowledge. *Contemporary Educational Psychology* 13(3): 229-235.

Reigeluth, R.M. (1980). *Meaningfulness and Instruction: Relating What Is Being Learned to What a Student Knows.* New York: Syracuse University, School of Education. (ERIC Document ED 195 263)

On advance organizers

Explorations on Learning and Instruction: The Theory Into Practice Database. Subsumption Theory. (2001). Available at http://www.tip.psychology.org/ausubel.html.

Schwartz, N.H., L.S. Ellsworth, L.S. Graham, and B. Knight. (1998). Accessing Prior Knowledge to Remember Text: A Comparison of Advance Organizers and Maps. *Contemporary Educational Psychology* 23(1): 65-89.

Stone, C.L. (1983). A Meta-Analysis of Advance Organizer Studies. *Journal of Experimental Psychology* 54: 194-199.

On image-rich comparisons

Ausubel, D.P. (2000). *The Acquisition and Retention of Knowledge: A Cognitive View.* New York: Kluwer Academic Publishers.

Clement, J.J. (1998). Expert-Novice Similarities and Instruction Using Analogies. *International Journal of Science Education* 20(10): 1271-1286.

Duit, R. (1991). On the Role of Analogies and Metaphors in Learning Science. *Science Education* 75(6): 649-672.

Chapter 8: Training Approaches and a Cornucopia of Learning Activities

[1]Clark, R.C. (2008). *Building Expertise: Cognitive Methods for Training and Performance Improvement,* 3rd ed. San Francisco: Pfeiffer-Wiley. This is an outstanding book for training professionals. See especially chapter 17 on learning architectures.

[2]A cursory examination of online "awareness" training programs and courses offered in a wide variety of subject-matter areas convinces us even more of the vagueness of what they purport to accomplish. We suggest that the reader examine some of these offerings to determine what the real, verifiable accomplishments might be.

[3]As an exploratory treat, visit Edmunds.com to simulate purchasing or leasing a new or used car. You will learn which models of vehicles are available; what the best price to pay will be in your zip code; and even, with step-by-step guidance, how to negotiate like an expert in purchasing or leasing the vehicle of your choice. Specific vehicle owners offer you their experiences, what they paid, and can even give you advice as required. What a learning experience! We actually did it with no initial training or guidance and ended up negotiating like pros and leasing a

vehicle at an excellent rate, as we later learned from other leasers, through the online information sharing function.

[4]Thiagarajan, S., and T. Tagliati. (2011). *Jolts*. San Francisco: Wiley-Pfeiffer.

Chapter 9: Testing or Examining—What's the Difference?

[1]There is a vast and growing literature on what is labeled as expectancy-value and achievement motivation. In essence, the theory is that how well one believes she or he will perform on a task and how much the person values successful achievement is related to performance. This has been demonstrated experimentally with young children all the way through adults in the workplace. For an excellent immersion into this interesting arena, read

Wigfield, A., and J.S. Eccles. (2002). *Development of Achievement Motivation*. San Diego, CA: Academic Press.

Wigfield, A., and J.S. Eccles. (2000). Expectancy-Value Theory of Achievement Motivation. *Contemporary Educational Psychology* 25: 68-81.

[2]There are a large number of opinions concerning the use of feedback to improve or maintain performance. The best and most complete resource on what research has found over the past 100-plus years is this wonderful article:

Kluger, A.N., and A. DeNisi. (1996). The Effect of Feedback Intervention on Performance: A Historical Review, a Meta-Analysis, and a Preliminary Feedback Intervention Theory. *Psychological Bulletin* 119(2): 254-284.

A more recent article on this is

VanDijk, D., and A.V. Kluger. (2010). Task Type as a Moderator of Positive/Negative Feedback on Motivation and Performance: A Regulatory Focus Perspective. *Journal of Organizational Behavior.* The volume and number and page numbers are not available as the article is in press at this time. An advanced online version was published September 6, 2010.

[3]Research on test anxiety and its effects both on test performance and individuals who experience this phenomenon has a long history. A recent study, available online, that deals with nurses provides some useful baseline information:

Driscoll, R., G. Evans, G. Ramsey, and S. Wheeler. (2009). High Test Anxiety Among Nursing Students. Available at http://www.eric.ed.gov/PDFS/ED506526.pdf.

A more comprehensive, recent study is a downloadable book containing a vast amount of information on test anxiety and ways of overcoming it. Although conducted at the high-school level, the findings and principles are generalizable across age groups:

Bradley, T.R., R. McCraty, M. Atkinson, L. Arguelles, R.A. Rees, and D. Tomasino. Reducing Test Anxiety and Improving Test Performance in America's Schools: Results From the TestEdge National Demonstration Study. Available at http://store.heartmath.org/s.nl/c.582612/it.A/id.311/.f.

[4]Oludipe, B.D. (2009). Influence of Test Anxiety on Performance Levels on Numerical tasks of Secondary School Physics Students. *Academic Leadership* 7(4), available at http://www.academicleadership.org/emprical_research/Influence_of_Test_Anxiety_on_Performance_Levels_on_Numerical_tasks_of_Secondary_School_Physics_Students.shtml.

Trudeau, T.L. (2009). Test Anxiety in High-Achieving Students: A Mixed-Methods Study. Doctoral dissertation, University of Alberta; NR55624.

[5]Stolovitch, H.D., and E.J. Keeps. (2003). *Engineering Effective Learning Toolkit.* San Francisco: Wiley-Pfeiffer.

[6]This is one of the best sources of information on testing and specifically on how to create criterion-referenced learning checks and more formal tests:

Shrock, S.A., and W.C. Coscarelli. (2007). *Criterion-Referenced Test Development: Technical and Legal Guidelines for Corporate Training.* San Francisco: Pfeiffer-Wiley.

[7]We are not offering any specific references on simulations for learning and assessment as this is such a growing field that new information and tools are continually popping up on the web. The world of Web 2.0 has us dwelling in and interacting with virtual realities. A quick browse on the Internet using terms such as learning, testing, assessment, simulation, and virtual reality will be sufficient to get you started. You can then add your own content interest areas to discover numerous resources and guidance.

[8]There is a wonderful, brief download with guidelines for writing tests. It is free and easy to use or share:

Cohen, A.S., and J.A. Wollock. *Handbook on Test Development: Helpful Tips for Creating Reliable and Valid Classroom Tests,* available at http://testing.wisc.edu/Handbook%20on%20Test%20Construction.pdf.

[9]The nature of this book is to provide useful information and guidance on a number of topics related to "telling ain't training." However, testing is so important as a means for reinforcing and strengthening learning that we feel it is necessary to provide additional references on the subject:

On the positive impact of testing on learning

Eilertsen, T.V., and O. Valdermo. (2000). Open-Book Assessment: A Contribution to Improved Learning. *Studies in Educational Evaluation* 26(2): 91-103.

Williams, L.P. (2000). The Effect of Drill and Practice Software on Multiplication Skills: "Multiplication Puzzles 'Versus' the Mad Minute." (ERIC Document ED 443 706)

On test anxiety

Cassady, J.C., J. Budenz-Anders, G. Pavlechko, and W. Mock. (2001). The Effects of Internet-Based Formative and Summative Assessment on Test Anxiety, Perceptions of Threat, and Achievement. *Proceedings of the Annual Meeting of the American Educational Research Association,* Seattle, April 10-14. (ERIC Document ED 453 815)

Spielberger, C.D., and P.R. Vagg. (1995). *Test Anxiety: Theory, Assessment, and Treatment. The Series in Clinical and Community Psychology.* Bristol, PA: Taylor & Francis.

Williams, J.E. (1992). Effects of Test Anxiety and Self-Concept on Performance Across Curricular Areas. (ERIC Document ED 317 554)

On criterion-referenced testing

Westgaard, O. (1999). *Tests That Work: Designing and Measuring Fair and Practical Measurement Tools in the Workplace.* Somerset, NJ: Pfeiffer and Company.

On test validation

Eyres, P.S. (1999). Legal Implications of Human Performance Technology. In H.D. Stolovitch and E.J. Keeps, eds., *Handbook of Human Performance Technology: Improving Individual and Organizations Performance Worldwide.* San Francisco: Jossey-Bass/Pfeiffer.

Gibbons, P.L. (1998). Are You Flunking Testing? *Inside Technology Training* 2(6): 24-27.

Gray, T.B. (1997). Controversies Regarding the Nature of Score Validity: Still Crazy After All These Years. *Proceedings of the Annual Meeting of the Southwest Educational Research Association,* Austin, TX, January 23-25. (ERIC Document ED 407 414)

On writing good tests

Hacker, D.G. (1998). Testing for Learning. *Infoline.* Alexandria, VA: American Society for Training & Development.

Osterlind, S.J. (1998). *Constructing Test Items: Multiple-Choice, Constructed Response, Performance, and Other Formats (Evaluation in Education and Human Services, 47).* New York: Kluwer Academic Publishers.

Wiggins, G.P. (1998). *Educative Assessment: Designing Assessments to Inform and Improve Student Performance.* San Francisco: Jossey-Bass Publishers.

Chapter 10: Training and Technology

[1]De Smet, A., M. McGurk, and E. Schwartz. (2010). Getting More From Your Training Programs. *McKinsey Quarterly*, October 2010. This report includes the findings of a McKinsey survey in which "only one-quarter of the respondents… said their training programs measurably improved business performance, and most companies don't even bother to track the returns they get on their investments in training."

[2]Arthur, Jr, WA., W. Bennett, Jr., P.S. Edens, and S.T. Bell. (2003). Effectiveness of Training in Organizations: A Meta-Analysis of Design and Evaluation Features. *Journal of Applied Psychology* 88(2): 234-245.

[3]Clark, R.E. (2001). *Learning From Media*. Greenwich, CT: Information Age Publishers. To summarize the author's position, here is a salient quote: "The best…evidence is that media are mere vehicles that deliver instruction but do not influence student achievement any more than the truck that delivers our groceries causes changes in our nutrition. Basically, the choice of vehicle might influence the cost or extent of distributing instruction, but only the content of the vehicle can influence achievement" (p. 13).

Media and Learning—Definitions and Summary of Research, Do Media Influence the Cost and Access to Instruction? Available at http://education.stateuniversity.com/pages/2211/Media-Learning.html#ixzz19ieTYCsy.

[4]K. Harman, and A Koohang, eds. (2007). *Learning Objects: Standards, Metadata Repositories, and LCMS*. Santa Rosa, CA: Informing Science. This book presents solid information on the technicalities of producing e-learning based on reusable learning objects. As you will note, the way training must be designed and produced requires a strong grounding in the technical knowledge and skills of instructional design for reusability.

Chapter 11: Learning With Technology: Making It Work

[1]As noted in chapter 10, a plethora of terms refers to the use of various forms of technology to support; present; and, in some instances, drive training-learning in the workplace. Currently, most of the terms imply use of computer technology, online learning, and the web in some form or another. Computer technology has allowed us to integrate video, audio, 3-D, simulation, virtual worlds, community forums, texting, and almost all other media and formats into one melting pot that can be delivered to terminals, telephones, tablets, and an ever-expanding array of devices. In *Telling Ain't Training: Updated, Expanded, and Enhanced,* we mostly use "training-learning technologies" as the umbrella term. However, we also use e-learning, collaborative learning, online learning, and other terms to break up the redundancy.

[2]Fallon, C., and S. Brown. (2003). *E-Learning Standards: A Guide to Purchasing, Developing, and Deploying Standards-Conformant E-Learning*. Boca Raton, FL: St. Lucie Press.

For a more recent publication that is available online, see

Laselle, J. (2008). *5 Steps to Developing E-Learning Standards*. Available at http://www .lr.com/Portals/61190/pdfs/eLearning_Standards.pdf.

[3]A fun, but informative read on this topic is "Converting Instructor-Led Training to E-learning or Distance Learning: Keys to Success" (2008) produced by Bottom-Line Performance, Inc. The brief article also includes readers' reactions and comments. Available at http://www.bottomlineperformance.com/lolblog/?p=1343.

[4]For a literature review on trainer resistance to technology-based learning:

Bozarth, J. (2006). *Classroom Trainer Resistance to E-Learning: Literature Review*. Available at http://www.bozarthzone.com/bozarth_classroom_trainer_resistance_lit_review_2006.pdf.

[5]This term has caught on like wildfire. See Cammy Bean's comments in her December 10, 2010, blog, "And a clicky-clicky bling-bling to you." *Cammy Bean's Learning Visions: Musings on E-Learning, Instructional Design, and Other Stuff*. A reference we provided earlier is also relevant here:

Thalheimer, W. (2004). *Bells, Whistles, Neon and Purple Prose: When Interesting Words, Sounds, and Visuals Hurt Learning and Performance—A Review of the Seductive-Augmentation Research*. Available at http://www.worklearning.com/seductive_augmentations.htm.

[6]Stolovitch, H.D., and E.J. Keeps. (2004). *Front-End Analysis and Return on Investment Toolkit*. San Francisco, CA: Wiley/Pfeiffer.

[7]Professor Michael Resnick of the MIT Media Laboratory has written a strong and persuasive article rejecting "edutainment," but favoring "playful learning." The article is illustrated with colorful photographs and can be accessed at http://web .media.mit.edu/~mres/papers/edutainment.pdf.

[8]This is the standard reference for creating valid tests and assessments for the workplace:

Shrock, S.A., and W.C. Coscarelli. (2007). *Criterion-Referenced Test Development: Technical and Legal Guidelines for Corporate training*, 3rd ed. San Francisco: Pfeiffer-Wiley.

[9]The University of Adelaide, Australia, Centre for Professional Development, provides a succinct explanation of online, synchronous learning in describing its programs: "Synchronous Learning is often referred to as 'live' learning and is used in conjunction with online learning. It means that the communications occur at

the same time between individuals and information is accessed instantly. People can communicate in 'real time' using their computers to both talk to each other as well as text chat. Presentations can be made using electronic whiteboards and electronic slides. This type of interaction is referred to as a 'virtual classroom.' Presentations, conversations, and text can be stored (archived) and made available online as a resource."

According to *The Webinar Blog* of February 11, 2009, several terms in the online synchronous domain require definition, including web-conferencing, webcasts, and webinars. Here is what this specialized blog offers:

Web conferencing is often used as an umbrella term for all web-based collaboration between two or more people over the Internet. As such, it may encompass webcasts or webinars depending on the context. But more specifically, web conferencing usually refers to interactive collaboration in work groups, such as brainstorming sessions between employees working on a new business strategy or product design. A typical web conference involves a relatively small number of participants, perhaps 15 as a maximum. Everybody is expected to contribute to the flow of ideas and information. You sometimes see the term "web meeting" used in exactly the same context.

A *webcast* refers to information dispersed to a large audience via the Internet. It might be just a simple audio stream, or it might include visual aids, such as PowerPoint slides, recorded video clips, or live software demonstrations.

A *webinar* expands the idea of a webcast into a more interactive format. The experience attempts to reproduce the benefits of attending a live seminar. Audience members can ask questions of the presenter, and the speaker can survey or poll the audience and get feedback as he or she delivers the information.

[10]This excellent article defines, albeit succinctly, synchronous and asynchronous learning. It goes on, however, to deal with research on both of these modes of online learning. The article contains a highly useful set of endnotes with research references. This is a recommended read for those who are interested in pursuing this topic further:

Hrastinski, S. (2008). Asynchronous and Synchronous E-Learning. *EDUCAUSE Quarterly* 31(4): 51-55.

[11]This wonderful expression appears to have had its origin in

King, A. (1993). From Sage on the Stage to Guide on the Side. *College Teaching* 41(1): 30-35.

[12]According to the American Society for Training & Development's *State of the Industry Report 2010,* "Employees in the surveyed organizations accessed an average of 31.9 hours of formal learning content in 2009, down from 36.3 hours in 2008. Although the number of hours of learning decreased, the amount still demonstrates that organizations expect employees to allocate a meaningful amount of time to formal learning and development activities."

[13]Estimates as to how much on-the-job learning takes place informally range from 58 percent to 86 percent. We examined a number of writings and supposed research and found that the methodologies for estimating the percentages varied widely and that authors criticized others' approaches. What we have seen leads us to believe that the general consensus is a 70/30 split between informal and formal learning. This reasonable book on the subject (that suggests the split is 80/20) explains the informal workplace learning process and helps capture its benefits:

Cross, J. (2007). *Informal Learning: Rediscovering the Natural Pathways That Inspire Innovation and Performance.* San Francisco: Wiley-Pfeiffer.

[14]In surveying a number of articles on both acceleration and obsolescence of knowledge, two findings emerge. The first is that, overall, the most frequently cited estimates suggest a doubling of knowledge every five years. Some state that the rate is every 10 years. Some even suggest that it occurs annually. The bottom line is that no one knows, but experts agree that it is rapid and increasing. In the second case, with respect to obsolescence of knowledge, the estimates are even vaguer. However, in the new technology specialties such as nanotechnology or stem cell research, the pace of new patents suggests that older ones are being replaced or outmoded by an accelerating stream of new ones.

[15]Brown, J.S., and J.P. Alper. (2008). Minds on Fire: Open Education, the Long Tail, and Learning 2.0. *EDUCAUSE Review* 43(1): 16-32. This article clearly explains the vision John Seely Brown and Ralph Alper have about how social media can and is transforming education and much more. An exciting read. Available at http://www.johnseelybrown.com/mindsonfire.pdf.

[16]The American Society for Training & Development has produced a useful report that speaks to this point:

Paradise A., L. Patel, H.B. Thompson, M. Vickera, and D. Wentworth. (2010). *The Rise of Social Media: Enhancing Collaboration and Productivity Across Generations.* Alexandria, VA: American Society for Training & Development.

Chapter 12: Hit or Myth: What's the Truth?

[1]Chapters 2 and 3 of the following reference explain differences between expert and novice learning, thinking, and information processing:

Bransford, J., A. Brown, and R. Cockey, eds. (2000). *How People Learn: Brain, Mind, Experience, and School.* Washington, DC: NAS Press.

The best source of information on this whole area of expert versus novice is, as noted earlier:

Ericsson, K.A., N. Charness, N. Hoffman, and R.R. Feltovich. (2006). *The Cambridge Handbook of Expertise and Expert Performance.* New York: Cambridge University Press.

[2]Geake, J. (2008). Neuromythologies in Education. *Educational Research* 50: 123-133. Geake also arrives at the same conclusion based on studies involving neuroimaging and tracking brain activity. He demonstrates, rather, the power of using multiple stimuli.

Massa, L.J., and R.E. Mayer. (2006). Testing the ATI Hypothesis: Should Multimedia Instruction Accommodate Verbalizer-Visualiser Cognitive Style? *Learning and Individual Differences* 16: 321-336. The authors arrived at the conclusion that the value of matching instruction to a specific style or attribute was not much more than folklore, with no true evidence to support the belief or practice.

[3]Coffield, F., D. Mosely, E. Hall, and K. Ecclestone. (2004). *Should We Be Using Learning Styles?* London, UK: Learning and Research Centre. Cited in Bishka, A. (2010). Learning Styles Fray: Brilliant or Batty? *Performance Improvement Journal* 49(10): 9-14.

[4]A great deal of material based on both research and enthusiastic opinion exists concerning the relationship between enjoyment or satisfaction and learning outcomes. Here is a recent list of more serious studies and works:

Blunsdon, B., K. Reed, and N. McNeil. (2003). Experiential Learning in Social Science Theory: An Investigation of the Relationship Between Student Enjoyment and Learning. *Journal of Further and Higher Education* 27(1): 3-14.

Fielding, M. (2006). Leadership, Radical Student Engagement, and the Necessity of Person-Centred Education. *International Journal of Leadership in Education* 9(4): 299-313.

Goetz, T., C. Nathan, B. Hall, C. Anne, A. Frenzel, and R. Pekrun. (2006). A Hierarchical Conceptualization of Enjoyment in Students. *Learning and Instruction* 16: 323-338.

Hartley, D. (2006). Excellence and Enjoyment: The Logic of a "Contradiction." *British Journal of Educational Studies* 54(1): 3-14.

Remedios, R., D.A. Lieberman, and T.G. Benton. (2000). The Effects of Grades on Course Enjoyment: Did You Get the Grade You Wanted? *British Journal of Educational Psychology* 70: 353-368.

Rieber, L.P., and D. Noah. (2008). Games, Simulations, and Visual Metaphors in Education: Antagonism Between Enjoyment and Learning. *Educational Media International* 45(2): 77-92.

This is an interesting study showing that law students, generally considered to be high-performing learners and capable of self-directed learning, strongly prefer structured instruction:

Boyle, R.A., and L. Dolle. (2008). Providing Structure to Law Students: Introducing the Programmed Learning Sequence as an Instructional Tool. Legal studies research paper series, paper #08-0113. Queens, NY: St. John's University School of Law. Available at http://ssrn.com/AbstractID=1103963.

[5]This study was sponsored by the U.S. Office of Education:

Means, B., Y. Toyama, R. Murphy, M. Bakla, and K. Jones. (2010). *Evaluation of Evidence-Based Practices in Online Learning: A Meta-Analysis and Review of Online Learning Studies.* Washington, DC: U.S. Department of Education, Office of Planning, Evaluation, and Policy Development–Policy and Program Studies Service. Available at http://www2.ed.gov/rschstat/eval/tech/evidence-based-practices/finalreport.pdf.

[6]The following two references are not only informative with respect to the value of worked-out examples for learning, but also are representative of the large number of studies demonstrating how worked-out examples in endless variations can be applied to improve problem-solving skills.

Kim, R.S., R. Weitz, N. Heffernan, and N. Krach. (2009). Tutored Problem Solving vs. "Pure" Worked Examples. In N.A. Taatgen and H. van Rijn, eds., *Proceedings of the 31st Annual Conference of the Cognitive Science Society, 2009.* Austin, TX: Cognitive Science Society.

Ringenberg, M.A., and K. VanLehn. (2006). Scaffolding Problem-Solving With Annotated, Worked-Out Examples to Promote Deep Learning. In M. Ikeda, K.D. Ashley, and T.W. Chan, eds., *Intelligent Tutoring Systems 8th International Conference Proceedings, Jhongli, Taiwan.* Berlin/Heidelberg, Germany: Springer-Verlag.

[7]Jennifer Herrod has produced a clear, brief tutorial on cognitive overload, how it affects memory, and what instructional strategies you can use to decrease the burden placed on the learner when there is a lot of content. Try it out: http://www.jchconsulting.com/fall2000/index.htm.

John Sweller also offers an online, brief introduction to cognitive load theory along with a good list of readings on the topic (http://www.scitopics.com/Cognitive_Load_Theory.html):

Clark, R.C., F. Nguyen, and J. Sweller. (2006). *Efficiency in Learning: Evidence-Based Guidelines to Manage Cognitive Load.* San Francisco, CA: Pfeiffer.

Geary, D. (2007). Educating the Evolved Mind: Conceptual Foundations for an Evolutionary Educational Psychology. In J.S. Carlson and J.R. Levin, eds., *Psychological Perspectives on Contemporary Educational Issues.* Greenwich, CT: Information Age Publishing.

Sweller, J. (2003). Evolution of Human Cognitive Architecture. In B. Ross, ed., *The Psychology of Learning and Motivation.* San Diego, CA: Academic Press.

Sweller, J. (2004). Instructional Design Consequences of an Analogy Between Evolution by Natural Selection and Human Cognitive Architecture. *Instructional Science* 32: 9-31.

Sweller, J., and S. Sweller. (2006). Natural Information Processing Systems. *Evolutionary Psychology* 4: 434-458.

Finally, for a short, fun article with a serious theme, read John Naish's article in the June 2, 2009, *The Times* (of London) titled "Warning: Brain Overload." In it he reports, "Scientists fear that a digital flood of 24-hour rolling news and infotainment is putting our primitive grey matter under such stress that we can no longer think wisely or empathise with others."

[8]Stephen R. Ruth, Martha Sammons, and Lindsey Poulin raise concerns about the quality of online or distance learning programs. In a well-documented argument, they point out that the quantity of e-learning, especially that offered by higher education institutions may be suspect:

Ruth, S.R., M. Sammons, and L. Poulin. (2007). eLearning at a Crossroads: What Price Quality? *Educause* 30(2): 32-39.

[9]Finding accurate information on costs and use of technology-delivered learning is difficult. Many of the costs are indirect ones and are therefore hard to capture (for example, updating of equipment, security, and maintenance). An interesting report that provides some benefits and concerns for technology-delivered instruction is a survey report of 110 professionals using technology for informal learning. Most of the survey respondents are IT sales and marketing professionals and turn to technology for acquiring product knowledge:

Training Industry Inc. and Intrepid Learning Solutions. (2010). *Effectively Using Technology-Enabled Informal Learning.* Cary, NC: Training Industry Inc. and Intrepid Learning Solutions.

[10]Shaw, S., and S. Sniderman. (2002). Reusable Learning Objects: Critique & Future Directions. In M. Driscoll and T. Reeves, eds., *Proceedings of World Conference on E-Learning in Corporate, Government, Healthcare, and Higher Education 2002.* Chesapeake, VA: AACE.

[11]This foundational book in human performance technology, the field concerned with obtaining valued behavior and accomplishment in the workplace details, with numerous examples, the many factors that strongly affect how people perform. It places skills and knowledge within the basket of other individual and environmental influences on obtaining "worthy" results:

Gilbert, T.F. (1996). *Human Competence: Engineering Worthy Performance.* Washington, DC: International Society for Performance Improvement.

The most up-to-date set of readings on what truly affects performance in workplace or organizational settings is the three-volume series of handbooks that not only deal with what makes for effective performance, but also provides cases, tools, and a great deal of evidence on the impact of individual variables influencing outcomes:

Silber, K.H., W.R. Foshay, R. Watkins, D. Leigh, J.L. Mosely, and J.C. Desinger, eds., *Handbook of Improving Performance in the Workplace,* volumes 1-3. San Francisco: Pfeiffer-Wiley.

[12]A great deal of controversy exists about the exact amount of training that gets transferred to the workplace. This is a futile argument as a number of factors affect transfer: utility of the training, the workplace environment, inhibitors and facilitators that occur posttraining, and even the attitudes of supervisors and colleagues. What appears to be the consensus of researchers is that the training event is one thing. The application is quite another. Some influencing factors relate to the quality and relevance of the training; most reside outside of the trainee. For a more rounded discussion of the important issue of transfer of training–transfer of learning, explore these publications:

Arthur, W., W. Bennett, P.S. Edens, and S.T. Bell. (2003). Effectiveness of Training in Organizations: A Meta-Analysis of Design and Evaluation Features. *Journal of Applied Psychology* 88(2): 234-245.

Bhati, D. (2007). *Factors That Influence Transfer of Hazardous Material Training: The Perception of Selected Fire-Fighter Trainees and Supervisors.* PhD dissertation. Orlando, FL: University of Central Florida.

Lim, D.H., and M.L. Morris. (2006). Influence of Trainee Characteristics, Instructional Satisfaction, and Organizational Climate on Perceived Learning and Training Transfer. *Human Resource Development Quarterly* 17(1): 85-115.

Morrow, G.M., M.Q. Jarrett, and M. Rupinsky. (1997). An Investigation of the Effect of the Effort and Economic Utility of Corporate-Wide Training. *Personnel Psychology* 50: 91-119.

Rodríguez, C.M., and S. Gregory. (2005). Qualitative Study of Transfer of Training of Student Employees in a Service Industry. *Journal of Hospitality & Tourism Research* 29(1): 42-66.

Subedi, B.S. (2006). Cultural Factors and Beliefs Influencing Transfer of Training. *International Journal of Training and Development* 10(2): 88.

Sugrue, B., and R.J. Rivera. (2005). *ASTD 2005 State of the Industry Report.* Alexandria, VA: American Society for Training & Development.

Tracey, J.B., S.I. Tannenbaum, and M.J. Kavanagh. (1995). Applying Trained Skills on the Job: The Importance of the Work Environment. *Journal of Applied Psychology* 80(2): 239-252.

Yamnill, S., and G.N. McLean. (2005). Factors Affecting Transfer of Training in Thailand. *Human Resource Development Quarterly* 16(3): 323-344.

[13]Dietrich, A., and R. Kanso. (2010). A Review of the EEG, ERP, and Neuroimaging Studies of Creativity and Insight. *Psychological Bulletin* 136(5): 822-848.

[14]Barnett, L. (2006). *The Universe and Einstein.* Mineola, NY: Dover Publications. The book is a reissue of the original published in 1957.

[15]*A Discourse on Method* was originally published by Descartes in 1637 in Leiden. This quote was drawn from

Descartes, R. (2004). *A Discourse on Method: Meditations on the First Philosophy—Principles of Philosophy.* London, UK: J.M. Dent. This translation by John Veitch was originally published in 1912. Of particular interest to anyone who would like to dig a little more deeply into what lies behind the quote, read the first part: Discourse on the method of rightly conducting the reason, and seeking truth in the sciences.

[16]Here is a list of references that were included in the first edition of *Telling Ain't Training* that we believe still make for good reading:

Phrenology

Chevenix, R. (1828). Gall and Spurzheim—Phrenology. *Foreign Quarterly Review* 2: 1-59.

Pearson, K. (1906). On the Relationship of Intelligence to Size and Shape of the Head. *Biometrika* 5: 105-146.

Riley, J. (1999). Did They Actually Really Believe This? Authentic Documents as a Window on the Past. *Social Studies and the Younger Learner* 11(3): 2-5.

Tomlinson, S. (1997). Phrenology, Education, and the Politics of Human Nature: The Thought and Influence of George Combs. *History of Education* 26(1): 1-22.

The brain as a muscle

Thorndike, E.L., and R.S. Woodworth. (1901). The Influence of Improvement in One Mental Function Upon the Efficiency of Other Functions. *Psychology Review* 8: 247-261.

Experts and unconscious competence

Bradley, F. (1997). From Unconscious Incompetence to Unconscious Competence. *Adults Learning (England)* 9(2): 20-21.

Ericsson, K.A., and J. Smith. (1991). *Toward General Theory of Expertise: Prospects and Limits*. New York: Cambridge University Press.

Specific aptitudes and learning

Snow, R. (1989). Aptitude-Treatment Interaction as a Framework for Research on Individual Differences in Learning. In R. Ackerman, R.J. Sternberg, and R. Glaser, eds., *Learning and Individual Differences*. New York: W.H. Freeman.

Tobias, S. (1985). Review, Other Macroprocesses, and Individual Differences. Proceedings of the 69th Annual Meeting of the American Educational Research Association, Chicago, March 31-April 4. (ERIC Document ED 258 134)

Enjoyment or satisfaction and learning

Bers, T.H. (1975). *The Relationship Between Learning and Enjoyment: A Study of Student Perceptions of Teaching Techniques*. Morton Grove, IL: Oakton Community College. (ERIC Document ED 119 764)

Clark, R.E. (1980). Do Students Enjoy the Instructional Method From Which They Learn Least? Antagonism Between Enjoyment and Achievement in ATI Studies. *Proceedings of the Annual Meeting of the American Educational Research Association*, Boston, April. (ERIC Document ED 188 601)

Media and learning

Clark, R.E. (1999). Media Will Never Influence Learning. *Educational Technology Research and Development* 47(2): 21-29.

Working out problems versus worked-out problems and learning

Van Morrienboer, J.J.G. (1997). *Training Complex Cognitive Skills: A Four Component Instructional Design Model for Technical Training*. Englewood Cliffs, NJ: Educational Technology Publications.

Van Morrienboer, J.J.G., and F.G.W. Paas. (1990). Automation and Schema Acquisition in Learning Elementary Computer Programming: Implications for the Design of Practice. *Computers in Human Behavior* 6(3): 273-289.

Too much content and learning: information overload

Clark, R.C., and D. Taylor. (1994). The Causes and Cures of Learner Overload. *Training* 31(7): 40-43.

Doring, A. (1999). Information Overload? *Adults Learning (England)* 10(10): 8-9.

Martin, D.W. (1980). Performance During the Stress of Processing Overload. *Proceedings of the 86th Annual Convention of the American Psychological Association,* Montreal, Quebec, September 1-5. (ERIC Document ED 195 892)

Sweller, J., and P. Chandler. (1991). Evidence for Cognitive Load Theory. *Cognition and Instruction* 12(3): 185-233.

Technology-based learning: need for evidence of effectiveness and cost savings

Bork, A. (1991). Is Technology-Based Learning Effective? *Contemporary Education* 63(1): 6-14.

Whalen, T., and D. Wright. (1999). Methodology for Cost-Benefit Analysis of Web-Based Telelearning: Case Study of the Bell Online Institute. *American Journal of Distance Education* 13(1): 24-44.

Technology: not necessarily the key to future workplace success

Ellis, R.K. (2000). Technology for Good/Technology for Evil. *Training and Development* 54(11): 32-33.

McCune, J.C. (1998). The Productivity Paradox. *HR Focus* 75(4): 4-5.

Weill, M., and L.D. Rosen. (1999). Don't Let Technology Enslave You. *Workforce* 78(2): 56-59.

Workplace performance: alternatives to training

Mager, R.F. (1992). *What Every Manager Should Know About Training or "I've Got a Training Problem"…and Other Odd Ideas.* Belmont, CA: Lake Publishing.

Mager, R.F., and P. Pipe. (1997). *Analyzing Performance Problems: Or You Really Oughta Wanna.* Atlanta: Center for Effective Performance.

Sanders, E.S., and S. Thiagargajan. (2001). *Performance Intervention Maps.* Alexandria, VA: American Society for Training & Development.

Stolovitch, H.D., and J-G. Maurice. (1998). Calculating the Return on Investment in Training: A Critical Analysis and a Case Study. *Performance Improvement* 37(8): 9-15, 18-20.

Successful performance during training and lack of transfer to the job

Baldwin, T.T., and J.K. Ford. (1988). Transfer of Training: A Review and Directions for Future Research. *Personnel Psychology* 41(1): 63-105.

Ford, J.K., and D.A. Weissbein. (1997). Transfer of Training: An Updated Review and Analysis. *Performance Improvement Quarterly* 10(2): 22-41.

Effect of pretraining activities on transfer of learning

Baldwin, T., and R.J. Magjuka. (1991). Organizational Training and Signals of Importance: Linking Pre-Training Perception to Intentions to Transfer. *Human Resource Development Quarterly* 2(1): 25-36.

Broad, M.L., and J.W. Newstrom. (1992). *Transfer of Training: Action-Packed Strategies to Ensure High Payoff From Training Investments.* Reading, MA: Addison-Wesley.

Cohen, D.J. (1990). What Motivates Trainees? *Training and Development Journal* 44(11): 91, 93.

Common sense versus science

Musgrave, A. (1993). *Common Sense, Science and Skepticism: A Historical Introduction to the Theory of Knowledge.* Oxford, UK: Oxford University Press.

Chapter 13: Concluding Reflections on Telling Ain't Training

[1]Jung, C.G. (1969). *The Psychology of the Transference*, 3rd ed. Princeton, NJ: Princeton University Press.

[2]Eggleston, E. (1943). *The Hoosier School-Master: A Story of Backwoods Life in Indiana.* New York: Books, Inc. Publishers. (Originally published in 1871.)

About the Authors

Harold D. Stolovitch and **Erica J. Keeps** share a common passion: developing people. Together they have devoted a combined total of more than 80 years to make workplace learning and performance both enjoyable and effective. Their research and consulting activities have involved them in numerous projects with major corporations such as Hewlett Packard, Sun Microsystems, Oracle, General Motors, Bell Canada, Telecom Asia, Canadian Pacific Railway, Canadian Business Development Bank, Bank of Montreal, Rio Tinto-Alcan, Prudential, Century 21, CDW, Canadian Navy, Chrysler, General Motors, International Association of Fire Fighters, Nissan, Pfizer, Southern California Gas, The Coffee Bean and Tea Leaf, USDA as well as the military, the police, government, counterterrorism agencies, healthcare institutions, and many others. Their dedication to improving workplace learning and performance is reflected in the workshops they conduct internationally on training delivery, instructional design, and performance consulting. Stolovitch and Keeps are the principals of HSA Learning & Performance Solutions LLC, specialists in the application of instructional technology and human performance technology to business, industry, government, and the military. In addition to the original edition of *Telling Ain't Training*, Stolovitch and Keeps are the authors of *Beyond Telling Ain't Training Fieldbook*, *Training Ain't Performance*, and *Beyond Training Ain't Performance Fieldbook* published by ASTD Press. Together, they are co-editors of two editions of the award-winning *Handbook of Human Performance Technology: A Comprehensive Guide for Analyzing and Solving Performance Problems in Organizations* and *Improving Individual and Organizational Performance Worldwide* and authors of the toolkit series, *Engineering Effective Learning* and *Front-End Analysis and Return on Investment* published by Jossey-Bass/Pfeiffer.

Harold D. Stolovitch, CPT, is a graduate of both McGill University in Canada and Indiana University in the United States where he completed a doctorate and post-doctoral work in instructional systems technology. With one foot solidly grounded in the academic world and the other in the workplace, he has conducted a large number of research studies and practical projects always aimed at achieving high learning and performance results. In addition to creating countless instructional

283

materials for a broad range of work settings, Stolovitch has authored more than 300 articles, research reports, book chapters, and books. He is a past president of the International Society for Performance Improvement (ISPI), former editor of the *Performance Improvement Journal,* and editorial board member of several human resource and performance technology journals. He has won numerous awards throughout his 40-year career, including the Thomas F. Gilbert Award for Distinguished Professional Achievement, ISPI's highest honor; Member-for-Life, the President's Award for Lifetime Achievements from the Canadian Society for Training and Development, their highest honor; and in 2004, he and his team won the ASTD Outstanding Research Award for their work on Incentives, Motivation, and Workplace Performance. Stolovitch is an emeritus professor, Université de Montréal, where he headed the instructional and performance technology graduate programs and was the School of Educational Sciences associate dean of research. He is also a former Distinguished Visiting Scholar and clinical professor of human performance at work, University of Southern California. Stolovitch is a principal of HSA Learning & Performance Solutions LLC.

Erica J. Keeps, CPT, holds a master's degree in educational psychology from Wayne State University, Detroit, and a bachelor's degree from the University of Michigan, where she later became a faculty member in the Graduate Business School Executive Education Center. Her 40-year professional career has included training management positions with J.L. Hudson Co. and Allied Supermarkets and senior-level learning and performance consultant positions with a wide variety of organizations. Keeps has not only produced and supervised the production of numerous instructional materials and performance management systems, but has also published extensively on improving workplace learning and performance. She has provided staff development for instructional designers, training administrators, and performance consultants. Keeps has been acknowledged by many learning and performance leaders as a caring mentor and major influence in their careers. She is a former executive board member of the ISPI; a past president of the Michigan Chapter of ISPI; and a Member-for-Life of the Michigan, Montreal, and Los Angeles ISPI chapters. Among her many awards for outstanding contributions to instructional and performance technology is ISPI's Distinguished Service Award for her extensive leadership roles. Keeps is the managing director and a principal of HSA Learning & Performance Solutions LLC.

The authors reside in Los Angeles and can be reached at
Website: www.hsa-lps.com
Mail: 1520 S. Beverly Glen Blvd., Suite 305, Los Angeles, CA 90024
Telephone: 1.888.834.9928
Email: info@hsa-lps.com

About Marc J. Rosenberg

Marc J. Rosenberg is a management consultant, writer, educator, and leading expert in the world of training, organizational learning, e-learning, knowledge management, and performance improvement. He is the author of the best-selling books *E-Learning: Strategies for Delivering Knowledge in the Digital Age* (McGraw-Hill) and *Beyond E-Learning: Approaches and Technologies to Enhance Organizational Knowledge, Learning, and Performance* (Pfeiffer). His column, "Marc My Words," appears monthly in the eLearning Guild's *Learning Solutions* online magazine. Rosenberg is a past president of the International Society for Performance Improvement (ISPI). He holds a doctorate in instructional design, plus degrees in communications and marketing, and the Certified Performance Technologist (CPT) designation. Rosenberg is a recognized thought leader in the field. He has spoken at the White House, debated e-learning at the Oxford Union, keynoted numerous professional and business conferences, authored more than 50 articles and book chapters , and been a frequently quoted expert in major business and trade publications. More information is available at www.marcrosenberg.com.

Index

Note: *c* represents a checklist, *f* represents a figure, *t* represents a table, and *w* represents a worksheet.